RACIAL EXHAUSTION

RACIAL EXHAUSTION

HOW TO MOVE THROUGH RACISM
IN THE WAKE OF DEI

RALINA L. JOSEPH

NEW YORK UNIVERSITY PRESS
New York, NY

NEW YORK UNIVERSITY PRESS
New York
www.nyupress.org

© 2025 by New York University
All rights reserved

Please contact the Library of Congress for Cataloging-in-Publication data.

ISBN: 9781479839995 (hardback)
ISBN: 9781479840007 (paperback)
ISBN: 9781479840045 (library ebook)
ISBN: 9781479840038 (consumer ebook)

This book is printed on acid-free paper, and its binding materials are chosen for strength and durability. We strive to use environmentally responsible suppliers and materials to the greatest extent possible in publishing our books.

The manufacturer's authorized representative in the EU for product safety is
Mare Nostrum Group B.V., Mauritskade 21D, 1091 GC Amsterdam,
The Netherlands. Email: gpsr@mare-nostrum.co.uk.

Manufactured in the United States of America

10 9 8 7 6 5 4 3 2 1

Also available as an ebook

For my family

CONTENTS

Preface		ix
Introduction: Racial Exhaustion		1
1	Radical Listening	31
2	Sitting with Discomfort	57
3	Radical Speaking	87
4	Reparative Dialoguing	127
	Epilogue: The Wake of DEI	155
	Acknowledgments	163
	Appendix: Sample Dialogue Prompts	167
	Notes	173
	Bibliography	205
	Interrupting Privilege Clip Bibliography	225
	Index	227
	About the Author	239

PREFACE

These days, the response I receive to the question "How are you doing?" is often, simply, "Tired!" To which I nod. Me, too. Amid the world-shaking events of the past few years—from the reverberations of COVID-19 and its disproportional racialized impacts to the state-sanctioned violence against Black people and the resulting "racial reckoning"—I, like so many friends, family, and colleagues, am working nonstop. This work for many means varying, unceasing, and often invisible forms of intellectual and emotional labor. Indeed, while many of us have been exhausted for years, those from 2016, when the forty-fifth U.S. president was elected, to 2024, when he was reelected, have been extraordinarily taxing. Those eight years also map onto the first eight years of a racial dialoguing project I created called Interrupting Privilege, which animates this book. Its aim is to help readers move through the deeply embodied experience of racial exhaustion, what this book explores as people of color feeling tired of talking about racism and white people feeling tired of listening, by learning how to practice the *critical communication of race*, a circuit of listening, holding discomfort, speaking, and dialoguing. This circuit is *critical*, meaning that it interrogates power in every moment. *Racial Exhaustion: How to Move through Racism in the Wake of DEI* will take you to stories of how academics and lay audiences, including my exhausted students, friends, research participants, community members, family, and I, interrupt privilege by critically communicating race from small, interpersonal, and everyday ways to huge, structural, and future-cast ones.

This moment exhausts many folks like me who are "the first." Like many faculty of color, I was hired to diversify my institution in scholarship, curriculum, and, of course, the unstated but perhaps most important mandate: in body. We have been—if tokenistically—included. Our bodies have been prominently featured in splashy PR stories, on highly publicized committees, and in expressions of the institution's fulfilment of its

DEI (Diversity, Equity, and Inclusion) mission. (I utilize the abbreviation "DEI" because it has gained popularity—and notoriety—not because I think it's better than any similar names and acronyms that have emerged in this time.[1]) Two decades into the game, I'm inured to this selective inclusion. But before I received the academic freedom that comes with tenure (in a state that still respects both academic freedom and tenure), I was particularly sensitive to the ways in which my colleagues—white men and women, senior and junior—expressed an uneasy relationship to my *inclusion* and, in textbook microaggressive ways, showed me in a myriad of subtle, and not so subtle, ways that I didn't belong.

Because of this experience I have a fraught relationship with fighting to join *existing* tables of power to make minoritized voices heard. I don't fight for my seat, but when offered, I do take it, sometimes reluctantly, and even when I understand the offer to be a tokenistic gesture. Like the great Shirley Chisolm, I might pull up a folding chair.[2] But I don't fight to be "included." At other times, similarly minoritized folks and I cobble together our own tables, craft our own chairs. Now, our wood is bought by the university, but I like to think that our labor and tools are our own (even if their purchase was university-subsidized). I have aimed to use my power for good: my efforts have been focused on crafting majority-minoritized spaces where change is possible, sometimes inside, sometimes outside the university. I understand that this, in and of itself, is one of my many privileges—a privilege that is also exhausting because the fight never feels reciprocal, never pauses, is even never-ending.

To be clear, my exhaustion might be exacerbated by geography. Seattle, Washington, a city with far more Black Lives Matter signs outside people's houses than actual Black people inside of them, has been home for twenty years. I crossed the threshold of time where I lived there longer than anywhere else. I first came to this town in 2005, lugging a rambunctious toddler over the shelf of my pregnant belly and magically transitioning within the span of two months from student to professor, from "Ralina" to "Dr. Joseph," and from scrappy dissertator to respectable young professional and homeowner. My California-bred, partner-in-crime met my side-eye with a buoying, crinkling smile.

My side-eye masked my nervousness about our change in fortune. It also masked my uncertainty about the oppressive, stultifying whiteness of our new space. Without sufficient reflection on neighborhood demographics, we had moved to the white(st) end of the city, the one close to the university that brought us here, and to my husband's new job. We found that whiteness was not just a numerical reality. Whiteness saturated the North Seattle air. White homogeny produced a white affect, including a peculiar white language—or rather, lack of language about race. In contrast, race was central to our lives, our family, and our work, and the language of race (our second, sometimes first language) carried us through the moments when we needed soul-searching and strategizing, when we needed laughter and relief, when we needed to feel seen and heard.

We wondered why white people in our new neighborhood remained so silent about race, why questions of demographics or disparities were verboten in so many polite conversations with white folks. Why, on a much more mundane level, white people couldn't use a racialized descriptor around us without stuttering, sweating, turning red, or figuring out a quick excuse to change the topic or leave the space. Why the eyes of white North Seattleites glazed over in the presence of my family's (mixed-race) light brown bodies when the topic of race emerged, then searched (nervously!) for a white person with a white topic. Never had I experienced race feeling so perpetually, purposefully absent from conversation and yet (or as a result) so present in communication. Never had we experienced white people so exhausted by the thought of communicating about race.

And not just any white people but so many white folks who described themselves as liberal purveyors of social justice, and yes, even anti-racist allies. Including the interracially married ones. Even they were afraid of race talk. Both my husband and I, sharing the experience of being raised as post-Loving, 1970s kids of interracial marriages,[3] were chagrined by the ways in which our own white family members communicated race in limited ways, celebrating that our very bodies transcended race, while talking too little about racism. Like our new white neighbors, we had grown up with too much racism, and too little race talk. But unlike them, we had learned that silence causes damage in the form of denying children the essential, indeed sometimes lifesaving, tools of racial socialization, which fundamentally means critically communicating race. For children of color, this damage can mean a diminished sense of self, a weaker alignment with their own communities of color, and a lack of preparation for experiences of racial bias.[4]

Let me be clear: I understand my family to be incredibly privileged in many realms, skin shade being one. My multigenerationally multiracial family is the beneficiary of a pigmentocracy that values light skin above dark. The research is overwhelmingly convincing that light-skinned people of color, including light-skinned Black folks, have a leg up in education, the criminal justice systems, job promotions, and even basketball referees' calls.[5] Here, as a first-generation college student–now professor I have experienced more class privilege than I ever imagined possible. We feel lucky not to have been on the receiving end of physical racialized violence. We have rarely (but not never) been met with racial slurs. Indeed, like all cities and towns in the United States, our city is not devoid of everyday explicit racialized violence.[6]

And yet . . . I heard race silence but felt racial animus in our children's schools. In our workplaces. In the grocery store. And our experiencing that silence and racism felt like a particular type of exhaustion I was coming to understand not as the white racial exhaustion of having to communicate about race, but the people-of-color exhaustion of having to hold white racial exhaustion. Our children were in for what we understood to be a very confusing sort of racialization, the living of race in everyday life, if we did not figure out ways to combat both forms of exhaustion.[7] That is, if we didn't do some serious extra-credit race work to counter the emotional, spiritual, and intellectual destruction that we knew silence around race would cause—especially when partnered with the proliferation of other kinds of racism.

And serious extra-credit race work with our kids is precisely what we did over the next decades as we settled into the Emerald City. While attempting to maintain a conscientious critique of Obama-era policies, we delighted in Obama's two elections and celebrated that a Black first family would be the first first family our children would remember. We unashamedly took pictures of their multigenerational multiracial, chubby cheeked selves cheesing next to the front page of our new hometown paper proclaiming Obama's victories: a not-too-subtle visualization of the change we all hoped for had finally come to fruition (Figure P.1). In this hyperwhite city, we lived in what critical race scholars deem *counterspaces*,

Figure P.1. Four more years. Photo courtesy of James Joseph.

"sites where deficit notions of People of Color can be challenged."⁸ We wrapped our children in counterspace bubbles of color, of difference. Our chosen Seattle family was comprised largely of similar transplants to the region who also balked at the culture of silencing race talk: other families of color, interracial families, gay and lesbian families, all of whom similarly spoke race-and-privilege as their first language. We regularly left Seattle for our previous hometown of Oakland, so that we would remember what it was like not to always be gazed upon as the onlies. A longtime Black Seattleite confided to me that such "visual relief" was the key to her sanity.

This work kept us from abandoning this city altogether. We also did something key: we moved from Seattle's north to the south end, where we joined far more Black and brown folks, and far more white folks speaking (sometimes awkwardly, often earnestly, but at least effortfully, and without exhaustion) about race. This in-city move when our kids were four and six made all the difference: suddenly race talk didn't only happen only within their counterspaces. With this move our children became true Seattleites, unfazed by the grey and drizzle and enthusiastic in their love of this clean-smelling, park-filled, multiracial child haven, this rapidly gentrifying city, politely proclaiming itself postracial.

And . . . then came the summer of 2020. The so-called worldwide racial reckoning prompted many folks to abandon the illusion of postracialism. We—race scholars, DEI practitioners, agitators of all stripes who never believed such lies—received more invitations to *their* tables, their grace said with mournful, prayerful, promise-ful proclamations. And as no one seemed to be checking for our collective racial exhaustion, how could we move through it? How could we tend to ourselves and our communities when the fight, we knew, was one of our entire lifetimes? How about those who invited us to their tables? Those white allies who embraced, preached, and proclaimed antiracism with the obsession of new zealots, but quickly lost their own racial stamina, returning to their same segregated tables?

The answers to these questions are those I explore in this book. The answers are incomplete and sometimes unsatisfying, but they do provide a way to practice moving through racial exhaustion. And I have not come to these answers alone. In addition to scores of brilliant race and communication scholars you will discover in the upcoming pages, alongside the astonishingly generous research participants, I cite here, first and foremost, my race-talking, now young adult children of whom I am embarrassingly proud. Their audacious racial fluency, their fearlessness of "getting it wrong," their understanding that racial communication is a journey not a destination help move me through my own racial exhaustion every day. And they teach me that the journey is not about critically communicating race as an end goal but using that communicating to move through their own racial exhaustion in order to care for themselves and create a more just world. Their journey through racial communication is emotional, intellectual, spiritual. I watch, listen, and endlessly converse with them about their intrepid forays into interracial, intra-racial, intergenerational, and critical communication about race. I crib from them as I teach, write, and learn to embrace failure as a byproduct of critically communicating race. You will undoubtedly learn some of their techniques here. This book is both inspired by and dedicated to them.

INTRODUCTION

RACIAL EXHAUSTION

Americans are tired of contending with race. After years, decades, and centuries of fighting racism, racial disparities remain intransigent, racial discourse devolves to hate speech, and racial divides persist. People of color are forced to address sideways racial comments, compelled to right racial injustice; they are tired of correcting, teaching, intervening—so tired that many of them, in fact, are giving up and losing hope that speaking up can change minds and right past and present wrongs. Simultaneously, white people are tired of talking about race. They feel uncomfortable or awkward having to listen to friends' and colleagues' stories of navigating racism. They feel like they must constantly defend their anti-racist credentials, while fearing that any off remark might be scrutinized as potentially racist. They are tired of being told they hold an innate privilege they might have never had to come to terms with—a privilege that may be inherited from the misdeeds of their ancestors. They feel shunned by conversations about race and agitated by the idea that their well-meaning contributions to these discussions are often seen as irrelevant.

We live these moments in our everyday interactions and see them reflected in our government, media, and educational institutions. So it's not a surprise that we are tired. But we rarely name or acknowledge our racial exhaustion. This book's goal is a lofty one: to help you work through interpersonal moments of conflict and exhaustion to create the stamina to stay in the fight for equitable, large-scale change.

And before I go any further, I want to be clear that I do not employ the phrases "people of color" (or BIPOC, or Black, Latine, Native American, Asian American, and Southwest Asian North African, also known as SWANA) and "white" for the purposes of essentializing experience or drawing a straight line between racialized groups and racialized communication. I believe, as race scholars have long established, that race is a construction. The historian Matthew Frye Jacobson, for example, writes of race scholars' "shaken faith" of the "biological certainty" that "race [is] . . . indisputable." Jacobson continues that, while race "frames our notions of kinship and descent and influences our movements in the social world," such notions reflect the "arbitrariness . . . of affixing racial labels."[1] The fundamental paradox of race is that it is "imagined but not imaginary." Thus, when I write "white," I am not arguing that *all* white people in the United States communicate in a singular white fashion about race, but rather that whiteness as a powerful construct produces white race talk (and racial exhaustion). Similarly, while *all* Black people do not communicate the same about race, the construct of Blackness in America produces Black race talk and racial exhaustion that, like whiteness, emerges from our shared histories. This is the process that sociologists Michael Omi and Howard Winant call racialization.[2]

To take on the exhaustion that emerges with racialized communication about race, this book will teach you how to listen to and dialogue about race, or what I call *critically communicating race*. The "critical" piece, meaning *with an ear and voice toward power*, is key here. I define power through sociologist and Black feminist scholar Patricia Hill Collins's concept of the "matrix of domination," which crosses structural (power through social institutions) and interpersonal (power through individual relationships) domains.[3] *Racial Exhaustion* offers up interpersonal power as a conduit of change for structural power: individual action is always impacted by and impacting institutions.[4] Our individual, interpersonal moments of communicating race—and our silence about race and racism—can shape or reshape the histories and structures underpinning our daily lives. In a variety of quotidian ways, we either lift up or shut down moments of racial changemaking, an individual-meets-structural means of more equitably reshaping our racialized world. We achieve racial changemaking by developing a critical communication fluency about race, which then enables individuals and communities to collaboratively construct solutions to racialized problems. Racial changemaking always holds individual experiences in relation to structural, historical, and institutional ones. In other words, experiences of racism are not random, but are rather reflections of racialized structures and racialized systems of oppression.[5]

First, let's look more closely at racial exhaustion, the phenomenon I examine where people of color are tired of talking about race, and white people are tired of listening. People of color experience racism daily, exacerbating their exhaustion. So does experiencing the silencing of racism, when white people, structures, histories, ideologies, and institutions fail to register, believe in, or work to change racism. This racial exhaustion comes after anger. Partnered with resigned frustration, racial exhaustion is the embodied, emotional experience of feeling done: lethargic limbs, exasperated sighs, closing eyes. Racial exhaustion means giving up: abandoning the practices of entertaining the "devil's advocate," of listening to counterarguments, of explaining race, of recounting racism, and of justifying the necessity for anti-racist action. And racial exhaustion is not incidental: racism, as Rochelle Walensky, formerly director of the Centers for Disease Control, declared in 2021, is a public health issue.[6] Race-based traumatic stress creates what sociologist William Smith calls racial battle fatigue (RBF), "the physiological and psychological strain exacted on racially marginalized groups and the amount of energy loss dedicated to coping with racial microaggressions and racism."[7] RBF produces health disparities ranging from headaches, backaches, ulcers, and high blood pressure, to psychological symptoms such as sleeplessness, "emotional and social withdrawal," and resentment.[8] Racial exhaustion is the everyday, emotional living of RBF.[9] It kills us slowly. And racial exhaustion is one of the hallmarks of being a person of color, and thus, of race itself.[10] Race—and not just racism—makes people of color tired. Further, the very DNA of racial exhaustion is the relationship between everyday and structural discrimination: we are so tired because we understand that the individual moments of discrimination that we might experience aren't one-offs. They're systemic. And they harm not just us but our community.

Racial exhaustion is not solely the purview of people of color. White racial exhaustion is also embodied. For allies, it can feel like frustration—muting screams while trying to hold other white people to account or a bracing for rejection while trying to prove their anti-racist bona fides to people of color. For racist whites, racial exhaustion can feel like the swallowed fury of having to fight to hold onto what has previously been unquestionably theirs and a hackles-up defense against the sense that they are unfairly accused of being bad people. However, in neither case is white racial exhaustion equivalent to the form that afflicts people of color. Interracial interactions can certainly impair the cognitive functions of white people,[11] but I've yet to find studies documenting that white racial exhaustion—being tired of listening to or talking about race and racism—increases the morbidity or mortality of white people. You might feel under threat, but you are very literally not.

In fact, white racial exhaustion can be a part of racism itself. White racial exhaustion has a long and storied history in the United States, where it is a willful, white-perpetrated race-silence that "protect[s] [white] interests, legitimate[s] the material conditions of racial inequality and the unequal social and economic status between persons of color and whites," in the words of legal scholar Darren Hutchinson, who coined the term "racial exhaustion," which he applies solely to white people. Hutchinson connects "individual opposition to race-based remedies, such as affirmative action" with "'classical racism' (or a belief in the superiority of whites) and a desire for in-group dominance."[12] In these moments, white people use the rhetoric of racial exhaustion to excuse away the very real structural, historical, and institutional reasons for racial inequality. This is a moment of moving from feeling racial exhaustion to iterating it, from silence about race to expressions of tiredness. Perhaps this means shrugging off racism with a "bad things happen to everyone and I'm tired of hearing Black people play the race card to make their bad things more important." For white liberals, expressions of racial exhaustion also fulfil another function: they "resolve deep contradictions between social norms favoring equal opportunity and justice and the vastly unequal social and economic status between persons of color and white."[13] In other words, the frame of exhaustion enables white people to both espouse high-minded and even egalitarian ideals and to ignore the realities of racial disparities. This might mean saying, "I believe deeply in equality, but reparations/affirmative action/structural racial change is simply going too far."

Racial Exhaustion: How to Move through Racism in the Wake of DEI names racial exhaustion as a central emotion-based frame that both white people and people of color get stuck in, and it shows you how to move through that frame with critical communication of race skills. I use the gentle phrase "move through" instead of more belligerent verbs such as "combat" or "confront" to gesture toward the more sustainable process of maintaining strength for the long fight, or developing resilience, as we'll explore later. For people of color, everyday racism already feels like a battle, and remaining in a perpetual state of combat only exacerbates exhaustion. In contrast, in *moving through exhaustion by critically communicating race*, we attend to the emotions that emerge from fighting or watching this battle.

Moving through takes some work. Here you will not only learn the steps but discern how your body handles this work. You will learn how to practice what elite athletes call training to a point of fatigue before leveling off to care for their bodies. Pushing too hard and too fast, you risk injury; not pushing hard enough, you risk never reaching your goal.[14] Those interrupting privilege must practice training up to a fatigue threshold in order to do this stressful work without recreating racial exhaustion. This book helps you understand how to identify this threshold and how to name and dismantle power to connect more equitably across, within, and among racialized identities. This book also looks at the underlying trouble of "grind culture," or never-ceasing work, that Tricia Hersey addresses in her "Nap Ministry," in which she teaches us that attending to our exhaustion is key to feeding our souls.[15]

Racial Exhaustion aims to accomplish two wildly different but intimately connected goals: attending to the racial exhaustion of people of color while also navigating the racial exhaustion of white skeptics and allies. Crucially, some of the ways in which Black folks, non-Black people of color, and white people *can* and *should* attend to their racial exhaustion are different. *Racial Exhaustion* asks, When, for people of color, racial exhaustion emerges from deep personal, familial, historical, and institutional experiences of trauma, but whites' racial exhaustion comes from viewing racial trauma from the outside, how do we radically listen to each other? How do we engage in equitable dialogue when the racial exhaustion of people of color arises from interrogating and resisting power in the face of racism, while white racial exhaustion comes from utilizing white power for or against itself, shoring up or contesting power? How do we foster everyday, respectful, and honest race conversations when everyone's racial exhaustion produces resignation? The *can* and *should* might differ for people of color and white people, but the answer for all of us is racial dialogue.

MOVING THROUGH RACIAL EXHAUSTION: HOW IT'S DONE

In a recorded session for a racial dialoguing project, Jordan, a Black high school junior, and Kalia, a Black high school sophomore, describe their experiences of race and racism at their large, racially diverse public high school. Their facilitator for the dialogue is Davarius, a Black college senior and communication major, who, in the fall of 2019, is one of a team of university students who meets up with pairs of Black Seattleites to talk about what it's like to be Black in various spaces.[16] Jordan explains that an everyday form of racism that he experiences at his racially diverse, large public high school is his white teachers failing to know about—or acknowledge—their school's celebration of Black History Month. Jordan is a leader in both the school's Black Student Union, which programs the Black History Month activities, and its student government, which runs assemblies. He recounts his experience with a resigned matter-of-factness about his teachers' failure to acknowledge the voices of Black students and community members inside and outside the school. His story and tone intimate that his resignation is a hallmark of his life as a Black high school student leader.

Jordan goes on to describe another variation on everyday racism, which occurs when one of his white teachers, Mr. New, "teaches to one part of the classroom at a time. He . . . talks differently when he's speaking to us [Black students]." In this honors class, Jordan explains, Mr. New assumes that the white kids are going to take the rigorous advanced placement exam, while the Black kids are not; thus, Mr. New does not give the Black students equitably attentive instruction. Jordan describes his frustration and explains that he respectfully shared his concerns with his teacher. Their conversation didn't change Mr. New's behavior, so Jordan asked for help from Mr. Barkley, a Black vice principal. Mr. Barkley dismissed his concerns, telling him, in Jordan's recounting, to "tough it [out]. . . . Get through it and you'll be fine." Jordan now says, simply, "I don't think they understood what I was trying to say." Moreover, the adults with power didn't do the necessary work to hear him fully, talk about his concerns, and create a change.

Davarius, a young man skilled at facilitating racial dialogues, nods along, feeling Jordan's frustration. With hope in his voice, he asks if anyone else—perhaps Jordan's white classmates—speaks up to the teachers or administration to protest inequitable classroom experiences. Jordan emphatically says no, white people don't stand up for students of color. Instead, "They pretty much stay to themselves when stuff like that happens. Like rarely would something like that—a white person standing up for a POC [person of color]—ever happen just because it's so rare. I'd say the most [that would happen is] a white person would *feel* or *have sympathy* [for us] but nothing would be done as far as standing up or trying to help or assisting or guiding a POC through anything that they go through."

Davarius takes a moment to appreciate Jordan's answer and then asks, what about white *friends* versus white *classmates*—the white kids Jordan chooses to be around, not just the kids he happens to be in class with. He asks Jordan: "Do you ever talk about race with your white friends?" Jordan quickly responds, "No I don't. I feel uncomfortable because I feel like they're going to say something and it's not going to be the right thing or something that's triggering toward me, I would say. I might lash out or something like that." Jordan is a student leader, an outspoken, quick-to-smile young man elected junior class president. He has white friends, but he can't trust them to hear his experiences of racism in the supportive ways he needs to be heard. Moreover, as a young Black man, he must enact greater control over his emotions as white peers might see his "lashing out" as not typical teen frustration but a sign of impending violence.

Davarius brings in the third member of this conversation, Kalia, prompting her to tell a story that occurs in another of Mr. New's classes. Kalia is quieter by nature than Jordan; in this conversation she has been verbally and nonverbally co-signing Jordan while letting him take the lead on answering questions. Now she's ready to talk. Kalia describes the everyday form of casual racism from her white peers she experiences in her classroom. In one example, the white students share resources, notes, and answers with each other, shutting Kalia and her Black classmates out of their study groups. Kalia imagines that if she were to tell her white *friends*—not just classmates but friends—about this experience that they would express sympathy for the white kids in class instead of her. She predicts her white friends would create excuses for the other white kids, envisioning dismissive responses such as, "'I don't really see it' or 'They like you.'" Kalia concludes, "I feel like they wouldn't be able to relate or feel for us." Jordan agrees with this idea, adding, "Kind of like they're oblivious." As the conversation moves on, more details about the myriad, everyday ways in which racism shapes the experience of Black high school students emerge, as does also the fact that no one—save themselves—will hear their stories, speak out about inequitable situations, or engage in dialogue to create a change. They make clear the toll that everyday, interpersonal racism takes on them. Yet this level of racism is rarely named or measured in headline-grabbing stories about the opportunity gap between Black and white students.

At the same time that Jordan and Kalia were participating in this racial dialoguing program, I had the opportunity to talk with Mr. New, who Jordan said refused to listen to him and Kalia said didn't intervene in her classroom's racialized resource hoarding. This teacher, a self-described progressive, anti-racist, was renowned for aiding his students in garnering high scores on their advanced placement exams for college credit; he bragged to me about the out-of-class study groups he required, which he noted were key to the students' testing success. But both Jordan and Kalia had told me that the study groups were segregated, denying entrance to Black kids, so white kids hoarded information. They also noted that many Black students could meet only infrequently in their own study groups because they commuted to school from much greater distances, a direct result of the racial gentrification that had displaced their families from the neighborhood of this school. Separate was not equal. I shared this information with Mr. New and suggested that perhaps he construct a different, integrated, in-class study group model. In a department meeting, his colleague Mr. Day, a Black teacher, shared his own strategies of inclusion. Mr. New thanked both of us. But the students reported back that nothing changed. Mr. New was undoubtedly tired of people demanding that he consider race where he had previously not; he was almost certainly experiencing a particular form of white racial exhaustion. Maybe Mr. New was feeling like some white skeptics who express racial exhaustion, saying that they are tired of hearing about race. Perhaps he was feeling uncredited, thinking about the hard work he did outside of the classroom. He might have felt tired from keeping other white people accountable for their racism, a kind of tax on their allyship.

But the story doesn't end with a depressing moment of high school kids sharing their experiences of racism with a college student in a university recording studio or with white racial exhaustion stymieing change. These three students—alongside seventeen other high school, undergraduate, and graduate students and another twenty community members—participated in a year-long, university- and community-based, critical communication of race program called Interrupting Privilege. They gathered in the 2019–2020 academic year to listen to stories shared by participants; engage in deep and sustained dialogues about race, racism, and its many intersectional iterations (racialized sexism, racialized homophobia, racialized ableism, racialized transphobia, racialized colorism, and so on); learn how to process their own discomfort around these topics; and construct solutions to each other's concerns.[17] Although we sometimes joked that we endeavored to "solve racism," the goal was never as lofty—or naïve—as that. Instead, we strove to move through moments of racial exhaustion by critically communicating with, for, and about race with our community.

So while Kalia relished the cathartic process of talking race in supportive spaces, Jordan had an additional solution. He asked me to share some of our group's lessons at a 2000-person high school assembly as part of a new program called Black Lives Matter at School Week. I said yes—if he would join me as co-presenter. Together we led the assembled high school students, teachers, and administrators through a listening exercise to gear them up to tune into voices more intently, and then we played Jordan and Kalia's recorded stories. Next, Jordan returned to the mic. While Kalia and other Interrupting Privilege participants watched supportively from the bleachers, Jordan's voice rang through the speakers, emphatically telling his assembled high school that they needed to listen better to Black students, acknowledge and work through their own discomfort with race, engage in supportive dialogue with Black students, and step up to create change with and for Black students.

This moment planted the seeds for structural change. Mr. Day cited Jordan's and Kalia's words as the reason for recommending that teachers in the school get their summer continuing education hours from a "teaching for liberation" summer institute he was involved in, where they would learn anti-racist classroom strategies.[18] The reverberations continued at the school district office, where Jordan's and Kalia's voices primed school leaders to rethink their policies and design a year-long professional development course on race and equity. They echoed through Parent

Teacher Student Association (PTSA) meetings, where members considered strategies for including families like Jordan's and Kalia's in the organization, starting with steps as simple as not having meetings during work hours. This is how interpersonal, critical communication of difference leads to structural change.

In this moment, for the entire assembled crowd, Jordan had moved through racial exhaustion—not only his own but that of others. That is, Jordan's intervention was two-fold: he traversed his own and Mr. Day's Black racial exhaustion from daily interpersonal racism, which collided with and amplified experiences of structural, historical, and institutional racism, and he also navigated Mr. New's white racial exhaustion from being challenged to hear or acknowledge complicity in perpetuating racism. Despite being resigned and shut down at various other moments, Jordan boldly shared his experience as a way to connect with fellow Black students and faculty. In speaking out, Jordan called on the white students and faculty who were tired of talking about race and were experiencing white racial exhaustion; his story remotivated white students and faculty to move through their exhaustion by illuminating the stakes of their silence for Black students. In telling his story, he also provided the opportunity for the assembled non-Black people of color to connect with each other around their experiences of racism and to seek alliances with Black students.

INTERRUPTING PRIVILEGE: THE CIRCUIT

The strategies in this book grew from the program that Jordan, Kalia, and Davarius were participating in: Interrupting Privilege. I designed Interrupting Privilege as public scholarship exercise that attends to the racial exhaustion of people of color such as Jordan, Kalia, Davarius, Mr. Day, and Mr. Barkley, as well as their white allies and could be-allies, like Mr. New. The program helped them all work through exhaustion to build stamina for the struggle against racism. My team of faculty, staff, and students launched the project in the fall of 2016, when so many of us felt overwhelmed and exhausted: newly elected President Trump and his party re-popularized and legitimized hate speech, and hate crimes rose at an unprecedented rate. The project expanded over the years: in 2020, COVID-19 ravaged BIPOC communities in devastating and disproportional ways, and the world reckoned with racial violence following the televised 2020 murder of George Floyd. Interrupting Privilege participants moved through exhaustion by practicing the critical communication of race. To date hundreds of participants have experienced Interrupting Privilege and the moments of racial healing, respite, and connection it proffers.

Racial Exhaustion braids three strands of narrative to bring you to your own moments of racial changemaking: my stories of facilitating the program; dialogues between program participants; and strategies for listening, holding discomfort, speaking out, and talking together. In the first strand, as a woman of color academic-activist in liberal white spaces, I describe how I try, and often fail, to traverse my own racial exhaustion while doggedly developing a racial dialoguing program. In the second strand, I share interviews from the Interrupting Privilege archive, in which participants, who range from teenagers through retirees, negotiate their racial exhaustion.[19] In these first two strands I connect everyday moments of *interpersonal* intersectional racism and resistance with *structural* intersectional racism and resistance. In the third strand, as I apply intersectional racial critique to scholarship on communication strategies, I provide tools for understanding, confronting, and navigating racial exhaustion. Into these three strands I crochet a fourth: addendums and interventions to those strategies through an intersectional critical race lens, which provides an interconnected, identity-based power analysis. Put another way, you're going to find personal essays, interdisciplinary research, a field guide, and actionable tools in every chapter.

Like the Interrupting Privilege program, *Racial Exhaustion* is grounded in interdisciplinary research with a critical race lens in the academic field of communication in partnership with education, social work, and more.[20] As emotion is central to this communication circuit, I draw particularly heavily on psychology. In fact I bring all of my training and experience to this book. After having studied intersectional race critique and after working and teaching the last two decades in a methodologically and theoretically diverse communication department, I have lived my way into becoming a race and communication scholar. I have immersed myself in other people's deep work on listening, dialoguing, discomfort, microaggressions, and community building. And I had to learn what communication scholars Robin Means Coleman and Jennifer Reyes note

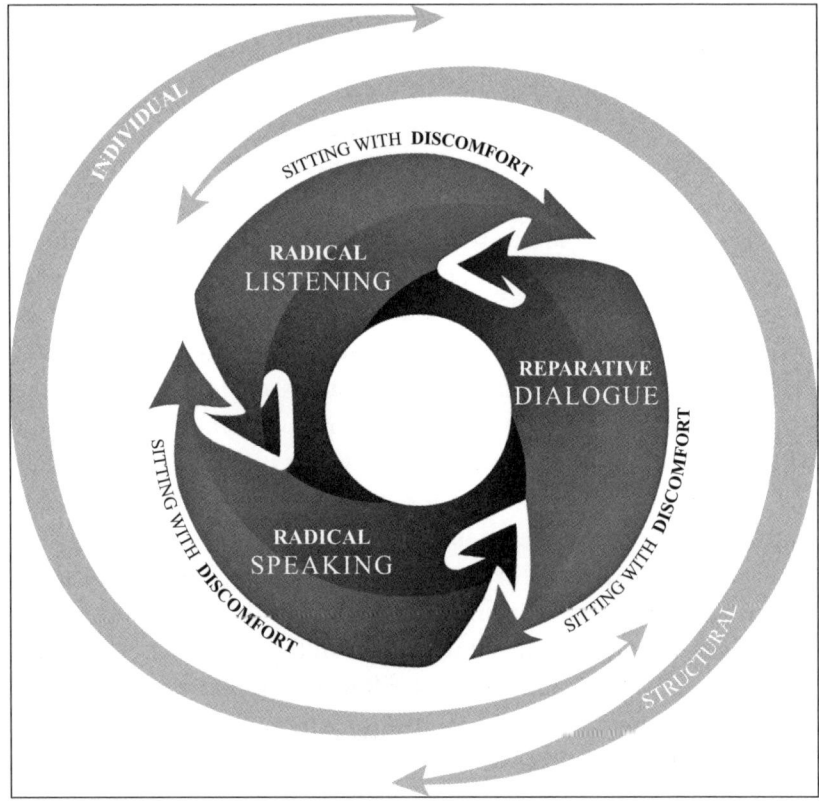

Figure I.1. Circuit of critically communicating race

are the strategies essential to navigate everyday racism in workplaces—namely, "skills and competencies in intergroup dialogue, bystander intervention, and allyship."[21]

Racial Exhaustion will help you develop these skills and competencies yourself, taking you through the four steps of the critical communication of race circuit:[22] *radical listening*, or hearing stories of racial exhaustion; *sitting with discomfort*, or attending to the emotions that arise from racial exhaustion; *radical speaking*, speaking forthrightly about racial exhaustion; in order to engage in *reparative dialoguing* and create true change in a community. This is illustrated in figure I.1, where the arrows demonstrate how these separate dynamics connect into a continuous circuit and how discomfort occurs at every step. One can begin at any place on the circuit and move through the different communicative moments in any order. In addition the graphic shows another key element of the circuit: individual change foments the work of structural change and vice versa.

The chapters in this book follow this circuit. To preview how it unfolds, let's return to Jordan's story. When he spoke in front of his all-school assembly, he exemplified the critical communication of race steps that structure this book.[23] As in Chapter 1, "Radical Listening," Jordan experienced both sharing deeply and being truly heard by his peers, which enabled him to identify when people were not listening to him and other Black students. People of color need spaces to share these stories, and white people need to practice the skills to fully hear them in the ways in which the speakers want to be heard, which is not necessarily in the ways in which the listeners desire to hear.[24] In this chapter I explore multiple modes of listening before moving to define radical listening as critical listening with an ear toward power. Radical listeners must work hardest to hear the stories that push against systems of power but have been ignored and silenced.

Despite being shut down multiple times because of others' distress (his classmates', teachers', administrators'), Jordan persevered, past his own and others' discomfort. Chapter 2, "Sitting with Discomfort," illustrates how those interrupting—or being confronted with—their own privilege must enact strategies to stay in the work. For most of us, the ability to do this work isn't innate—it's something we must learn and practice. So our work starts with the understanding that the discomfort can be a positive sign that the speaker or listener is confronting biases and learning from this confrontation. Psychologist Jennifer Eberhardt calls it "friction."[25] We will learn how to lean into *pedagogies of discomfort* in order to increase *distress tolerance*.[26] This chapter will also discuss the ways in which mindfulness and self-compassion, especially as articulated by meditation teacher and race scholar Ruth King, can combat racialized stress, including the stress of racial exhaustion. Notably, discomfort circulates through all of the other chapters as each step isn't possible without experiencing and managing some distress.

Jordan emphasized that non-Black members of the school community should participate in supportive dialogue with Black students. Chapter 3, "Radical Speaking to Interrupt Microaggressions," posits that people must practice radical speaking about race and its intersections. People of color and white people need supportive spaces to share their difficult-to-tell, often unasked-for, and sometimes previously untold race stories in free and unguarded ways. Radical listening opens the opportunity for radical speaking in order to interrupt the everyday forms of discrimination enacted through microaggressions, what microaggressions guru and psychologist Derald Wing Sue defines as "the everyday slights and indignities, insults, put-downs and invalidations that people of color—when we talk about racial microaggressions—experience in their day-to-day interactions with oftentimes well-intentioned individuals who are unaware that they have engaged in a demeaning or offensive manner towards the individual."[27] This chapter stresses that minoritized people, especially those who must daily combat microaggressions, have the option to resist everyday discrimination, whether by responding in the moment or later, calling on an ally to speak for them, creating official documentation of the offense, or simply walking away. This chapter also aims to help allies think about when to speak up, when to let the person who's experiencing the microaggression speak for themselves, and when to create a change that doesn't burden the minoritized person. In this chapter I'll also address some myths surrounding microaggressions, such as why the "micro" in "microaggressions" doesn't mean small and why, as Derald Wing Sue notes, as "almost any marginalized group in our nation can be the object of microaggressions," the term applies to the experiences of minoritized people alone.

The book arcs toward the final chapter on "Reparative Dialoguing." Jordan ended his assembly speech by saying that listening and talking are not enough; the school must engage in reciprocal, changemaking dialogue with the Black students who bravely share the harm they experienced. Reparative dialogue must happen with and for Black students in order to create a more just community. Change happens in individual ways, but these individual moments of changemaking-through-dialogue resonate more widely and impact structures of privilege. The location of this discussion at the end of the book is not accidental: people must learn how to listen differently and speak differently—and combat their discomfort with race stories differently—before springing into dialogic action. Reparative dialoguing is the collaborative moment of changemaking in which radical listening meets radical speaking. Here is where we can see the cumulative effects of the circuit. Radical listening, sitting with discomfort, and radical speaking provide the opportunity for those whose identities confer outsized power to consider the disproportionate amount of discursive space they might take up, and then, in the next step of reparative dialoguing, choose to build community through truly reciprocal, changemaking conversations.

DEFINING TERMS: INTERRUPTING AND PRIVILEGE

Jordan's actions demonstrate that *to interrupt privilege* means to resist coded, casual, explained-away everyday inequalities.[28] Broken down further, to interrupt is to "interfere with action or speech," "break . . . the continuity or uniformity of (. . . a process)," "stop (a person) in the midst of doing or saying something," or "cause a . . . discontinuance."[29] The action verbs "interfering," "breaking," "stopping," and "discontinuing" denote explicit, dramatic motion; they connote urgency and a cleavage from socially acceptable flows of communication. If the sender-receiver model of communication theory tells us that communication is a "transmission or exchange of information between senders and receivers through certain channels, and subject to noise and feedback loops, with the functional purpose of achieving some sort of instrumental goal or outcome," then interruption operates as a breaking of the loops, an increase in noise that drowns out the original.[30] Further, such broken loops and increased noise are not heard or understood equally: as Stuart Hall notes in his classic "Encoding, Decoding" model of communication, our positions in relation to power dictate the ways in which we hear a message such as an interruption.[31] More on interrupting in Chapter 4.

Like "interrupting," "privilege" is a far-from-neutral term that also illuminates how individual experience maps onto structures, institutions, and histories. Using this word enables one to name inequality in order to eliminate it. Spotlighting privilege, not simply discrimination, illuminates how systems of power—not individuals' work habits or cultural conventions or genetics—create and sustain inequality. In other words, focusing on privilege helps uncover the how and why of racism, and not just the what.[32] For those who hold privilege, the word can feel emotion-laden; the intonation "check your privilege" can activate emotions ranging from the offensive—irritation, denial, shame—to the defensive—resignation, pride, embarrassment. For those who hold the race privilege of whiteness, the going-on-the-offensive emotions of irritation, denial, and shame might present privilege as an excuse, an unfair way to concentrate too much on history (as the past should be left in the past—how many years ago was slavery?), too much on identity (as individuals shouldn't be weighed down by perceived privilege—how can you assume my whiteness plays any role in my life?), and not enough on individuals pulling themselves up by their bootstraps (just work harder). Widespread—and misguided—protests about critical race theory in schools emerge from these urges.[33]

Lamentations about privilege are in fact a hallmark of one kind of white racial exhaustion, and they echo with the defensiveness of resignation, pride, and embarrassment. These emotions might sound like the disingenuous question, "What can I do about the privileges that I have?" They might sound like the ahistorical claim that "I—and I alone—worked hard for all that I have—I'm proud of what I have meritoriously earned." Or perhaps they might sound like the whispered shrug of "What's the point of me admitting that my great-great grandparents were slaveowners, my grandparents bought their home in a redlined area, and that I am now inheriting their racialized wealth?"

Expressions of white privilege are, as Ruth King writes, "the privilege of not knowing or caring."[34] Even the coupling of "white" and "privilege" "turns off white individuals or makes them angry. While some white people can relate to being white, many have difficulty relating to the term *privilege* because it has not been their 'individual' experience. Whites would say that their success is the result of hard work."[35] Such protests illustrate what race commentator Jay Smooth describes as the urge for white people called on their racism to defensively cry out, "Are you saying that I am a racist? How can you? I am a good person! Why would you say that I am a racist?" These emotions, Smooth continues, turn "what started out as a what-you-said conversation . . . into a what-you-are conversation, and what-I-am conversation which is a dead end that produces nothing except mutual frustration, and you never wind up seeing eye-to-eye and finding any common ground."[36]

Separated from emotion, privilege is "immunity or benefit enjoyed by a particular person or a restricted group of people beyond the advantages of most"; "the unearned and mostly unacknowledged societal advantage that a restricted group of people has over another"; "a special right [or] advantage."[37] Privilege, in other words, is a power relation.

When I provide these definitions in Interrupting Privilege sessions, most participants nod along: yes, privilege has benefits, yes, it is unearned, and yes, it confers a special right. But inevitably participants will pause and push back on the word "immunity." In response, I tell the story of learning to drive in Washington, DC, where cars with diplomatic plates abound. My driver's ed instructor intoned to my class of teen drivers that we needed to give those special-plated cars wide berth; they had "diplomatic immunity." Were we to get into an accident, we would be responsible for any damage caused to their cars, while a bubble of diplomatic immunity protected them from experiencing the same penalties.

I shared this dictionary definition with one group of K-8 parents at an evening session of Interrupting Privilege arranged for a PTSA that consisted of mostly white women. Janet, a white woman in the audience gasped out loud about ten minutes in. As we were many slides past the topic of her gasp, she asked me to go back and please put my definition of "privilege" back on the screen. Janet smiled, emphatically saying, "Special! I always tell my [white] daughter that she is *the most special* girl, the *most unique* person in the *whole wide world*." She looked at the dictionary definition on the screen in the front of the room, paused, and asked me, "Does that have anything to do with whiteness?" I instinctively nodded yes. (I probably did that way too quickly; I should have bumped it back to her with a "tell me what you think," but her response was so unguarded and genuine that I matched her in openness.) I jumped to a yes not because whiteness is synonymous with specialness or uniqueness, but rather because I had experienced white parents creating such equivalencies with unselfconscious praising; Black and brown parents just didn't seem to do this. Janet made this connection as well, and described how the language she used to praise her daughter was laden with privilege, and racialized privilege in our culture amounts to white privilege. The PTSA that evening was grappling with the privileges of their whiteness: how whiteness in their school community, their households, and their neighborhood remained, like Janet's words to her daughter, unnamed, while celebrated. Their privilege was guarded by insulating and isolating their community from racialized and class difference. Their privilege was unearned while conferring the greatest advantages to members of their community.

Driving home from that evening session, I pondered the way in which the white mothers—who had invited me in to provide an Interrupting Privilege workshop as a part of their new commitment to becoming more anti-racist—described parenting their white children. Their bolstering of privilege through unselfconsciously praising their children stood in marked contrast to so many of the other Black and brown mothers of similarly aged children I know (myself included). Now this isn't to say that my Black and brown mother friends don't support and love and even slather their children with compliments. But it felt different—I suspected because of racial exhaustion—and the work of psychologist Joy DuGruy helped name it for me.

DuGruy describes the difference in Black versus white mothering practices as ones based in critique versus celebration of the child. She notes, for example, that while "the Black mother . . . standing in line at the bank . . . chastises her daughter for leaving her side, . . . a white mother lets her own daughter explore to her heart's content." Likewise, compare a white mother propping her child up as "the most unique" with the way a "Black mother . . . denigrates her high-achieving son in front of a white female friend, saying he drives her so crazy, 'I could just strangle him.'"[38] DuGruy links such public denigration to what she calls Post Traumatic Slave Syndrome, where the threat of a child being snatched away was always imminent. The freedom of a white parent to uncritically praise a white child ignores the context of racialized danger, and the very real need of Black and Brown parents to keep our children safe. It also ignores the Black mother's racialized exhaustion that emerges from living in fear.

Beyond the definition of "privilege" and Janet's illustration of the ways in which the "the most special" aspect of the definition resonates with racialized parenting, my favorite reading of "privilege" comes from Janelle, a fifty-something Black woman tech worker from the Seattle area and an Interrupting Privilege participant from an all-tech-workers session. She participated in an Interrupting Privilege session that involved a recorded online dialogue with her sister Michele, an elementary school teacher on the East Coast. The sisters spent an hour talking about the racially exhausting ways in which a lack of privilege infiltrated their work lives. They experienced violations of their physical space, where they endured colleagues touching their hair without invitation, and observations about their physicality, where they grimaced through comments such as, "I've never met a Black woman with freckles." Such interpersonal violations are not just irritating, but consistent with the myriad ways in which individuals devalue Black women through, for example, lower salaries.[39] Toward the end of the session, as they talked about larger structural iterations of privilege, including police violence, Michele incisively defined privilege as that which "wipes away restraint." Those who don't face consequences have the luxury of being careless, impulsive, and thoughtless, but at the same time, their interpersonal expressions of privilege are not one-off irritants for those whom they mistreat. They foment structural inequality and erode Black women's well-being. Janelle agreed, sighing that such a lack of restraint means that privilege will disappear "not in four years, not in four hundred years."[40]

Those who have privilege may not recognize that they do. The author David Foster Wallace was getting at something like this when he advised new graduates that they need to be the fish who see the water,[41] a metaphor Robin DiAngelo explicitly uses to illustrate privilege. Sociologist Michael Simmel describes privilege as running with the wind at your back, so that "you do not feel how it pushes you along; you feel only the effortlessness of your movements. . . . Only when you turn around and face that wind do you realize its strength." It is, Kimmel writes, both "ubiquitous and invisible."[42] Whiteness studies scholar Peggy McIntosh's canonic essay on the invisible knapsack illuminates not just a wide variety of often unnamed privileges (from buying band aids that match one's skin tone, to reading books at school that reflect one's culture), but argues that one needs to examine the contents of the knapsack—make them visible—in order to confront privilege.[43]

At the same time, making privilege visible does not alone create greater equity. Some might feel helpless when they realize that individual, unconnected action cannot systemically combat privilege. Some are just fine with having privilege over others; it makes them happy about winning. White racial exhaustion emerges not simply when white people process that their racialized identity provides unearned benefits, and when they realize that they must deal with their guilt, or anxiety, or embarrassment in order to make a change. And casting off white racial exhaustion could let people use their privilege for good. After the PTSA session Janet told me that moving through her own racial exhaustion involved first seeing her privilege, then acknowledging her very personal and mundane manner of conferring unmerited power to a child. Once she saw through this, she was able to act. After our session she told me that she was going to work to make change by joining the volunteer search committee to vocally advocate for teachers of color, as she was deeply influenced by the research I shared with her group that teachers of color are vital for the success of all students and especially students of color.[44] Janet also changed the morning PTSA committee meeting times to accommodate those without flexible morning schedules and led an effort of direct outreach to families of color to welcome them to the PTSA. That school year the search committee hired their first administrator of color, and the PTSA committees included more families of color than ever before.

CREATING INTERRUPTING PRIVILEGE TO COMBAT RACIAL EXHAUSTION

Kalia, Jordan, Davarius, Michele, Janelle, and Janet are six of the hundreds of participants who have experienced the Interrupting Privilege project, which was launched at the University of Washington, Seattle's Center for Communication, Difference and Equity in the fall of 2016. At that time, we started bringing together interracial, intergenerational groups of people to practice learning about, listening to, and talking about race, racism, and its intersections. Our listening and talking was goal-oriented: we collaboratively and collectively conspired about how to fight everyday racism in our everyday lives. The participants ranged from high school students such as Jordan and Kalia—student leaders who signed up for the project after hearing about it through a Black student-support organization at their high school—through undergraduate and graduate students such as Davarius—who took classes with me and in the process sharpened their racial dialogue facilitation skills. Our community members first came from the UW's alumni association and quickly grew to include non-university-affiliated participants from all over the greater Seattle region—like Janelle—and beyond, through Zoom—as with Janelle's sister, Michele.

The project has expanded to profession-specific groups including librarians, K-12 teachers, Special Education administrators, attorneys, and

Figure I.2. Interracial meeting of Interrupting Privilege. Photo by Gina Aaftaab

corporate folks of all ilk, including (as Seattle is home to several tech companies) many tech workers. My team and I conduct both inter- and intra-racial versions of the program (see figures I.2 and I.3) with our Seattle-based Black-community versions run in collaboration with Seattle's Northwest African American Museum (NAAM). Their members have included police officers, hairdressers, social workers, college professors, philanthropists, deacons, artists, librarians, alongside high school, undergraduate, and graduate students. Interrupting Privilege has grown in theory, practice, and method: students' deep and honest engagement with race and its intersections continually shifts and re-shifts the direction of the program. The life experiences of many elders, including their having lived through the better part of a century as racially minoritized people in the United States, further grounds the work.

From its inception this program did not take the form of a traditional class, neither in composition nor curriculum, in that it takes place both inside and outside of the university, with many versions being a hybrid of the two. In the first class of Interrupting Privilege, launched in September of 2016, twenty-five undergraduate and graduate students joined with an equal number of community members. About 70 percent of students were people of color (POC), with about half of the POC group identifying

Figure I.3. Intra-racial meeting at Seattle's Northwest African American Museum. Photo by Ralina Joseph

as Black. Black experiences were split between what, at the time, some students were calling "legacy Black," also known as American Descendants of Slavery or ADOS,[45] and the children of African immigrants, primarily from Somalia, Eritrea, and Ethiopia. The rest of the students of color were Asian American, Native Hawaiian, Pacific Islander, and Latine, with a handful having Native American and Southwest Asian and North African (SWANA) backgrounds. Reflective of the region and Generation Z, a good number of the students were also mixed-race. Of the white students, the majority identified as LGBTQ+. In other words, the student group was heavily minoritized. Our youngest undergraduates were eighteen-year-old first-year students, and the oldest graduate students were in their early forties.

The alumni group had opposite racial numbers, with straight white participants in the majority, and fewer Black, Latine, Asian American, Native Hawaiian, Pacific Islander, SWANA, Native American, and LGBTQ+ alumni. While we had alums as young as thirty, the majority were Baby Boomers. In that fall of 2016, we dove into our first month of programming together and prepared ourselves for what we were convinced was the inevitable change in the Democratic guard from Obama to Hilary Clinton.

Some of our members experienced great excitement, predicting gleefully what the Clinton presidency had to offer—a Democratic build on Obama—changed in particularly interesting ways with the promise of the first (white) female presidency. Other more pessimistic folks—further to the Left—steeled themselves for their fears over what Clinton's presidency portended, particularly in the realm of race. Not one member of our group believed that Trump would win. No one expressed an alternate political view in the group, much less support or enthusiasm over the Republican nominee. Subsequently, no one was prepared for the results of November 8, 2016.

The morning after the election I was scheduled to give a lecture for a (majority white) women's philanthropic group at Seattle's Town Hall. It had been billed as a day of celebration of our first female U.S. president. I, in typical fashion, had planned on bringing the doom and gloom by providing a lecture I had tested out the week before in the seminar, "Structural-to-Interpersonal Iterations of Interrupting Privilege." I was planning a rumination on white-perpetrated race-silence, everyday racism, and the connections between interpersonal inaction and structural and institutional stasis. In advance of the day, I worried my talk would be poorly received in the room of mostly white women who would be celebrating the victory of their sister president. It turned out that being called on their privilege was just what these Democratic women philanthropists wanted when the results came out. Like many progressive cities, Seattle, 87 percent of whose residents voted for Clinton and 8 percent for Trump (the percentages were more lopsided only in Detroit and Washington, DC[46]) went into mass mourning after the 2016 presidential election. People wore black. Sobbed openly. Screamed out, "Not my president!" Tacked up countdown clocks proclaiming, "days out of office." The women that day loudly lamented their silence-around-politics with their families, which resulted in 47 percent of white women voting for Trump, compared to white women voting 45 percent for Clinton.[47] Looking out at the audience, filled with lots of tears, I felt as if, for once, they saw that race was *their* issue and not simply that of people of color. Returning to the seminar, I feared that our group would similarly be frozen with grief.

Amazingly, our Interrupting Privilege group remained a space of hope. Amid nationwide (and yes, primarily coastal, but because of increased population on the coasts) teeth-gnashing and chest-beating, Interrupting

Privilege participants recalibrated. Harold, a retired African American senior business exec, husband, father, and grandfather in his seventies chuckled to the group—but especially to our students—during just about every session that fall, "I've seen this before, I'll see this again. We are going to be ok." We took on Harold's words on as a mantra. Our space remained one of steadiness, optimism, and pragmatism. We had work to do, and the work started with listening to and speaking about race across generations, race, class, and gender. Because of the change in regime, our goals were clearer, and our stakes were higher. Our race talking and listening was not the end goal: we had to work to create change interpersonally, structurally, and not in some imagined hypothetical, someday-to-be deployed way. Such change had to happen within our communities, within our very personal spheres of influence, and it had to happen right now.

For four years—from 2016 to 2020—we grew this program in various physical spaces—in the university, in corporations, in K-12 education. The inside-the-university iterations of Interrupting Privilege changed themes from year to year, from simply "Interrupting Privilege" to "The First Time You Remember Experiencing Discrimination," "Generation Mixed Goes to School,"[48] and "Black Seattle." As our minoritized participants requested affinity exercises, or grouping around the same identity as spaces to combat their own racial exhaustion, we launched additional intra-racial versions of the program. Until March of 2020 we met exclusively in person in locations such as NAAM, all over a vast university campus, and in Seattle's downtown public library. In every room we arrived early to move desks and chairs around so that each person could see faces, and no one faced a back. We alternated our small group "turn and talks" with listening exercises and lecture content. As we often met at an after-work time convenient for our community members, we provided *bánh mì* and easy-peel mandarins. Participants munched and learned, passed along tissues and dabbed away tears, laughed together and exchanged raised eyebrows with kindred spirits at the absurdity or resonance of another participant's comment. People hugged often—in greeting, in support, in farewell.

Then, in the late winter of 2020 our group at the time—an intra-racial one of Black community members, high school, and college students including Kalia, Davarius, and Jordan–had to cancel a meeting at NAAM when we heard news of a new transmissible virus. Two weeks, we approximated, then we'd be back together. Two weeks became a month, and we soon realized that we couldn't keep canceling our program in the beginning of not just COVID-19 but what the news began calling the "dual pandemics."[49] Reckoning with the disproportional impact of COVID-19 on historically underserved communities fundamentally changed the ways in which our groups interacted with each other. And we needed to talk about that. So Interrupting Privilege, like much of the world, moved online. We were online together when George Floyd was murdered. We were online together when Jacob Blake was paralyzed. We were online together when Breonna Taylor was ambushed. We met to cry and curse and strategize. To learn about local protests and discuss national efforts for change. And fundamentally, to move through the circuit of critically communicating race to combat our own rapidly increasing racial exhaustion.

And as we met together, the world around us—corporate, retail, governmental, nonprofit, educational, healthcare, media, and otherwise— began translating activism and protests like ours into calls for organizational change in the name of what was beginning to be popularly called "DEI." High-profile calls in all of these industries rang out for Diversity (demographic change, and specifically the ushering in of racially minoritized bodies), Equity (the understanding that not all people have the same needs and that minoritized people need different and appropriate resources and opportunities), and Inclusion (changing organizational culture to welcome minoritized people). In the DEI era, organizations scrambled to create racial justice missions and vision statements; to hire more and publicize the existence of their current BIPOC employees, especially executives; and to consider their own pasts. This time was marked by the splashy and often highly publicized creation of executive positions.[50] Public proclamations and one-off training sessions were hallmarks of the height of DEI.

Representationally, the DEI era featured an explosion of BIPOC imagery in mainstream media, the greenlighting of POC-helmed media creations, and the growth of academic positions addressing race across disciplines. Visual culture scholar Rizvana Bradley describes DEI-era representational change as surface-level—and often maddening— moments of inclusion such as a new Netflix BLM genre alongside the very vehicles of racialized violence, "police cars . . . adorned with historic

Black political leaders and Pan-Africanist colors for Black History Month."[51] Because high-profile companies and high-profile individuals publicly decried racism and vowed to embrace DEI, media labeled the moment as one of "racial reckoning."[52] For some, this was a corrective era, a time to right historical wrongs; for others, it was a time to feign this urge. Those like me, who had been instigating for institutional changes in racial equity long before 2020, met the DEI era with a paradoxical mix of incredulity that the public proclamations would lead to actual changemaking, and a feeling of hope that change was finally happening. In other words, our racial exhaustion both ebbed and flowed as we knew that symbols and representations only matter if they are accompanied by structural and institutional change. Nurse Sheena S. Williams asked what many of us thought: "Are [DEI] actions for optics, or are we really taking a deep dive into change?"[53]

Exhaustion reigned in a variety of fields and areas. Williams put it this way: "I am exhausted from having to do so much more than others to be perceived as half as good. I am exhausted from having to educate my oppressor with regards to implicit bias and why their actions are offensive."[54] Racism did not end with the rise of DEI. It translated to the continued exhaustion of holding white emotions. White liberals who felt distress about their new knowledge of racial inequality imposed that distress onto their Black colleagues. Kimberly D. Manning, a professor of medicine, describes receiving, via text from colleagues (not friends), "paragraphs of questions, reflections, and personal thoughts . . . about ways to navigate doing better after all that they had been missing from their position of privilege."[55] People of color became racism priests and gurus, the sacred beings specially ordained to guide America out of its original sin through a melanin-based specialized knowledge and imagined ability to host racism confessions and absolve America of racial sins.

A swift and fierce backlash stopped true changemaking. Just six months into the public launch of DEI, on January 6, 2021, white supremacists stormed the U.S. Capitol, toting Confederate flags and hurling racial slurs.[56] The racist backlash continued apace at schoolboard meetings where parents agitated against curricula that aimed to tell the real story of American history. Florida Governor Ron DeSantis signed a bill known as the "Stop WOKE Act" to prevent public universities from, in its wording, funding DEI.⁵⁷ In addition to outlawing colleges from providing general education classes that "are based on theories that systemic racism, sexism, oppression or privilege are inherent in the institutions of the United States and were created to maintain social, political, or economic inequities," the bill specifies that colleges cannot "advocate for diversity, equity, and inclusion, or promote or engage in political or social activism." In its prohibition of critically educating students about race, the bill worked to shield white people from emotions, including white racial exhaustion: Stop Woke prevented schools or workplaces from providing curriculum or training that calls attention to "personal responsibility" of whites who must be shielded from "feel[ing] guilt, anguish, or other forms of psychological distress." White people, especially white students, needed protection from negative emotions. Further, the word "woke," once the linguistic purview of Black activists, was coopted by whites wanting to signify as allies, and demonized by those experiencing white racial exhaustion.⁵⁸ These were the very conditions that presaged re-election of Trump in 2024, and the complete and utter drowning of DEI that left all of us in its wake.

APPROACH

At the heart of *Racial Exhaustion* lies the very secret of how to swim through the wake of DEI: dialogues about race. In the Interrupting Privilege program, in order to keep our conversations from "float[ing . . .] away, seem[. . .] more entropic, and far more difficult to pin down,"⁵⁹ we began recording our dialogues in 2017 and created a publicly available archive in 2021. The possibilities of digital archives seem endless. They let white people confront white racial exhaustion by learning about race without requiring racially minoritized participants to retell racially traumatizing stories; by the same token, also they head off POC racial exhaustion by freeing minoritized participants from having to endlessly, and in potentially unsupported ways, share their stories over and over again. Those experiencing similar forms of everyday racism don't have to constantly re-narrate their experiences to prove the existence of racism; they can simply share a link and invite someone to listen. In community, we play a clip and simply ask participants, "What did you hear?" In Chapter 3 I go into the specifics of the community engaged, participatory

Interrupting Privilege methodology we began practicing in 2016 and have honed with every iteration of the program.

A caveat: *Racial Exhaustion* is not something to be picked up in lieu of or even as part of DEI training. We now know that such training sessions don't create anti-racist change.[60] While they exhort participants to create such change, they fail to provide all the tools necessary so participants can safely jump off the edge of discomfort into a new reality. The approach itself is often flawed: trainers might lecture at folks, sometimes shame them, even shock them. Then, they leave. Instead of walking with participants towards the precipice of change, the unidirectional bullhorn of such a training session can cause people to either retreat from the edge or stumble into the abyss without a support harness—or a buddy to save them from plummeting. Stumbling can happen when vulnerability is exposed and a passion to change is ignited, but no adequate tools to create sustained changemaking are in place. One-off trainings shock participants, then leave them without guidance to process their emotions and translate them into action; many participants back away and recede into themselves.

What works instead is what structures this book: the sustained practice of learning how to practice critical communication of race skills. A practice (as noun) or to practice (as verb) is not a one off, a check box; it's a constant development of skills building, strength, resilience, and stamina. This book illuminates the practice that happens within Interrupting Privilege sessions—and through the critical communication of race scholarship—in order to illustrate a way to move through racial exhaustion in real life.

This book's approach unabashedly and unapologetically validates and amplifies the stories of racially *minoritized* people, the intersectional term that I use to denote smallness of power but not size of groups (often also deemed historically underrepresented or historically underserved), while striving to illustrate the vital role that white allies can play. Power stratifies our world through difference: our interpersonal experiences of race, gender, sexuality, ability, and class reflect the structural, historical, and institutional ways in which we live our identities. Difference, or broadly, a "deviation from an assumed norm," helps us to "re-think ... communication with equity central."[61] We don't all speak and hear equally. And power is invisible: those with power must work harder to recognize power differentials, and then even harder to create the type of change that will uproot power.

Reflecting the Interrupting Privilege archive, most of the stories I draw on feature Black and white participants. And to be clear, the focus of this book is on *racial* exhaustion. While wholeheartedly acknowledging the constructedness of race, I home in on race because of the ways in which this fiction structures our life chances and choices. Indeed, as anthropologist John L. Jackson Jr. writes about "the slippery links" between Blacks and Jews, "Race [i]s one of the modern world's fundamental constitutive elements, inextricably central to future understandings of how biopolitical, nanopolitical, and necropolitical strategies constrain the hopes and dreams of national citizenries."[62] Further, I am inspired by the words of Ruth King in her book on race and mindfulness: "To give this book the focus and shape it needs," she writes, "I have had to isolate race, carving it out from the gestalt of social oppression, all of which are worthy of attention and care. Racism, however, is the ism that I feel is the most insidious and the most enmeshed with our sense of social normalcy—and insanity. It's been discussed the longest, yet has not penetrated the global heart in ways that uproot its poisons."[63] Because of this centrality of race, racial exhaustion is not the same across racialized identities: the ways in which Black folks, non-Black people of color, or white people *can* and perhaps *should* critically communicate about race looks very different across our various spheres of influence—a phrase the Interrupting Privilege program uses to talk about the ripple-out effect of individual action.[64] And race is essential for all of us to communicate. "All of us" includes white people because white people have a race.[65]

This book responds to Jordan's and Kalia's stories of having to fight anti-Black racism alone, especially when—even at their young ages—they are used to white people denying the reality of their experiences. Thus, *Racial Exhaustion* offers a way for white people to practice race talk, a way to combat uncomfortable white silence around race. It's an invitation for white people—including, in the high schoolers' words, white *friends*—to listen and respond differently to their Black friends' stories of racism, and not, as Kalia notes, dismiss their accounts with a flip "I don't really see it." It's an intervention for white people to not just "feel" for or have "sympathy" for, in the words of Jordan, those experiencing racism. It's an invitation for them to fight their white racial exhaustion by choosing, also in

Jordan's words, to "stand up" or "help" or "assist" or "guide." Interrupting privilege necessitates action that is guided by open and honest race talk.

But *Racial Exhaustion* isn't just for white folks. It's for people of color who want to figure out when we want and need to say something and interrupt, and when we want and need to preserve our energy and choose silence. Jada, a Black woman social work graduate student in her twenties, put it this way in an Interrupting Privilege dialogue: "I've always had a fight and a need to speak up for things like injustices or just even ignorance and that's why . . . I . . . speak up." This "fight" is something that lives inside Jada. However, the fight gets more urgent for her, and she says she feels "most empowered when I know that [*long pause*] . . . when I think about whose life is on the line." Jada notes, connecting interpersonal racism and police violence, "I have to address [racism] because . . . people's lives are on the line, mothers are dying, sons aren't coming home. This is not a trend. This is an epidemic. This is . . . a genocide." But Jada also notes that the urgency of experiencing, addressing, and combatting everyday racism is, at times, unbearable: "I think the fact of the matter is that as a Black or Brown person it's draining. It's emotionally draining to walk in our shoes every day." Because of this exhaustion, sometimes she needs to not respond, to rather "sit back and marinate on it because it's hard."[66] *Racial Exhaustion: How to Move through Racism in the Wake of DEI* will help all folks think through when (and why and how) to interrupt privilege and when (and why and how) to rest.

1

RADICAL LISTENING

In the year and a half following George Floyd's murder, my inbox overflowed with requests from organizations—overwhelmingly corporate—asking me to come in and address the questions about racialized violence that their workers were now asking. One of these happened about six months into the pandemic, in the autumn of 2020, when I gave a talk to a multinational tech company on understanding race in the United States. This was a broad intro talk that covered everything from the history of the term race itself (*rasse*, France, 1512) to the racist theories of polygenesis (that different races had separate origins, and thus different races must be different species) through the codification of racial categories in the U.S. Census (racial categories created for political means).[1] The talk was scheduled for synchronous, online sessions that would occur early morning U.S. Pacific Coast time so that mid-morning U.S. East Coasters, afternoon people in Europe, and late evening folks from Asia could join; the online audience was around two hundred people.

Immediately the audience was engaged—asking me questions, making comments, blowing up the chat. I feed off that type of energy so I was happily toggling between my scripted materials and answering live questions, riffing, talking about history, the events of the moment and new scholarship—mine and others'—that could help provide the group with the answers they were seeking. It was one of those magic "on" moments. The moderator of the event had set the online meeting platform's participant settings to open, meaning that individual participants could unmute themselves at any point in the session. Nevertheless, they were instructed to either raise their digital hands or post questions on the system's question-and-answer function. The moderator would then let me know who was next in the queue and call on them. We had a nice rhythm going.

Then, in the middle of this magic, as I was mid-sentence, I heard an audience member talking, a regular occurrence for sure. I paused, reflexively saying, "Someone's mic is on, please mute," before registering the content. Then I heard a high-pitched voice filled with incredulity trilling, "Do you really think she got into Brown on her own? On her own?" A second voice interjected, "I don't know but—" At this point, all of four seconds had passed, but that flash of a moment felt like four minutes to me. I was briefly stunned into silence as my moderator jumped in and repeated, "Hot mic, you've got a hot mic. Please mute yourself!" I was stunned—shocked into silence—as I realized that the person had, indeed, been talking about me. Although my undergraduate degree isn't a part of my intro bio, I know it's easily discoverable online. I grasped—what felt like very slowly—that I was the one under suspicion for not getting into my alma mater "on my own." I suspect the "on my own" wasn't a comment stemming from assumptions that I received a boost from the largest "push" factor in college admissions, legacy status (which, in admissions data from 2017, demonstrated a thirty-one-point boost for the children of alumni[2]), but from another more unquantifiable but clearly discomfort-causing factor, affirmative action based on skin color.

I had been laboring under the illusion that everyone on the other side of the computer was rapt in the conversation . . . or at least not harboring the type of animus—I quickly assumed was racial—that dictated disbelief at my academic credentials. Instead, at least two people (working at home together? roommates? partners?) were distracted not by their email or their laundry or their pet or their homeschooling child but by the apparent contradiction between my academic pedigree and my skin color. These two audience members told me in that moment that they were not engaged in my lesson on race, its origins, and the history of racial categorization. They could hear me only through the audio filters—racialized cotton balls in their ears—of their own biases. I later shared this story with one of my best friends and collaborators, a Black, straight cis woman, diversity practitioner, and Ivy League grad. She said that what she heard in the story was fear. "They're scared of you," she said. "They're scared that you might be smarter than them." And maybe that's true.

Certainly, that's what a sista-friend is for—to lift you up when racism smacks you down. I find that remaining mired in the mud of racialized rejection can feel easy because of its familiarity. It's that bruise you keep pressing, the barely healed scab you keep picking. This is, for me, the process of giving in to racial exhaustion. However, hearing a friend affirm my feelings prompted me to rise up, hear, and hold her affirmation. With her voice in my ear, I could hear those two people's fear, but also their distress at my providing them with some real truths about race. These truths are so uncomfortable that listeners need to immediately pull their focus away from the topic of race, reject diving into the work of anti-racist education, and cast aspersions on anything else, including the credentials of the person sharing said truths. Such a pull-away allows the listener to debunk all the content without listening to a word. Those listeners (who never identified themselves, much less by race) were experiencing their own racial exhaustion in refusing to hear how race operates.

I began to understand a lesson: *The easiest way to refuse to listen is to keep talking.*

Ironically, I chose to enact that truism in that very moment. I refused to hear the echoes of that hot mic. It felt impossible to instantaneously process a personal moment of racial animus in a public forum. I had neither the magic words nor the surety of my emotions. So I stopped listening because of my own racial exhaustion, refusing to acknowledge my feelings of vulnerability (at least while on the virtual stage). Later, as I thought through what happened, I also imagined a different outcome in which I reframed the interaction by calling attention to racial exhaustion: mine, activated in this moment, and the listeners', expressed in their prejudice. I considered what it would have felt like to acknowledge that moment instead of wishing it away. I could have paused, taken a breath, maybe allowed myself to tear up and embrace my vulnerability in that space. I could have garnered strength from the audience while shining a light on prejudice. I could have experienced a moment of pride for calling this moment out, instead of dwelling on the embarrassment I felt for being targeted. I could have called the two speakers into conversation, to ask them simply, "Please explain." I could have set the table for a respectful, engaged conversation that could prime the speakers to be vulnerable enough to admit or name their prejudice, and I could have been vulnerable enough to express my hurt. But without foregrounding a circuit of critically communicating race, I fundamentally questioned whether *listening* to experiences of racial hurt change a listener's limited, defensive, solipsistic, or even downright racist views. Could all parties have laid down their racial exhaustion?

So I stopped Monday morning quarterbacking this event to see what I should have done and started thinking about what I would do next time. Before I could bring audiences to any "intro to race" content, I first needed to teach the critical communication of race skills. And the first step of critically communicating race is radically listening. Radical listening combats both POC racial exhaustion (feeling tired of not being heard) and white racial exhaustion (feeling tired of having to listen). Radical listening steers people away from listening selfishly or selectively; radical listeners do not listen to rehearse or create an argument, or perhaps, even a response. Radical listening starts with the listener tuning in to the speaker with careful attention, an open heart and mind. Listeners give speakers the respect of not interrupting them and of providing nonverbal affirmations such as encouraging head nods. Radical listeners work to hear the speaker in the ways in which they want to share. In radical listening, people listen with what communication scholar Stella Ting-Toomey describes in terms of the Chinese word *ting*, or "attending delicately with our ears, eyes, and a focused heart . . . to the sounds, tones, gestures, movements, nonverbal nuances, pauses, silences, and identity meanings in a given intercultural situation."[3] Listening with *ting*, social work scholar Michael Spencer adds, means that you give the person you're listening to the respect you'd give to royalty.[4]

Radical listening also means attending to power, to difference, and to race. In working to hear racialized power differentials, a radical listener strives to understand a speaker's truth, without assuming the speaker is representative of all "their people," and, in the process, the listener busts their own assumptions of who the speaker's people might be. Radical listening tunes into hearing people differently, deeply, and with an ear toward power. To hear power, one must listen for when a speaker slows down or speeds up, overenunciates or mumbles, becomes quieter or louder, reiterates or omits a word. Radical listening means hearing silence and working to understand why people are or are not speaking. It's listening to the interweaving of personal story with history, structures, and institutions of power even when those connections haunt the space, but do not emerge in a narration. It's listening to race. Radical listening is hearing speakers' retold, reclaimed counter-histories—those histories that investigate incorrect or silenced stories.[5]

Radical listening can bring speakers to the moment of openly sharing their racial exhaustion and listeners to points of being able to hear racial exhaustion, sometimes for the first time. One example of such a first time happened between an Interrupting Privilege student, Jackson, and his seventy-something white female dialogue partner, Sue. The year he participated in Interrupting Privilege, Jackson was also doing research for his senior honors thesis, interviewing fellow football players about how university instructors treated Black male student athletes, like him, in the classroom. He was an affable young man whose long experience in this PWI (Predominantly White Institution) aided him in creating a series of strategies for his daily dose of microaggressions. I witnessed him, for example, skillfully dodging the white women's hands—of all ages—who attempted to caress his six-foot-five frame.

One evening, Jackson arrived at our Interrupting Privilege gathering visibly upset and asked to speak with me outside. He told me that Sue, with whom he had been partnered the previous week for two hours of dialoguing, had just met him at the door with a disapproving look and asked, "Do you go to school here?" Not only was Jackson upset that he was once again not being recognized as a student, but that he was not being recognized by someone he thought had been radically listening to him. I asked him what he wanted to do: head home and make up the work later, go back into class and ignore the comment, or make another attempt to have Sue radically listen to him. Jackson chose the third option.

Our classroom warm-up exercise involved participants sharing a mundane story of living race that week for an uninterrupted two minutes with a partner. In one pair a white female student reflected on the privilege of arriving late to class without worrying that the instructor would stereotype all white girls as time-challenged, while a Pacific Islander community member described having a perpetually open bus seat next to him even on the most crowded North Seattle busses; he perceived that white Seattleites didn't feel safe sitting next to him. Jackson, paired again with Sue, spent his speaking time slowly narrating what she said to him before class and how he felt disappointed and dismayed to be unrecognized as a student in a space where he had allowed himself to be so vulnerable. As instructed, Sue enacted radical listening, not responding verbally; but she flushed bright red in what Jackson told me he thought was a combination of embarrassment and guilt. After class, Jackson, relieved, described to me some of his racial exhaustion ebbing away because he felt fully heard, and Sue, chagrined, whispered to me that she needed to double down on her work to dismantle her own white racial exhaustion, which had prevented her from fully seeing and hearing Jackson. She told me that she was "too embarrassed" to apologize to Jackson, but that she would work up to it, which she did at the next gathering. Today, almost a decade later, Jackson's career in fitness—catering to Black professionals—incorporates radical listening to race and racism stories in training sessions, while Sue holds listening at the center to attend to multifaceted questions of the power that she holds as a philanthropist. This regenerative moment of growth exemplifies what moving through racial exhaustion can proffer for all of us for individual change and structural reverberations.

This is not to say that radical listening is easy. One of the biggest challenges is not rehearsing a response while listening. For Sue, this might have been quieting her urge to jump into fix-it mode (I can't wait to share my solution. When is he going to stop talking so I can fix this problem?), or what-about-me mode (Now how long do I have to wait before I share my story?), or incredulity mode (Did that really happen? Why do people like this always claim an offense?), or disagreement and defensiveness mode (I don't agree with their reading of the situation at all. When can I tell this kid that I am the opposite of a racist?). Instead of listening to respond, radical listeners listen to understand. In a radical listener's internal dialogue, "fix it mode" might become "It's not my job to fix the problem. Just listen." "What about me" mode turns into, "Focus on Jackson's words. It's about him, not me." Incredulity mode becomes, "Believe this young Black man." And disagreement or defensiveness mode might sound like, "This is hard to hear, but I know that I've been wrong before, and I need to listen to hear that possibility." Indeed, radical listening is the essential baseline for all the other practices addressing racial exhaustion, the first tool in our critical communication of race toolbox.

At the same time, the concept of radical listening itself builds on and with many other more "neutral" forms of listening. The field of listening is currently experiencing an explosion: listening scholars have named 289 different styles of listening.[6] Listening research, which now flourishes in disciplines as far flung as communication, linguistics, psychology, anthropology, political science, and management, dates to post–World War II studies on classroom listening and university students' comprehension in classrooms.[7] This work rings with optimism, the belief that human connection itself can be enriched by better listening.[8] Such scholarship describes listening as a neutral endeavor in which individuals are "listen[ing] from a space of emptiness and unknowing."[9] After discussing this important scholarship, as well as the ways in which listening has made its way into popular discourses, this chapter reviews critical listening scholarship, which posits that to hear race and other forms of power, such "emptiness" is impossible: we carry our identities into every encounter. This journey through listening will bring us to radical listening, or listening with and across difference to hear race with the respect connoted by *ting*. Wedding together the connection-based elements of "neutral" listening with the power-conscious elements of critical and radical listening provides all of us with the first step to help us move through our racial exhaustion. The chapter closes with a story of radical listening literally saving a life.

(TALKING ABOUT) "LISTENING" IS ALL THE RAGE: THE LIMITS OF INSTITUTIONAL LISTENING

Over the past two decades "listening" has become a hot topic in popular as well as scholarly worlds, with institutions both listening to individuals and providing guidance for individuals listening to each other. "Listening tours, listening sessions, and town hall meetings are commonplace at all levels of government, from local parent-teacher organizations to state and federal political operations," organizational communication scholar Laurie Lewis notes.[10] As constituents, we have come to expect the institutions in which we participate to create some sort of official mechanism to listen. In these institutional spaces, listening sessions might mimic the older form of the public forum, where citizens air their grievances with hopes of creating new solutions in addition to critiquing old approaches. But attending to the emotions—the exhaustion people express about fraught issues, including racially fraught ones—isn't a part of the standard structure of institutional listening sessions.

And just as institutional listening struggles with holding emotions, it also struggles with holding power differentials. Various large nonprofits such as the American Association of Retired Professionals (AARP) and

National Public Radio (NPR) provide free online toolkits to aid their constituencies in listening, but without offering any insight into the ways in which listening is governed by power. For example, while NPR's "Six Ways to Run a Listening Session" states that listening sessions should enable workplace leadership to "get constructive feedback and share best practices," they also note the importance of short sessions. And yet, truly listening needs time. Further, while a facilitator should be attuned to "moments at which a participant might get defensive or feel attacked," the connection to very real dynamics of power and privilege are not stated as a concern.[11]

In addition to not supporting emotions and failing to see power, institutional listening also fails to provide accountability in listening, or creating a mechanism to solve the problems addressed. Part of this inability to provide accountability emerges through institutional listening feigning listening. The format for listening forums is often for leaders to take in information and not respond, a process that in public policymaking is called inviting "public comment." Constituents hope that leaders will incorporate the listening session feedback when addressing problems and crafting solutions. And yet this hope is not often realized. Some who have attended listening sessions say that they feel as though it is a checkmark for leadership, a pretense that constituent concerns have been taken into consideration. In the business realm, too, listening tours can similarly function as a strictly controlled feedback mechanism, where, in the words of Lewis, businesses leaders put "on a public show" to "merely listen in respectful tones." This is a "'check the box' of listening and consideration," in which to "manage the appearance of listening, leaders are advised to make eye contact, paraphrase what has been said, express empathy and understanding . . . , ask questions to demonstrate interest . . . [and] avoid . . . the appearance of distraction."[12] In other words, sometimes listening signals no more than a performance.

For example, in February 2018 President Trump held what the White House branded a "listening session" for Parkland High School students after the mass shooting at their Florida high school. While he largely (and uncharacteristically) remained silent, *appearing* to listen, critics noted two things: first that his response after listening was to promote the arming of teachers, something the students categorically did not endorse

Figure 1.1. Trump holding a cheat sheet on listening

(you might remember warrior Emma Gonzalez's echoing response, "We call B.S.!," to such an idea) and second that he was caught with a crib sheet whose last point was a note for him to say, "I hear you" (figure 1.1).[13] As his policy ignored the wishes of those most impacted by gun violence, his listening session was a sham, and the cheat sheet a bitter reminder that he lacks even the most basic empathy. He could not even pretend to listen without being prompted.[14]

FROM HEARING TO ACTIVE AND ATTENTIVE LISTENING: NEUTRAL (POWER-EVASIVE) LISTENING

Scholarly theories of radical listening help make sense of such a brazen refusal to listen (in the midst of performing listening) by illuminating how power can prevent true listening. But to make our way there—and fully understand how radical listening combats racial exhaustion—we first need to understand the process of neutral (or power-evasive) listening, beginning with understanding the difference between listening and hearing. While all the forms of listening I discuss in this section evade attention to power, they start to bring in elements that are a part of radical listening: agency, attunement, and attention to body language.

Hearing is an involuntary physiological process; listening is a voluntary emotional, intellectual, and sometimes spiritual one. Hearing is the passive process of taking in sound,[15] while listening involves turning sound into meaning, what the International Listening Association describes as "the process of receiving, constructing meaning from, and responding to, spoken and or nonverbal messages."[16] And there are so many ways to listen. This includes discriminative listening, or ascertaining what sound (and sight) is coming from where, comprehensive listening, or discerning meaning from that sound (and sight),[17] and, appreciative listening, or simply "listening to enjoy."[18] Listening does not happen in a vacuum but, as Lewis describes, is "part of an active social process of knitting together meaning with others."[19] And yet, in the process of turning sensory input into meaning, many of us create incomplete or incorrect meanings because we don't listen fully.[20] Listening fully, as fields as diverse as psychology, medicine, education, social work, and journalism,[21] assert, comes about through "active listening."

Active listening means filtering out other noise—both around us and in our brains—by focusing on the person speaking, and not simply decoding the meaning being conveyed. Psychologists Carl R. Rogers and Richard E. Farson coined the phrase in their 1957 book of the same title as a supportive therapeutic technique in which a listener must work to hear both meaning and emotion, to "actively tr[y] to grasp the facts and the feelings in what he hears." Rogers and Farson describe active listening as a keen "responsibility" whereby listeners must "help the speaker work out his own problems."[22] They assert that active listening is counter to a lawyerly urge to listen for "contradictions, irrelevancies, errors, and weaknesses." While all active listeners might not (and probably should not) embody the stance of a therapist, what connects active listening to radical listening is Rogers and Farson's emphasis that listeners should not passively let language wash over them but instead tune into both the information and the emotions shared. This definition of active listening begins to take us toward action-oriented listening in radical listening.[23]

In a connected vein, active listening does not necessarily mean silent listening. As a listener you might need to paraphrase, ask clarifying questions, validate someone as they're narrating an experience, perhaps verbally and nonverbally (i.e., through a co-sign or a head nod). But your moments of paraphrase, questioning, or narration should never intrude on the speaker's story. In other words, active listening is connected to but distinctly separate from dialogue, which we'll delve into in Chapter 4. Active listening also means allowing a speaker to complete their full thought, perhaps with accompanying verbal co-signs (which can be culturally specific). The classic nonverbal communication studies by psychologist Albert Mehrabian have echoed around the world as the "7-38-55" mantra, which refers to the finding that only 7 percent of what a listener takes in is verbal messages, while 38 percent is tone of voice and 55 percent is body language.[24] Although these famous studies were shown to be flawed, our bodies speak just as our words do.[25]

Because we strive to hear power through radical listening, I caution against romanticizing active listening as some sort of pure entryway into another's consciousness; following a check list of active listening steps doesn't ensure that one is thoughtfully taking in another person's words, much less that one is hearing power imbalances or abuses. Further, active listening alone is not, in the words of listening scholars Penny O'Donnell, Justine Lloyd, and Tanja Dreher, "a benevolent gift, a cure and even a cure-all." O'Donnell and colleagues are skeptical of a "romance of listening," in which "talk of listening regularly seems to find itself rooted in naïve faith that listening is a good in itself."[26] Listening for power addresses this pitfall.

LISTENING FOR POWER

What active listening doesn't explicitly consider is difference and power. Considering such elements means that active listening accompanies a culturally inflected head nod or verbal co-sign to show that you are taking in a speaker's words and feelings. It's not interjecting or dissenting; it is attempting not to judge.[27] Further, while active listening, for many, means making eye contact, a marker of "seeing and being seen,"[28] eye contact might not feel possible for all. For example, in Interrupting Privilege workshops, Black and Brown men have shared they are cognizant of racialized and gendered stereotypes misconstruing them as physically or sexually aggressive, and they consciously limit their prolonged eye contact accordingly. Moreover, in some cultures it's considered rude to make eye contact, while some religions hold that women should avoid eye contact with men.[29] In addition, some individuals' challenges with holding eye contact are a marker of autism.[30] Further, when listening scholar Elizabeth Parks assessed her research participants on the importance of eye contact, they were split on their comfort level with both giving and receiving eye contact, particularly the prolonged kind. Some of these participants interpreted lack of eye contact as rude and not listening, and others considered prolonged eye contact as too intensely intimate.[31]

Culturally inflected expectations around eye contact can also dictate how, and in how much detail, a speaker speaks. In cultures where eye contact is expected, a listener's lack of eye contact (and other gestures of preoccupation) can cause a speaker to "slow down, stumble, and leave out more than they ordinarily would."[32] In contrast, an audience's listening attentively helps speakers to better remember what they've shared. Truly active listening that considers difference and power also facilitates attunement, or attentive connection, which communication scholar Elizabeth Molina-Markham writes is "listening together," which is similar to the Quaker decision-making process of tuning in to the inner light, as Laura Helper puts it.[33] Likewise, Poppy de Souza and Tanja Dreher describe attunement as "a practice that comes before decision-making, setting the conditions for listening together that are simultaneously responsive and responsible."[34] And in another vein, Sara Ahmed describes attunement as a form of emotional labor marked by "openness to what is around us."[35]

Connected to attunement is what Stella Ting-Toomey deems mindful listening, or "listening attentively with all our senses" to help us "notic[e] and check . . . responsively for the accuracy of our meaning decoding process on multiple identity and contextual levels." Mindful listening "involves a fundamental shift of perspective . . . [from] not only how things look from my identity perspective, [to] how they look and feel from the other's identity framing perspective."[36] To identify how our identities frame listening we must develop what Lisbeth Lipari describes as insight into how we are "shaped by our social conditioning and our places and relations in the social world." Lipari describes this listening orientation as a "listening habitus," which dictates "whether we ignore or notice a sound, whether we find it pleasing or jarring, or whether we welcome silence or find it uncomfortable."[37] Our listening habitus thus emerges from our identities and cultures.

Listening for power is a move away from the romance of listening and a move toward the radical listening that helped Jordan and Sue address their racial exhaustion.[38] Three themes in the critical listening scholarship will become key aspects of radical listening: listening for silenced voices, listening to dissolve hierarchies, and listening without othering. The theme of listening for silenced voices emerges from the simple therapeutic notion that we must listen differently to hear silence, articulated most extensively by psychologist Carol Gilligan and her colleagues' feminist, "voice centered" 1980s-era Listening Guide (LG).[39] Accordingly, researchers must be attuned to their own auditory filters, which they analyze to assess their own listening biases.[40] Researchers must also work to hear "contrapuntal voices," the moments of discordance instead of coherence. While gender is a central analytical lens for Gilligan and those who follow the LG, it falls short of providing the most fitting theoretical model for Jordan and Sue because it does not take into account race and other identity categories outside of gender.

Rhetorical theorist Krista Ratcliffe moves further toward the model of radical listening when she uses the phrase "rhetorical listening" to highlight the fundamental step to make power "more audible ... and then perhaps more visible" to both listeners and speakers in a classroom space. Rhetorical listening is "listening to discourses not *for* intent but *with* intent"[41] to dismantle power by explicitly putting power on the table. Just as Gilligan encouraged LG listeners to engage in their own self-reflexivity, rhetorical listeners utilize self-reflexivity to identify what they want to receive from the listening encounter. Rhetorical listening, Ratcliffe writes, "may be employed to hear people's intersecting identifications with gender and race (including whiteness)."[42]

"The Listening Project" of critical media scholars pushes Radcliffe's emphasis on "difference and inequality" toward radical listening's moment of action through its aim to "dissolve entrenched hierarchies of listening and speaking."[43] Centering justice means that listening is never a neutral endeavor.[44] It also means that we must enter into listening with "openness, receptivity, attention, engagement, duration, continuation, and recognition."[45] But these qualities are not sufficient by themselves to dissolve hierarchies. For example, such critical listening would lead those undergoing white racial exhaustion to hear and experience "refusal [and] discomfort," in addition to "attunement and yielding."[46] In other words, listening to dismantle hierarchies demands disruption. And listening to dissolve hierarchies represents a change in critical media studies scholarship from a "politics of expression" (speakers) to a "politics of impression" (audiences).[47] This shift moves critical listening scholars toward the larger goal of unsettling stagnant structures of power by hearing underrepresented voices.[48] This work can be thought of as listening *without* othering.[49] This moves us toward radical listening.

By the same token, listening without a critical race lens can amount to listening by othering. In Interrupting Privilege sessions, I've witnessed a white listener overidentify with a speaker of color sharing a story of racial exhaustion, saying "I understand exactly what you mean. I've experienced the same." After listening to that white interlocutor tell a story that is very much *not* the same, the partner of color will then shut down, perhaps smiling politely, perhaps giving a blank look, or perhaps just shaking their head, no. That smile, blank look or head shake shows that they do not feel as though they have been radically listened to. Overly identifying listeners don't listen to their partners with malicious intent. In fact, that listener might be experiencing empathy (what we will explore in the next chapter as feeling *with* someone), but that empathy might well be contingent on imagining the speaker as a version of themselves (so feeling more deeply for themselves). When a speaker is on the downside of power and the listener is on the upside, a well-meaning "I can identify" can silence an already hard-to-tell story. To avoid the automatic process of othering the listener and reproducing power hierarchies, allied listeners must enter into a "contract of listening," says communication scholar Wendy Chun, one that opens our ears to a past and present that might well be ugly, violent, and painful.[50] As part of this contract, Chun notes, the listener "must constantly question" how they might be eliding, forcing, or feigning their identification with the speaker and thus potentially erasing the speaker's complex, intersectional identities.

Without inserting these questions during active listening—including during moments of "interpretation, appreciation, validation, disagreement, reformulating, or mirroring"—one risks abusing power; such practices, psychiatrist Janeta Tansey writes, are "invitations to mutuality and may distort or affect the other's unique momentum and trajectory."[51] Instead, listeners should "pull . . . back . . . the watchful gaze, the nonverbal cues of nodding and receptivity, the verbalizations of assent or mirroring or repeating." This gives speakers the space to iterate their full stories (but also ignores the cultural imperative of some to create such co-signs). Tansey proclaims that the most equitable forms of listening are "not for the sake of love, empathy, understanding, or mutuality," but "for the sake of humility, courage, justice, and metamorphosis."[52] The listener must abandon their own desires to hear coherence, identification, connection, or any number of listener-identified wants. Instead, holding the moments of difference is the very goal of listening.[53] The listener thus commits to both hearing power and creating change. Further, truly equitable listening calls for a conscientious holding of difference, what philosopher Megan Laverty describes as "a willingness to imagine others as independent centers of reality" instead of versions of ourselves. This kind of listening allows listeners to "simply dwell with the questions and the impossibility of solving them."[54]

We have arrived at radical listening, the first step in critically communicating race.

RADICAL LISTENING

Radical listening puts into practice the tenets of active listening—agency and attunement—plus the tenets of listening for power—listening for silenced voices, listening to dissolve hierarchies, and listening without othering. Radical listening also unapologetically centers listening with, to, and for difference, including racialized difference. In addition to these ideals, radical listening highlights the transformational, revolutionary possibilities that can emerge through this mode of taking in information. Radical listening provides a way for listeners to hear and speakers to iterate racial exhaustion.

"Radical" has at least three meanings in the context of radical listening. The first one, defined by Angela Davis, is simply "grasping things at the root."[55] Radical listening takes us to the very core, the foundation, the essence of listening. Second, "radical" homes in on the ways in which interpersonal interactions meet structural iterations of power in the listening encounter.[56] The third definition of "radical" centers on action, the type of revolutionary transformation that begins with listening.[57]

TO THE ROOT

The phrase "radical listening," which has been adopted by scholars and practitioners across disciplines as diverse as business and psychology, was coined by critical pedagogy scholar Joe Kinchole in 2009. Listening to the root formed his idea for radical listening, or "consciously valuing others by attempting to hear what the speaker is saying for the meaning he or she intends, rather than the meaning the listener interprets through his/her own view of the world."[58] The listener does not filter what is being said through what they want to hear, which takes insight, on the listener's part, into their own filters. The root of listening is thus consciously *not* superimposing one's one worldview onto the speaker; as Kinchloe's colleague Ken Tobin instructs, "Listen to what a speaker [is] saying without projecting [one's] own ideas and identity." By removing listening filters and not projecting one's thoughts and desires, radical listeners uplift, or "consciously value," the speaker—particularly the minoritized or too-little-listened-to speaker—by hearing them in their own terms.

Recall the earlier story of Jackson and Sue. In practice, Sue's listening—radically—means that she hears all of Jackson's story, including "the kernel of an idea" that provides her with the opportunity to "encourage the speaker to grow that idea in his or her own way." There is fundamental good will here, or as Tobin puts it, "a serious endeavor to explicate others' good ideas."[59] The first step of hearing "to the root" is simply slowing down to hear what a speaker intends as their meaning, not what you, the listener, desires; Sue hears Jackson's experience without shutting down because of her own guilt or shame. This slowing down invites in the process of what we will explore in the next chapter as a productive discomfort. Such deep listening can also ease the racial exhaustion of a speaker of color like Jackson, giving him time and agency to freely share his truth.

POWER AND DIFFERENCE

The second definition of "radical" in radical listening entails hearing power and difference. Radical listening, as Sue experienced, enables listeners to "gain . . . new perspectives . . . from a different locale in the social world of reality."[60] But humans are trained to hear sameness, which can shore up our understandings of our identity. Listening for difference, Kress notes, can "destabilize" one's sense of self and "leave us vulnerable." This vulnerability pushes us to "reframe so-called battle grounds as fields of listening and learning." [61] In the case of Sue and Jackson, the moment flips from Jackson's distress in experiencing a microaggression to Sue's vulnerability in hearing (and owning up to) this microaggression. Yet radical listening doesn't mean abandoning, in Winchell and colleagues' words, "our sense of self and our convictions." In other words, we hold each other's stories, but we don't become those stories. This holding moment enables "knowing [to be] forged in the spaces between the self and other."[62]

If you are the one who holds greater power, then you give the mic to those who are often silenced; you practice your own silence, and you use your privilege to take that mic from those who jealously guard it. In other words, if you are someone, like Sue, who takes up a lot of space because your identity confers unearned power, you must consciously try to listen. Power is situational and contextual. As an older white woman, Sue might experience sexism and ageism in various spaces, but in her before-class interactions with Jackson her privileged racialized identity clouded her vision and clogged her ears. In addition, radical listeners are patiently listening for silence, which isn't the absence of meaningful communication, but what Molina-Markham describes as "generative."[63] Silence, whether held intentionally in a listening dyad or as an entire group, brings listeners to listening differently, which is fundamental to moving toward different, more equitable action. In Quaker meetings, for example, Molina-Markham writes that "communal silence plays an active role in decision-making through a process understood to take precedence over its outcome.... Silences serve to prepare participants to take part in decision-making process, as participants wait and listen for guidance."[64] Silence frames the process of changemaking.

LISTENING TO CREATE CHANGE

As a strategy in the critical communication of race, radical listening builds toward collaborative changemaking. In the third definition of "radical," radical listening is listening for, in Tobin's words, "potential" and not "pitfalls and shortcomings"; radical listeners focus on "making sense and exploring possibilities." Radical listeners build together, though this does not mean that every idea or every positionality is championed. Fundamentally, "to undertake radical listening is to open the door to transformation, and to act in new ways of being, doing, and understanding." Radical listening is not bound to the here and now, but rather "is a praxis of celebration of the world that is yet to be."[65]

Radical listening enables us to hold difference, interrogate power, and create structures of change. This means that there is an action component to radical listening. The listener cannot remain content with accepting a story of inequity. However, any action must be in concert with the speaker's desires as the listener aids in this transformative process. The listener must ask permission for interventions if possible. In the case of Sue and Jackson, Sue's action item, which Jackson directed her toward, was two-fold: to take radical listening out of the classroom and radically listen in her everyday encounters with people of color and to work harder to acknowledge Black male student athletes as students first and foremost.

Radical listening is a step toward righting the wrongs of power inequalities through easing and combatting racial exhaustion. The Interrupting Privilege program's practice of radical listening instantiates this building by connecting groups of people together to listen not just as isolated individuals, but as connected collaborators.[66]

A RADICAL LISTENING SESSION IN ACTION

Radical listeners actively listen for agency and attunement; they tune in for power to dismantle hierarchies, hear silenced voices, and avoid othering; they hear *to the root* by putting aside their own preconceptions and desires and focusing all their attention and intentions on the speaker and their chosen words. In radical listening we allow our conversation partner to express themselves fully, without interruption. We push ourselves to completely absorb their words. To hear *difference and power*, we as radical listeners do not immediately process our own feelings; we acknowledge our discomfort but push past it to stay with the listener. Perhaps most challenging, and most rewarding of all, radical listening provides an opportunity for a form of *action and changemaking* that must emerge in concert with a conversation partner.

Radical listening is the first tenet of the Interrupting Privilege program. Part of our radical listening happens live in the space, as in the sharing exercise between Jackson and Sue, and some of it happens through hosting recorded dialogues. We audio record conversations between groups of two or occasionally three; from its beginnings as a part of Anjuli Brekke's dissertation research,[67] this project has been a voice-focused one. We showcase our participants speaking without visuals because of the ways in which isolating the aural can prompt greater focus, partly because featuring the visual more immediately stokes racialized assumptions. This is not to say that voice is not racialized—it most definitely is—but, for the most part, we make people work a little harder with just voice to make meaning of race. Almost all of the people who sign up to share their stories are people of color; those who volunteer to have their conversations recorded often jump at the opportunity to do so because they are accustomed to being quieted, ignored, or shut down. Our radical listening dialogues follow an array of community-based research principles, including having participants choose with whom and about what (within a broad frame) they want to dialogue.[68] When participants don't want to speak about their racial exhaustion with someone they know, we provide a partner. We offer a list of questions and topics as suggestions (generated by the research team), and the participants pick and choose which ones to cover, sometimes adding their own questions and topics as well (see the appendix).

The participants co-interview each other, with members of our research group inserting ourselves for the most part only if they ask us to do so (the exception being when we host dialogues with children and youth, in which case we more actively facilitate). After recording the dialogue, we share the transcript of the session with participants, instructing them to redact what they don't want included and highlight what they do. Our team then makes audio clips of the highlighted portions, which we play in further radical listening sessions of assembled groups ranging from ten individuals to hundreds, and we host the clips on our website for all types of folks interested in stories of experiencing and moving through racial exhaustion. Our first invitations for these live sessions are to the dialogue participants, who are asked (but not required) to speak to their clip and who often bring friends and family to the event. Radical listening

Figure 1.2. Radical listening session at the Soul Collective Salon. Screenshot of video courtesy of Victor Leak

sessions take place out in the community (a hair salon, a community center; see figure 1.2), at schools and universities (a gym, a lecture hall; see figure 1.3), or at various workplaces, and since COVID, often online. The radical listening sessions begin with a teaching section on how to be a radical listener, in which we prime participants with lessons on listening to the root, listening for difference and power, and listening to create change. We structure a listening environment that shakes listeners out of their usual distracted forms of listening. We, in Brekke's words, "remove listeners from habituated patterns of unreflexive and non-reflexive listening by encouraging them to engage in the rare activity of listening together to mediated sound."[69] We then play selected clips that have been pre-approved by participants, listening together—some with eyes closed, some taking notes, some staring off in the distance. We instruct participants to turn to each other and talk in small groups, answering the question, "What did you hear?" We then invite any of the recorded dialogue participants who are in attendance to share their thoughts or feelings before opening the room to general comments. Here we put our radical listening theories into practice by always uplifting minoritized voices. For example, when we hosted dialogues featuring children's voices, as in our Generation Mixed project that was focused on amplifying the voices of mixed-race kids ages 5–19, we reflected the reality that the children in our space are those on the downside of power: "Our rule was that any child or youth in the space could 'cut the line' and grab the mic. . . . Throughout

Figure 1.3. Radical listening session at the University of Washington. Photo courtesy of Gina Aaftaab

the session, the children and youth participants ruled the spaces, with even the youngest ones grabbing the mic to share their thoughts. The adults practiced their radical listening."[70]

Without question, radical listening is hard. Most listeners struggle to hear fully and openly in a way that enables other voices to ring out louder than their own, or what Brekke describes as "tuning in to multiple voices in relation to each other and in relation to the self." Sue, for example, had to acknowledge her own feelings of guilt but not let them distract her, and she had to recenter her full listening on Jackson. Listening in this intersubjective manner, Brekke says "is both labor intensive and risky; it requires vulnerability without offering guarantees of solidarity."[71] In radical listening, listening to a live story in a small group or a recorded one in a large crowd, can be both exhilarating and exhausting. It lays bare our own stakes and confronts us with our limitations in our collective work toward the liberatory practice of moving through racial exhaustion.

A particular difficulty in radically listening to people's stories of racial exhaustion is engaging with emotionally heavy issues, for example, those of racial trauma. For people of color, the "race-based stress" of racial trauma, as psychologists Lilian Comas-Diaz and colleagues write, communicates "threats of harm and injury, humiliating and shaming events, and witnessing harm to other POCI [people of color and Indigenous people] due to real or perceived racism."[72] Thus, bringing together dyads for Interrupting Privilege recorded dialogues requires great care and attention to not reactivate or exacerbate our participants' racial trauma. When we create the conditions for people who experience similar forms of minoritization to speak with each other, those participants can, as Brekke, anthropologist Gina Aaftaab, and I write, "be seen, heard, and fortified." But centering minoritized voices—asking Jackson, for example, how he wanted to proceed following Sue's microaggression, and then, when he wanted to speak, having him speak first—helps everyone. Then, "listening dyads create moments of reciprocal communication by allowing us to talk through the trauma of racism."[73]

Radical listening is a strategy for all who seek to critically communicate about race. However, it might not feel equally easy for all of us to undertake. My experience in leading radical listening exercises is that radical listening is a form of resilience that comes with everyday living as a minoritized person. So those who listen most deeply are also accustomed to experiencing vulnerability, are minoritized, experience having less power, and are accustomed to not being heard and feeling as though their words—in concert with their presence—are often unwelcome. It's easy for the disempowered to be quiet and disappear into another's story. Jackson, for example, came to our very first gathering already well-skilled at being a radical listener; his twenty years of life as a young Black man in predominantly white institutions taught him how to effectively utilize this skill. This strength in the face of erasure is part of the skill set I have elsewhere called "strategic ambiguity," or playing the long game of watching, listening, and learning about structures of power, and strategizing about when to intervene at a later moment.[74] But to right unequal power relations, being heard is even more important for those who disproportionately lack power.

Here is a story illustrating how radical listening can literally save lives—in this story, my husband's life.

RADICAL LISTENING TO SAVE LIVES

A failure to radically listen almost killed the love of my life. I am moving through my own racial exhaustion to tell this story. The attempted murder didn't come about through police violence or racist vigilantes trying to regulate his use of public space. Instead, it came at the hands of the very people who should be improving the quality of his life: his doctors.

My husband doesn't like to go to the doctor. His mantra when it comes to medicine is "They don't do anything." He says this because he has experienced a medical industry in which doctors and nurses don't spend the time necessary to see him, to listen to his pain, to diagnose his illnesses, and to constructively devise solutions. As decades of research now show,[75] medical interactions are "racially discordant" for patients like him, a six-foot-six Black man. His doctor's visits are characterized by medical personnel moving him out the door of the examination room as quickly as possible. Such racial discordance means that patients like my husband will have shorter, less informative, less patient-centered, and fewer relationship-building experiences in a doctor's office.[76] He is a former athlete who has many persistent and sometimes excruciating pains, but because of his alienating experiences with doctors, he chooses to deal with them alone. This is racial exhaustion. He just feels too tired to always fight it.

Seven years ago, however, his pain led him to the place he avoided most: the doctor's office. My golden-skinned man was starting to lose his color. His strong gait was becoming labored. His breath was slow. He wasn't himself. When he went to the doctor's, they quickly examined him, taking less than five minutes he estimates, and then sent him off with a diagnosis of seasonal allergies. Doubling up on over-the-counter allergy meds, he shook his head and soldiered on.

But he got sicker. Over the next weeks he struggled to walk across a room without holding onto furniture for support. His breath came out ragged. His skin had become grey. I was terrified, staying up at night listening to his breath, and despite his "they don't do anything" mantra, I successfully harassed him into returning to the doctor. This time he received a few more minutes of examination and a chest x-ray, but left feeling brushed off again. He came back with a diagnosis of walking pneumonia and prescription for steroids. He took his pills. And still he got sicker. And sicker. Looking into my then-forty-three-year-old husband's face, the man who had been my center for over half our lives, I thought he was going to die.

At that point he had been going to a branch of the large HMO his work subscribed to in the overwhelmingly white end of our city, near his work but not our house. He saw whatever (white) doctors were on the docket that day. Now we needed an immediate appointment. We found one at the care clinic on the far more Black and Brown end of town, just a couple of blocks from our house. This time my husband was not the only BIPOC person in the waiting room; Black and Brown office staff, nurses, caregivers, and other patients surrounded him.

A young, white, nine-month-pregnant resident saw him this time and knew that he wasn't well, that he didn't have pneumonia, and that the problem certainly wasn't allergies. She spent time with him, asking questions, taking tests, waiting for results, and ordering additional tests when she wasn't getting the answers she needed. In other words, she radically listened: she heard *to the root* of his problem from the very beginning of his sickness, she listened to the *difference* that my husband experiences in medical settings, she heard and refuted the *power* that hadn't heard his pain, and she worked to create a *change* in his life. When she let him go, it was with a promise to call as soon as the rest of the tests were in and with instructions for me to watch him closely.

Early the next morning my husband handed me the phone as her voice soothed, "Don't panic, but drive him directly to the ER." Pulmonary emboli (PE)—blood clots—straddled both of his lungs in a saddle formation. The condition had been developing for months, since before his first diagnosis of "allergies," since before he had "walking pneumonia." Why had the two previous doctors not seen the signs? They had not radically listened to my husband or indeed the racially discordant research: that Black people suffer from deep vein thrombosis, including PE, at rates 30–60 percent higher than whites.[77] Had the doctor who saved his life not taken the time to radically listen to him, to hear his distress, to confront the implicit bias that keeps so many other white caregivers from hearing Black people's pain, he wouldn't be here today with me.

Throughout his sickness the racism continued, during his hospital stay and in follow-up appointments. He recovered, but we came to understand that a PE diagnosis dictates a mortality rate twice as high for Black than for white patients.[78] And even though that one lifesaving doctor (who went into labor a handful of days after diagnosing my husband) was wonderful, he left that healthcare system so that he could choose his doctors outside of the HMO's roulette wheel. We are privileged that my job provides us with that choice.

When our white friends and family hear this story, I feel their pause: "Was it *really* racism that almost killed your husband?" they ask. After all, they point out, my husband is a K-12 educator who has worked in DEI; an Ivy league graduate with multiple degrees; a light-skinned, soft-spoken man who escapes into his fantasy books, cooks five-star meals, and revels in family game nights. In short, he isn't their stereotype of a Black man. How could he have received the same racism that paralyzed Jacob Blake, that killed George Floyd, that murdered Breonna Taylor? Implicit in their skepticism is that my husband couldn't have experienced such racism because he's done everything "right." And by this they mean he is "like them." But just as they refuse to listen to the racism he experienced, they deny the racism they express. This might not be the explicit kind (they swear they're not that kind of folks), but rather the implicit type. And the implicit kind kills people too. By denying it, they also reject their own role in perpetuating that racism.

I am a race practitioner and scholar of communication—my whole professional life is dedicated to the eradication of racial disparities through critically communicating race—yet I found myself unable to even pen a letter to the doctors who failed my husband. My husband and I were unable to document the very types of complaints I help others process, script, and register daily. What good would it do, we have told ourselves. Instead, we spend our days grateful that he is alive, unlike Eric Garner, who was murdered by the police who refused to radically listen as he cried out "I can't breathe"; unlike Andre Maurice Hill, who was murdered by the police who refused to identify their biases and killed him as he investigated a noise outside his garage; unlike Dr. Susan Moore, who was murdered by racist medical neglect as she cried out for doctors to radically listen to her as she was dying.

But more recently, I have found ways to express my gratitude for his life in telling my husband's story. My small spark of hope has been that by critically communicate race myself and by providing the skills to others of how to critically communicate race—beginning with radical listening— his story might just trigger transformations and help save lives.[79]

And I think that it just might have. I first shared this story in print with the local POC paper, intentionally placing it in a space where it would resonate the most with my community. After it circulated, I took a hard copy of the story, with a thank you card, to the doctor who saved my husband's life. She shared the story with the rest of the clinic staff. And—although I usually avoid social media—I shared the piece on Twitter and tagged the healthcare HMO. Within a day their DEI folks had reached out to me, and we met a couple of days later to talk about what had happened to my husband and what changes they could work to make. Forcing this institution to radically listen to my husband's story became one of the many push factors that got this HMO to create the changes over COVID to eradicate health disparities.[80]

Radical listening, as the first step in the critical communication of difference circuit, is also the first step in addressing and soothing racial exhaustion. And it demonstrates that individual action is necessary to move through racial exhaustion for structural change. Striving for change fuels the discomfort that is the topic of the next chapter.

2

SITTING WITH DISCOMFORT

Jean and Zoe, two white women attorneys in their thirties, reached out to me during the summer of 2020's "racial reckoning" to learn strategies for talking about race with their children. As Jean put it, she was concerned that in her household, "We were not racist but not antiracist and we need to start changing that conversation."[1] Zoe and Jean represented a small networking and mentorship group of mother attorneys—almost all white women—who were coming to a racial awakening and wanted to discover, in Zoe's words, "how to talk to my fellow white women [about race] without being a total jerk about it." As we brainstormed, I shared a collection of previously recorded Interrupting Privilege clips—including the one of Jordan, Kalia, and Davarius—to play for their community so that they could radically listen to them and engage in dialogue. But Jean and Zoe decided that instead of listening to strangers' stories, they wanted to record their own radical listening dialogues and then host a session in which they shared the recordings with their group.[2] This is how we came to host our first dialogue between two white people. Since the Interrupting Privilege program began recording dialogues, we have overwhelmingly showcased voices of color, with white voices featuring in conversation with partners, children, and best friends of color.

Jean and Zoe are colleagues, not close, but friendly, and aligned in the earnestness with which they approached their dialogue. When I presented them with consent forms, for example, Zoe proclaimed that having her voice featured in research on the critical communication of race is akin to, she said with an excited laugh, "donating my body to science." Their conversation circled around how they negotiate the uncomfortable topic of race with their spouses, parents, and children. Jean lamented that she and her husband "have not made a conscious effort" to talk about race. A "conscious effort" means, in an active and often uncomfortable way, working through white racial exhaustion to "stand up [to] what our kids hear," especially when they hear racism.

They acknowledged that their children were absorbing the messages around them—largely, in Jean's house, from the TV news in the background, but also including intimate conversations with loved ones. Jean and family often talk with her father on speakerphone, with her early elementary- and preschool- age children passively taking in the conversation but not participating. Jean recalls telling her dad that as in many U.S. workplaces, her work was closing in 2020 for the first time to commemorate Juneteenth (before it became a federal holiday in 2021). Over the Zoom dialogue with Zoe, she paused and sighed, "This is horrible to repeat for my poor dad," but, she continued, "he made a comment. . . . Don't they already have MLK [Day]?" Without letting the uncomfortable weight of this statement stand, Jean's words quickened, her voice rising in pitch: "I was like, 'they'! Don't 'they'? Dad, come on! We have every other holiday!" She adds, "It's very important to recognize [Juneteenth]. it's very important to talk to my kids about it, because prior to this year I'm not sure I understood it." Zoe nodded, adding that she had not even heard of Juneteenth prior to 2020. While I was witnessing their dialogue with my own camera off (as is our practice for our researchers during online dialogic interviews), I felt Jean's emotions—her frustration with her father; her embarrassment at sharing this story with a fellow white woman who also aspired to be anti-racist; her shame at having me and my then-graduate student Anjuli Brekke, race researchers and women of color, present; and fundamentally, her exhaustion at having to enter, again, into such moments of racial discomfort with someone she loves.

Jean continued, her voice strained, noting that "standing up" to her father was new because "I've always deferred to my dad. I'm always just like, ok dad, you're an adorable farm boy." She said that previously she thought, "Right, you're not going to change and that's how I've always took it is, he's not going to change." Zoe nodded along, listening radically, supportively emoting, and adding that she made concessions for her father's similarly biased comments because he's in his seventies and "not going to change now." But with Jean's own racial awakening, she realized that silently dismissing his biased views was insufficient: "Now I'm looking at it as he might not change, but I need my children to understand in a loving way Papa doesn't always have it right."

The conversation continued in this vein, with both Zoe and Jean stalwartly pushing themselves to stay in an uncomfortable conversation. During our planning sessions both Zoe and Jean had been eager to participate in the dialogue but given the exhausting reality of talking race for an hour—something they admitted they rarely did—they ended up pushing to end their session as quickly as possible. This thirty-five-minute conversation was the shortest I had facilitated up to that point (three years into recording interrupting privilege dialogues), and it remained the shortest for more than a year after; by comparison, other pairs of participants regularly continued their conversations well past the allotted hour mark.

In dialogic, self-directed interviews such as the ones we record for Interrupting Privilege, the participants draw from a list of questions that the organizers provide: they can choose from this list, add to it, or ignore it entirely in lieu of exploring the conversation they want, and they can go for however long they choose (you can see a sample list of questions in the appendix). Zoe and Jean's questions included ones such as, "How racially diverse is your immediate family? Extended family? Is race something you discuss with your family?" and "How diverse are your children's friend groups? How often do you host children of color at your house? How often do your children spend time at a friend of color's house?"[3] While choosing their questions, I noticed they brought up moments such as the one Jean shared—in which she remained the antiracist hero—but not moments where they got caught in their own racism and would risk their *own* vulnerability.

But moving through white racial exhaustion means leaning into vulnerability and uncomfortable emotions. And not just ones that are displaced onto others. In the next section we'll see what happened when I pushed Jean to do just that. While many people of color are well-practiced at negotiating racial discomfort (and so need to practice how to move through and release that discomfort), some white people like Jean need to practice staying with such discomfort to build up their stamina to continue to move through their white racial exhaustion. This chapter explores how to weather uncomfortable moments of critically communicating race to move through racial exhaustion, both for white people tired of being called on their—or their father's—racism and people of color tired of experiencing, explaining, and combatting racism. I frame discomfort through two different modes: the philosophy of engaging in a *pedagogy of discomfort* and the practice of providing skills of *distress tolerance.*⁴ These similar-sounding phrases differ in the mental and physical degrees of intensity they connote: discomfort is an uneasiness,⁵ while distress is pain or suffering.⁶ A pedagogy of discomfort provides a set of theories that enable us to glean lessons for both inside and outside the classroom. Distress tolerance is a set of tangible skills that enable us to practice this theory in real life.

As neither of these theoretical models explicitly discuss race, I layer lessons about mindfulness and compassion—two key strategies for managing discomfort and distress—alongside racial dialoguing, and this chapter mirrors that bridging. I learned these lessons through a partnership between Interrupting Privilege and the University of Washington's Resilience Lab which aims to build wellbeing at the UW and beyond. We called the project "Resistance through Resilience" to suggest both the struggle and the moments of working through struggle. The Resistance through Resilience group of faculty, staff, students, and community members held the advice of meditation teacher Ruth King as a beacon: while "racial distress is a real experience, . . . how we relate to racial distress is a habit."⁷ Keeping King's lessons in mind, this chapter draws on the models of a pedagogy of discomfort and distress tolerance to frame the differences between experiencing discomfort in confronting your own privilege (white racial exhaustion as in the example of Jean) and experiencing discomfort at experiencing discrimination itself (racial exhaustion of people of color [POC], which we'll explore in a moment). These are clearly not the same.

HEARING RACIAL EXHAUSTION OF WHITE PEOPLE AND PEOPLE OF COLOR

When white people "share that they have experienced racial trauma," King notes, they mean that "they feel shocked and frightened by the rage or other emotions expressed by POC."⁸ Because of the bubble that surrounds whiteness, white people are often not familiar with examining their racial assumptions and prejudices, and they find it exhausting. The discomfort of being called on your own expressions of racial discrimination comes about because of managing this racial exhaustion. Such management means regulating your emotions in order to not lash out or escape. It means feeling your guilt, your shame, your utter dismay, without taking it out on the person calling you out or shutting down completely. All this is the discomfort of being called into self-examination, and perhaps not liking what you see in the mirror. Here managing racial exhaustion also means using these very same emotions to change your own behaviors and to work to create change in your sphere of influence and beyond.

In stark contrast, POC racial exhaustion emerges from the sometimes painfully frequent discomfort of experiencing discrimination, the repeated emotional distress of not being treated as fully human. Fighting this distress raises not just the question of how to respond (as we will focus on in the last chapter on interrupting microaggressions), but also the question of how to honor your feelings without exacerbating your pain or not directing your pain inward. Further, while those who experience discomfort because of discrimination might be distressingly used to racial exhaustion, they do not have the luxury of turning it off, and the accumulated stress takes an incredible health toll.

Let's hear some of these differences between kinds of racial exhaustion. Even though Jean and Zoe avoided talking about their own vulnerabilities, they were noticeably uncomfortable, and, perhaps, necessarily so: sitting in discomfort is key to critically communicating race. Their discomfort grew past the dialogue itself. In preparation for the session with their full group of mother attorneys, I met for a third time with Jean and Zoe to discuss what clips we would share. At first Jean didn't want to play the clip of her father speaking as she was concerned that he would be demonized by her peers. We talked through her apprehension, and after I addressed Jean's fears of publicly labeling her father a racist, I set the table for what I hoped was a more nuanced conversation about not just her father's racial bias, but the (non-heroic) role that *she* played in the triangulated interaction of herself, her dad, and her kids and in her own narration of it during her dialogue with Zoe.

I asked Jean to focus in and listen radically to her own words, to fight her own exhaustion with her father, and shift her energy to look inward. We listened to the clip together again over Zoom. She first insisted that she didn't hear anything different, so I probed, "Did you notice that when you described your conversation about Juneteenth with your dad, you said, '*We* have every other holiday'? I'm wondering who the *we* is?" Jean turned red and stuttered a few times, exhibiting the rhetorical incoherence that sociologist Eduardo Bonilla-Silva describes as a hallmark of white people talking about race.⁹ It was immediately clear that she understood my question, and she responded slowly, "I guess I meant white people." Jean then paused, laughed with some chagrin and then, changing the tenor of our exchange, continued with an uplifted tone, "But of course! Duh! White people aren't the only ones who celebrate Halloween, Christmas, Memorial Day." I nodded and suggested that perhaps the clip that demonstrated how she confronted her father's prejudice should also be about confronting her own implicit biases—how they emerge in her everyday talk with her children, even, and perhaps especially, in the moments when she is working to critically communicate race—and how she confronts them. She agreed, and her modeling how to fight her own white racial exhaustion—with her father and me challenging her in different ways—enabled the session to proceed with honest and uncomfortable race talk.

Talking and listening in a way that interrogates power can be uncomfortable whether you are listener or speaker, or on the upside or downside of power.¹⁰ I give Zoe and Jean a lot of credit for choosing to participate in an Interrupting Privilege dialogue that directly raised and combatted their white racial exhaustion. In fact, they are outliers in their desire to volunteer for a forthright conversation about race. Developmental psychologist Brigitte Vittrup found that in talking (or refusing to talk) about race, only 30 percent of the 107 white American mothers in her study utilized what she calls a "color conscious approach," while 70 percent had a "color blind or color mute approach."¹¹ In their conversation, Jean and Zoe noted the prevalence of this colorblind/color mute tactic in their own growing up experience of avoiding conversations around race and how they were working to change this approach in favor of a more egalitarian and color-conscious one with their children.

Discomfort in racial dialogues is one of the hallmarks of white racial exhaustion. That exhaustion doesn't mean anyone is bad or lazy or irreversibly prejudiced. Rather, just as Jean reverted to an "us" that included only white (or perhaps non-Black) people in her imaginary of Americans celebrating holidays, our minds revert to biased thinking, particularly when we are stressed or in a hurry.¹² Moreover, uncomfortable topics—those that push against hearing a version of a story or iterating a point of view counter to ours—can prompt the listener or speaker to escape. Further, POC speakers' anxieties about listeners' discomfort also make it difficult for them to share their truths: speakers might battle anxiety or guilt over sharing a story they know others will have a hard time hearing. They might struggle with showing their vulnerability for fear of being judged. It also means that people of color understand the intimate connections between individual and structural inequalities and privileges. Wiradjuri scholar Robynne Quiggin asserts that dwelling in discomfort should be the norm for non-Indigenous people who seek to "ask themselves about the kind of benefit that they receive from the history and the present day."[13] This means that we must "live, at least momentarily, with painful or uncomfortable feelings that emerge when we understand that systems that have violated others have benefited us."[14]

The challenge for white racial exhaustion, as exemplified by Jean's defaulting to thinking about her father when pushed to examine herself, was to stay in the work—to, as I urged Jean, not just work to change others but first change ourselves. In contrast to the racial exhaustion white people experience, King writes that racial exhaustion (although she doesn't use that phrase) for people of color emerges from "individual and generational trauma—the unnerving vulnerabilities that follow us around like a shadow." This vulnerability, King notes, is "pointedly about race. Racism was and continues to be the injury on top of more commonly shared social sorrows." Further, the spaces for people of color to attend to this "social sorrow" are themselves constrained by emotions and, indeed, racism itself.[15]

In contrast to Jean and Zoe, Janelle and Michele, two Black sisters, had no problem talking race fluently throughout their Zoom dialogue. The discomfort they felt, instead, was that of racism. Janelle is a tech worker in her fifties, who, as I shared in the introduction, incisively named privilege as that which "wipes away restraint." She must perform restraint at the very moments when she is experiencing what King names "the injury" of racism, which for her includes her work colleagues

> pat[ting] me on the head or put[ting] their hands in my hair or ask[ing] me about my skin color and if I tan and are those moles or are they freckles or, you people do such and such a thing, don't you? Or, well, I knew that you couldn't really speak with that voice all the time, do you? That's not really who you are, is it?

Janelle chuckles a bit ruefully as she casually rattles off a laundry list of the everyday moments of racialized aggression that she experiences, what she identifies as "when people would say or do racist things or what we call microaggressions." These daily microaggressions are the same as what she has experienced for decades "twenty, thirty years ago . . . [when] people tended to make you feel grateful that you even had a job." As a younger woman she feared responding "because you were always afraid, oh my gosh, if I got angry, what if lose my job or if I say anything to HR, what if they retaliate?" Janelle knows that others' fear of Black women's anger will rebound in her direction. She notes that her discomfort emerges when she feels compelled to quiet her anger and mete out her response, "considering how it would be received." Black women automatically pay what her sister Michele refers to as the "Black tax," a demand to be superhuman—including never responding to racism with anger—in the workplace in order to survive.[16] In this dialogue we get a glimpse into older sister Michele's role in supporting her younger sister through her distress; Michele radically listens, affirms, and adds to Janelle's experiences.

Janelle no longer puts up with such behavior, noting that today she fights her discomfort with racism by speaking up for herself and "politely put[ting] those [racist] people in their place." Another way for Janelle to move through her own racial exhaustion from microaggressions is to mentor younger co-workers, telling them that "it's ok to talk with HR about those situations. It's ok to talk with your manager." However, Janelle is clear that being more direct and more senior in her career doesn't mean that the risk of being labeled an Angry Black Woman disappears. Thus, Janelle coaches a young Black woman at this tech company that while she should validate her feelings—"It's ok to be angry"—she should also understand that anger has disproportional consequences, which particularly impact Black women and require a different level of self-regulation, of learning how "to diffuse the situation."

PEDAGOGY OF DISCOMFORT FOR MOVING THROUGH RACIAL EXHAUSTION

Janelle has tolerated the discomfort of everyday racism for decades by daily practicing what Megan Boler calls a pedagogy of discomfort. But

Janelle practices it with a Black feminist twist. Boler's theory of sitting in discomfort in order to learn is aimed at white allies experiencing racial exhaustion, which is a useful formulation to further understand Jean and Zoe. But like so many communication theories, it forgets that minoritized people, including people of color, sometimes make moves that are similar to those made by white people, but in a way that reflects strikingly dissimilar power relations. Let's explore how the pedagogy of discomfort might work for both white people—in our example, Jean—and people of color—here, Janelle.

The pedagogy of discomfort is a pedagogy because Boler designed it for the classroom ("pedagogy" refers to teaching). Boler writes, "A pedagogy of discomfort begins by inviting educators and students to engage in critical inquiry regarding values and cherished beliefs and to examine constructed self-images in relation to how one has learned to perceive others. Within this culture of inquiry and flexibility, a central focus is to recognize how emotions define how and what one chooses to see, and conversely, not see."[17] A culture of inquiry enables students and teachers to "examine when visual 'habits' and emotional selectivity have become rigid and immune to flexibility; and to identify when and how our habits harm ourselves and others."[18] In her dialogue, Janelle demonstrated that she was keenly aware of how her discomfort looped her back into an exploration of her racialized and gendered beliefs and values—those of her colleagues granting her basic human dignity. The habit she sought to change was continuing silence in the face of racism. Such awareness of her discomfort provides Janelle with an opening up to move through her racial exhaustion and to create change for other young Black women at her work. In contrast, in her dialogue, Jean had more difficulty seeing her racialized beliefs and values. Without being directly presented with her own racial assumptions, she could only see her father's, but not her own, "habits and emotional selectivity."

Janelle exhibited what Boler deems "inquiry and flexibility" as she acknowledged the anti-Black women stereotypes that spring up in her everyday life and also govern her ability to respond to the stereotypes themselves—an intersectional animus that Moya Bailey coined misogynoir.[19] With my guidance, Jean also practiced inquiry and flexibility when sharing her (previously unconscious) orientations toward whiteness with her group of white women colleagues. Self-reflection does not dwell so long that it becomes "a form of solipsism, a kind of 'new age,' liberal naval-gazing."[20] Rather, a pedagogy of discomfort "requires that [the] individual ... step outside of their comfort zones"[21] by positioning themselves as a "witness," one who "undertakes our historical responsibilities and co-implications," instead of a "spectator," one who inhabits a "position of distance and separation."[22] As a witness to her own experiences of misogynoir, Janelle moved through her racial exhaustion by staying present in her discomfort, nurturing communication with her sister, naming "the Black tax" and mentoring young Black women at work. Jean moved through her own racial exhaustion by also staying present in her discomfort, nurturing vulnerable race-conscious conversations with her white colleagues and family, and pushing to recreate her peer-mentoring network by recruiting women of color.

For listeners of color and white listeners alike, moments of hearing stories such as Janelle's and Jean's provide an opportunity to practice moving through discomfort. Different elements of the Interrupting Privilege program practice this life skill through small and intimate sharing moments, such as the dialogue between Michele and Janelle and between Jean and Zoe, with researchers (in this case, Anjuli Brekke and I) present, or in large assemblies with a variety of participants listening in community. Both opportunities to work through discomfort are acts of "collective witnessing" in which we are "always understood in relation to others."[23]

In the Interrupting Privilege program, the first level of witnessing happens with dialogue partners and facilitators, and the second level occurs when the dialogues circulate beyond the initial participants. Witnessing grounds larger listening and learning sessions, and witnesses maintain a responsibility to the dialoguers' stories. Witnessing means eschewing passive empathy, or benignly "feeling sorry" for those experiencing suffering or pain, and instead allowing ourselves to be uncomfortably changed in such a way that we can be a part of the changemaking that resists and reconstructs structures of power.

On an individual level, a pedagogy of discomfort "may lead to a greater sense of connection, a fuller sense of meaning, and in the end a greater sense of 'comfort' with who we have 'chosen' to be and how we act in our lives."[24] This comfort is what emerged for Janelle and Michele in the moment of sharing microaggressions and witnessing each other's racial exhaustion. The sisters demonstrated how to create a dialogic space that combats racial exhaustion.

On a structural level, illustrating the discomfort that Janelle names provides opportunities for larger institutions (like her large tech company, which assembled in groups of hundreds to listen to her clip) to hear and sit with the discomfort of misogynoir. What this produced, in one of the solutions the company named, was an augmented "sponsorship"—not just "mentorship"—program to bolster the executive pipelines of Black, Latine, and Native American employees. Whereas mentorship is the "relationship between someone sharing knowledge and providing guidance (the mentor) and someone learning from that person's experience and example (the mentee)," sponsorship is when "the mentor can become an actual advocate for the mentee."[25] Paradoxically, then, a pedagogy of discomfort is a way of gaining comfort in the very face of discomfort. This is particularly true for those who are minoritized, those who will benefit the most from sponsorship because their race, gender, and other identity markers do not match up with those in power.

As we build the critical communication of difference toolkit, understanding the distinction between white and POC experiences of discomfort is key. And when scholars around the world apply a pedagogy of discomfort to analyses of everything from trigger warnings, to teaching evaluations, to racialized emotions, to community, to literacy, to critical pedagogy, to peace education, the orientation is on confronting the discomfort of those in power.[26] Each of these applications shares a tenet of the pedagogy of discomfort of confronting one's own deeply held beliefs as well as naming the discomfort—through the lens of power—in order to enable scholars and practitioners to engage more fully in learning for changemaking.[27] The application of a pedagogy of discomfort doesn't ignore difference. For example, Poppy de Souza and Tanja Dreher cite Boler's "pedagogy of discomfort" to "provoke critical reflection, social transformation, and action" while also rendering difference visible. In this definition, where power and privilege are front and center, the pedagogy of discomfort is "an ethical imperative."[28]

Further, holding discomfort is key to anti-racist changemaking as it embodies what psychologist Jennifer Eberhardt calls "friction,"[29] or is the productive heat that arises when we hold someone's story that grates against our own. Inviting moments of friction enables you to learn how to interrupt your own implicit bias. For white allies, for example, friction isn't necessarily the heat of getting into a debate; it might instead be the heat of hearing a racist story and not interrupting it. This is why once one feels discomfort, radical listening can easily stop. We have to fight against what emerges, which is a type of critique that Shari Stenberg notes "offer[s] . . . justification for the reader" or listener "to remain squarely in his or her current position." Stenberg stresses that true listening is based on curiosity and that when discomfort arises, the listener loses curiosity and instead jumps to a "monolithic and thus immediately knowable" position of the speaker.[30] The converse is also true. The previous chapter on radical listening demonstrated that listening without attending to power reproduces power inequities, but critical listening, or listening for power, makes equitable listening possible.

Sitting with discomfort—as with all of the critical communication of difference skills—threads the needle between the role of the individual and the structural in changemaking. Just as in critically communicating race, embracing a pedagogy of discomfort does not allow for an individual to erase their personal responsibility in the face of structural inequality. Such an understanding of inequality is fundamentally uncomfortable and laden with complex emotions.

What are the emotions animating such discomfort, and how do we move through them to ease our racial exhaustion?

FEELING DISCOMFORT: SHAME, GUILT, AND BURNOUT

For white people and people of color, a range of emotions, from shame to guilt to empathy, both provoke and emerge from racial exhaustion. For those who are invested in colorblindness, naming *race* can be difficult. And even more difficult can be the moment of naming *racism*, as we'll see in the next chapter on radical speaking. In fact, moving through racial exhaustion is challenging because of what happens in our bodies when we simply hear the word "racism." King writes,

> Something deep within us is awakened into fear. All of us, regardless of our race and our experience of race, get triggered, and more than the moment is at play. That word picks at an existential scab—some level of dis-

ease at the mere insinuation of the word, some itch that we can't seem to scratch, or some fear we believe will harm us. . . . Regardless of how we look on the outside, we turn into frightened combatants and suit up for war. The heart quakes, and the mind narrows to its smallest, tightest place—survival.³¹

Racism activates all of our base emotions, or what King calls our "weapons of choice—aggression, distraction, denial, doubt, worry, depression, or indifference." King also notes that our emotions are stimulated to the point that they might feel "intolerable" and even "life-threatening."³² Thus, the social support that Janelle calls on—her sister and her mentees—helps create a way to move through such feelings of threat.

But again, the experiences of POC and white racial exhaustion are profoundly different. King adds that white people describe their emotions when considering racism to be "uncomfortable, confused, numb, and vague. One white woman described it as haunting, and a white man said it felt like flu symptoms."³³ In King's words, white people do not "vet" their racial exhaustion, meaning they dwell in the privilege of never examining their relationship to racism. And being pushed into self-examination—moving through racial exhaustion—prompts a variety of emotions, causing racial exhaustion even when they are trying to move through it. For example, the emotion that I heard in Jean's voice was shame. Psychologist Paul Gilbert asserts that "the fear of shame . . . can be so strong that people will risk serious physical injury or even death to avoid it." Shame is a "social threat" to one's sense of self that can impact both acceptance and relationships.³⁴ Jean felt ashamed of her father's comments, particularly when considering that her peers would be listening to them. Even so, social threats can be productive and even necessary if they prompt reparative action.

In Jean's comments, I also heard guilt. Guilt, Gilbert writes, evolved from caregiving and emerges from "some concern with the welfare of others, such that the (distress) experiences of others matter." Gilbert notes that "unlike shame, guilt is not associated with anger at others and reparation is chosen over concealment."³⁵ Following Gilbert's logic, where Jean's initial shame manifested in frustration toward her father and a desire to conceal his comments, her guilt prompted her to choose a reparative moment of discussion. Conceivably, had Jean not moved out of shame to guilt, then she might not have had the courage to engage in these difficult conversations about race.

For white people and people of color alike, this guilt/shame dynamic in response to the stress of naming racism can occur in a variety of places, including inside a therapist's office. When white therapists address issues of racism and race with their clients of color, for example, psychologists Saiqa Naz, Romilly Gregory, and Meera Bahu describe how without careful work, white therapists will themselves exhibit emotions of guilt and shame. They can inadvertently shut their clients down by creating "avoidance behaviours" including "avoiding mentioning issues of racism, ethnicity or culture with BAME [Black, Asian, and Minority Ethnic] service users in case they make mistakes."[36] This means that the therapists' inability to manage their own racial exhaustion ends up creating racial trauma and further exacerbating racial exhaustion for their clients of color.

Silence feeds racial exhaustion, while talking about race combats it. Consequently, Naz and colleagues suggest "rais[ing] and discuss[ing] issues related to ethnicity and culture, different experiences and values."[37] For example, "a white therapist gave an example of working with a black British service user who was worried about the way her teenage son behaved when angry. She expressed concern for his safety and said, 'He's going to be a big man.' The therapist reflected back, 'A big, black man,' opening up an opportunity for discussion of the service user's worry that her son needed to be extra careful with anger management to avoid triggering mainstream stereotypes of black men."[38] Both the white therapist and the Black client combatted their racial exhaustion with their forthright naming of race.

When not addressed, guilt and shame can also produce the emotional exhaustion of "burnout," what organizational behavior researchers call "a particular type of stress reaction or strain, . . . a syndrome of emotional exhaustion and cynicism."[39] Emotional exhaustion is a "unique quality of working life indicator. . . . One is most vulnerable to emotional exhaustion during the first one to two years on the job."[40] Interestingly, another group of physician researchers correlate white emotional exhaustion with implicit bias. In measuring the emotional exhaustion of non-Black physician residents, they found that "higher emotional exhaustion and depersonalization scores were associated with more unfavorable attitudes towards black people" and that conversely, residents who did not exhibit the same emotional exhaustion also did not exhibit the same anti-Black biases.[41] This tracks with the literature on implicit bias: as Eberhardt puts it, "When we are forced to make quick decisions using subjective criteria, the potential for bias is great."[42] Non-Black emotional exhaustion—in this book, white racial exhaustion—is thus linked to anti-Black bias.[43]

Such biases activate our emotions whether we are the ones at the giving or receiving end of them. Thus, dealing with these emotions—critically communicating race—is exhausting because such communication stimulates our emotions. And emotions are not incidental, but, as Sara Ahmed writes, "align individuals with communities—or bodily space with social space—through the very intensity of their attachments." Ahmed notes that "rather than seeing emotions as psychological dispositions, we need to consider how they work, in concrete and particular ways, to mediate the relationship between the psychic and the social, and between the individual and the collective."[44] As the examples of Janelle and Jean show us, processing the ways in which emotions connect us to our communities, whether they be Janelle expressing the racial bias she experiences at work, or Jean expressing her own racialized assumptions, provides a way to move through our racial exhaustion.

IS EMPATHY THE ANSWER?

As the circuit of critically communicating race wraps around, the emotion of empathy—which first surfaced in Chapter 1's discussion of active listening—returns again. There we considered how empathy could be feigned in order to act out the pretense of active—much less radical—listening. Here we look at how moving through racial exhaustion also connects to empathy. But first let's slow down to pause on the definition of empathy. My definition, which I date to an elementary school lesson by Sister Irene (starring in my memory as Maria from *Sound of Music*), has always been in tandem with sympathy: while sympathy means feeling *for* someone (in the dictionary definition, an "affinity"), empathy means feeling *with* someone (the action toward such affinity).[45] This echoes with the words of Jordan, the Black high school student who featured in the introduction. Jordan said that when racism occurs at his high school, white students "pretty much stay to themselves. . . . Like rarely would something like that—a white person standing up for a POC—ever happen just because it's so rare. I'd say the most [that would happen is] a white person would *feel* or *have sympathy* [for us] but nothing would be done as far as standing up or trying to help or assisting or guiding a POC through anything that they go through." Jordan's words illustrate that those who are disempowered live with a full understanding of other's humanity. Jordan doesn't need coursework in empathy: it's key to how he negotiates his daily racial exhaustion. Instead, it's those who live with outsized privilege who need to activate their empathy.

My basic understanding of empathy from Jordan illuminates how empathy can lead to action. Scholars also consider how empathy is key to moving through other emotions that can get in the way of action. "Empathy" comes from an early twentieth-century German art historical term meaning "in feeling," a type of empathetic witnessing. Then the term extended to a "stunning number of fields from aesthetic psychology to social work and psychotherapy, to politics, advertising, and the media," according to historian Susan Lanzoni.[46] In these contexts, empathy involves understanding, feeling, sharing another person's world, and maintaining self-other demarcation,[47] all of which are both emotional and cognitive and can be learned by working through the critical communication of race circuit.

Empathy "requires an exquisite interplay of neural networks and enables us to perceive the emotions of others, resonate with them emotionally and cognitively, to take in the perspective of others, and to distinguish between our own and others' emotions," writes psychologist Helen Reiss. It isn't, as scholars once believed, an "inborn trait that could not be taught," but is instead a "mutable . . . vital human competency."[48] Hearing others in an empathetic fashion thus requires the flexibility of radical listening which might mean hearing moments of change. Such mutability unfolds in interpersonal relationships when people are supportively hearing each other and working through discomfort together— through, for example, the conversations Jean and Janelle have—and also by engaging deeply in stories about someone from a different perspective.[49] Radically listening across difference and moving through discomfort provide the opportunity to redirect someone's notions of whom they see as "my people."

But the research on getting folks to such an expansive notion of "my people" through empathy is mixed. Philosopher Paul Bloom's book *Against Empathy* argues that empathy is a limited and perhaps even dangerous concept because it does not track well with moral reasoning, and his cautions echo the difficulties of sitting with discomfort particularly when it comes to critically communicating race. Bloom discusses the limitations of both "cognitive empathy"—what can be thought of as a type of perspective-taking, an intellectual understanding someone is in pain— and "emotional empathy"—tuning in deeply to the experience of someone's hurt, a type of imagining the pain and feeling with them. The concept is limited, he says, because in either of these types of empathy, we might be attuned to the suffering of an individuals, but we are inured to the suffering of large groups. Further, without radically listening and sitting with discomfort, activating racial empathy can mean largely imagining the suffering of individuals we envision to be "like us." For example, white women might feel *with* Jean (empathize) as she shares her father's racism but feel *for* Janelle (sympathize) as she shares the daily microaggressions she encounters. Because of these problems empathizing with larger groups and those unlike us (in race, nation, religion, and other modes of difference), Bloom argues for "conscious, deliberative reasoning . . . [where] we should strive to use our heads rather than our hearts"[50] to stoke greater cognitive rather than emotional empathy.

Indeed, dwelling in discomfort to strive for ethical, anti-racist action is not just an emotional exercise, but an intellectual one.[51] Moments of "conscious, deliberative reasoning," Stenberg writes, enable people to embrace discomfort, to "dwell" in or "linger . . . on . . . discomfort . . . long enough to allow oneself to be changed by one's hearing." The experience of "dwelling in rather than defending" means moving away from the "dysfunctional positions" of "denial, defensiveness, and guilt/blame" and toward "functional stances" of "recognition, critique, and accountability."[52] Dwelling, which necessitates a moment of pause, of standing still in contemplation, provides a way to eschew what Boler describes as "passive empathy," or "when our concern is directed to a fairly distant other, whom we cannot directly help."[53] This form of empathy "does not contribute to social change but rather encourages a passive form of 'pity.'"[54] Empathy can thus create a type of "fantasy space" in which a person can feign a positive desire to change without engaging in action. Boler goes on to assert that she is "not convinced that empathy leads to anything close to justice, to any shift in existing power relations."[55] She asks, "What is gained by the social imagination and empathy, and is this model possibly doing our social vision more harm than good?"[56] Fundamentally, without a way to move through discomfort, the concept of empathy might not be able to provide, in the words of de Souza and Dreher, a "sustained engagement" with discomfort, which is what is needed in order to create "justice . . . even when the form and shape of justice is not yet known."[57]

Yet I'm not ready to throw empathy out altogether. When empathy is in the realm of emotional empathy, we can foster "a connection and communication we don't want to lose."[58] Returning to psychologists Naz and colleagues—they urge white therapists' who work with clients of color to activate their own empathy by "tolerating uncertainty and vulnerability, bringing up clients' individual and cultural identities, inquiring about clients' experiences of racism in therapy, continuing to work with racially marginalized communities despite feeling a lack of confidence, utilizing supervision, and attending workshops to develop confidence."[59] Activating deep empathy beyond a group "like me" (i.e., across racial identity) also means that therapists need to lean into their own discomfort by first recognizing that they, too, have implicit biases.

People can recognize their biases not just in the therapist's office, but in a wide variety of other spaces, including classrooms. During Interrupting Privilege's "Resistance through Resilience" project, two participants and teachers, fifty-something Native Hawaiian Mele and thirty-something Korean American Chelsea evoked the notion of empathy-into-action by describing how they coach their students to look inward in order to understand their own communication styles and power.[60] They took on the issue of white students' racial exhaustion. Mele expressed frustration at how white students' racial exhaustion and their "sense of white privilege" leaked out in their saying, "I don't know what to do, I don't want to say the wrong thing." Mele tells them to combat their inaction with two emotions: "You have to be brave and you have to be humble. That's it." Students need to realize, Mele continues, that "you will say stupid things, you will make mistakes." The key is that "you just have to be humble enough to acknowledge and to make amends for what was hurtful or had an effect on others that was not necessarily what you thought it would be.... You have to stand up for something."

Mele acknowledges the role of fear—stemming from guilt and shame—in the discomfort that stops people from acting. But she says that students must push past it: "If you're always afraid you're going to say the wrong thing, that's where the humility comes in. Because you will say the wrong thing. Just be humble and say I didn't know that, I'm sorry, I learned, I'm going to try not to do that again." Mele teaches students to lean into "risk-taking"; she says "the worst thing to do is to not do anything. That is not acceptable. You must do something." Chelsea agrees, and shares that she teaches her students that "sometimes it might feel like the most important step is the first step, but the most important step is the next step. You have to keep on moving. Getting started is important but there's going to be problems and there's going to be hurdles but it's about making the next step every time. Even though it's scary and even though we make mistakes."

Moving through racial exhaustion and its discomforts—past guilt, past shame, even past empathy—is the fight for "the next step." The next step is where actionable change happens. When negative emotions such as guilt and shame arise, psychologists Naz and collaborators argue, "emotional withdrawal" partnered with a "reduction in empathy" can develop.[61] This can happen when someone is forced to confront their own prejudice. But, as Jean demonstrated when I gently pointed out her racialized assumptions to her, it doesn't always need to happen this way if one can practice the skills of sitting with discomfort.

DISTRESS TOLERANCE

Distress tolerance—or sitting with discomfort—is a primary skill in the behavioral modification therapy program psychologist Marsha Linehan created in the late 1970s called Dialectical Behavioral Therapy, or DBT. Linehan designed DBT to treat highly suicidal patients, and it has since been embraced around the world as a verified lifesaving technique. Within DBT, the goal of distress tolerance is to become more aware of how our emotions influence our response to difficult, upsetting, or uncomfortable situations, or in Linehan's words, to learn how to "bear pain skillfully."

Linehan notes that we all have the ability to bear this pain, but that we just don't all have the skills.[62] The very definition of distress tolerance, the "ability to persist in goal-directed behavior while experiencing affective distress,"[63] psychologist Stacey Daughters and colleagues write, is a way to understand how in moments of stress one can choose negative instead of positive actions. Linehan writes that DBT skills "are aimed at teaching a synthesis of how to change what is and how to accept what is. Skills teach you . . . how to change unwanted behaviors, emotions, thoughts, and events in your life that cause you misery and distress as well as how to live in the moment, accepting what is."[64] We will pause to consider some DBT skills that are particularly suited to combatting the distress of racial exhaustion. While Linehan's strategies do not explicitly address race or questions of racial exhaustion, the skills-based model of distress tolerance provides much insight into how to move through the uncomfortable moments of racial exhaustion.

Linehan's DBT workbook suggests four different ways that a person might react to emotional distress: change the situation (solve the problem), change your emotional response to the situation (feel better about the problem), tolerate the situation (accept the problem without action), or ignore or exacerbate the situation (feel worse about the problem). These can be applied to racial exhaustion. For example, Mele's description of her white student's white racial exhaustion—their "whining" and "tears" about what she names as their "white privilege"—fits into this fourth category of inaction, and subsequently feeling worse, about the problem. Mele promotes being brave and humble instead, which might mean attempting Linehan's option one, changing the situation (by, for example, apologizing) or option two, changing their own emotional response (from fear to bravery and humility).

Linehan and her co-author Chelsey Wilks call for people to enact a "synthesis of both acceptance and change."[65] This is radical acceptance, in which one fully acknowledges the realities of the present moment. When applied to racial exhaustion, radical acceptance means recognizing and assessing one's own emotions when it comes to race, including, perhaps, guilt and shame. This is a clear-eyed inventory of your racial exhaustion in which you don't hide from your emotions or throw up your hands in frustration or remain mired in a moment of feeling overwhelmed.[66] The change is also radical: it means not remaining content with this emotional response and instead "pushing for progress," which first and foremost is moving through these emotions. However, arriving at the acceptance/change synthesis of radical acceptance can be, in and of itself, distressing, as merely acknowledging that you're in the midst of racial exhaustion can feel overwhelming. Through radical acceptance, DBT provides concrete actions for how to confront the distress that might emerge by moving to that place of bravery and humility. Radical acceptance is again necessary to combat the distress of this new round of racial exhaustion. And refusing to accept the reality that you are feeling distressed "leads to increased pain and suffering." One can't ignore away discomfort as "pain and distress are a part of life; they cannot be entirely avoided or removed."

Thus, to critically communicate race, one of the first steps must be understanding that discomfort is a natural response. Race and meditation scholar Rhonda Magee puts it this way: "Because there are so many rivers of pain joining and forming the ocean of racial suffering in our times, personal awareness practices are essential for racial justice work. In order for real change to occur, we must be able to examine our own experiences [and] discover the 'situated' nature of our perspectives."[67] Wedding together distress tolerance (from Linehan) and racial justice as a practice (from Magee), we can see that sitting with discomfort is not a quick fix or a one-time proposition. Indeed, working to increase "distress tolerance, at least over the short run, is part and parcel of any attempt to change oneself."[68] This change, as de Souza and Dreher note, is fundamental for those with racial and colonial privilege, insofar as "the notion of dwelling in discomfort . . . offer[s] a way of sitting with unsettling truths and histories that does not seek an exit from them."[69]

Here is where another set of DBT skills comes in: observe and describe. One of the initial steps of DBT is naming a problem in a nonjudgmental manner. Observing and describing enables all of us to be more cognizant of our own reactions, including those spurring from our racial exhaustion. Linehan calls observing a "what" skill of experiencing or sensing without labeling. "Observing inside your mind," Linehan writes, "can be like sitting on a hill looking down on a train that's going by. . . . Some of the train cars are emotions, feelings. Each thought and feeling arises, coming closer, then passes and goes away down the tracks and around the hill out of sight. The trick is to not get caught in the content of the thought or feeling. Watch, observe, but do not get on the train."[70] Not getting on the train might be noticing the urge to avoid talking about race and also noticing where in the body one can feel that urge. Mindfully observing might be opening your mind "to each sensation arising, not attaching, letting go of each." Observing in a nonjudgmental manner enables one to narrate one's own thoughts "without minimization, justification, or other statements influenced by heightened emotional reactivity," as Ashley Pierson and colleagues note.[71] Linehan partners the skill of observing with that of describing or labeling without judgment. This means giving name to what is outside of your body as well as your feelings, sensations, and thoughts.

The best way to practice observing and describing nonjudgmentally is through mindfulness. King calls mindfulness the way to "get still and simply receive the present moment without preferences." Following King's words, the Interrupting Privilege Resistance through Resilience curriculum we developed explored how mindfulness, compassion-based, and other distress tolerance practices can help people move through racial exhaustion. As Resilience Lab director Megan Kennedy said in one of our radical listening sessions,

> Mindfulness helps to increase our capacity to be present in the moment to what's happening externally—as well as what is happening internally (such as paying attention to our thoughts, feelings, and emotions).... Mindfulness is simply paying attention, on purpose, with an attitude of friendly, open, nonjudgmental curiosity and a willingness to accept (at least for now!) what arises. Mindfulness is essential for developing the capacity to respond, rather than simply react as if on auto pilot, to what we experience.[72]

At one evening's listening party, in preparation to listen to and have dialogues around racial issues, Kennedy led our assembled group in a meditation that began with instructions for us to ground ourselves. Kennedy explained, "In dialogue, mindfulness allows us to notice when we might need to become grounded, for example placing our feet on the floor, taking a breath, sitting in our chair differently, saying something or not saying something." Kennedy taught the group that mindfulness entails taking a pause and asking "ourselves what we need in any given moment to be effective and compassionate to others or ourselves." Kennedy's exercises help both those being called to confront their own biases and those whose listening to stories of racial distress might reactivate their own experience of bias. Kennedy was drawing her practice that evening from the words of Ruth King: "The best tool I know of to transform our relationship to racial suffering is mindfulness meditation."[73]

Mindfulness involves the process of naming. As Janelle said to her sister Michele, responding immediately to a microaggression is a way of naming racism as something real, something occurring in the moment. So does Mele's urging her students to see their white privilege, or the ways in which they benefit from racism. Identifying moments of racism—as Janelle and Mele do—and accepting such naming moments—as Janelle encourages her mentees and Mele encourages her students to do—both happen by observing and describing with a nonjudgmental stance. A nonjudgmental stance is neutral; it is not an "evaluative judgment about good and bad or right and wrong, which are subjective and vague in their factual meaning." Factual naming—as of racism in action—is necessary for change.[74] While part of the naming might be internal for some (naming it for oneself), for others it might be external.

Another DBT skill that helps a person enact a nonjudgmental stance is adopting a beginner's mindset, which entails focusing on the present, as opposed to the past or the future. "In 'beginner's mind,' each moment is a new beginning, a new and unique moment in time." As a beginner you approach emotions with the openness of a child for whom every experience is new. This Zen practice can work to "increase curiosity and reduce assumptions about a universal, shared experience that denies realities of race and racism."[75] A related DBT skill is "checking the facts," or homing in on one's feelings of "guilt, shame, reactivity" as well as adopting a nonjudgmental stance that might even be a part of a "radical acceptance of past racist behavior."[76] All of these DBT skills provide tangible ways to deal with the discomfort of racial exhaustion.

Facing racial exhaustion is hard, but the consequences of not doing so are, among other things, poor health outcomes. In studies of adolescents, psychologists Daughters and colleagues describe people with low distress tolerance turning to troublesome coping techniques that can be "internal (e.g., isolation, worry)" or "external . . . (e.g., substance use, aggression)";[77]

these are linked to a slew of behavioral issues, "including depression, anxiety, and substance abuse."[78] One negative form of distress management that disproportionately impacts Black women is cigarette smoking. As psychologist Jennifer R. Dahne and colleagues note, this is a coping device that helps mitigate racial stress.[79]

By the same token, practicing DBT's distress tolerance skills can combat racialized stress, or racial exhaustion, in ways that improve our health. A "delay of gratification" is at the heart of distress tolerance, a pause during which you mindfully feel the discomfort or friction. In this pause you can also turn to DBT's healthy self-soothing techniques to ameliorate rather than exacerbate the situation. Interrupting Privilege participants learn to practice what DBT refers to as "TIPs" (*t*ip your face into cold water, *i*ntense exercise, *p*aced breathing/paired muscle relaxation), which "activates the body's physiological nervous system for decreasing arousal . . . through temperature, exercise, effective breathing, and muscle relaxation."[80] This means reducing the emotional dysregulation that in very real ways can help you attend to microaggressive moments—whether experienced or caused—and move through the resulting racial exhaustion.[81]

RESISTANCE THROUGH RESILIENCE: RACE + PEDAGOGY OF DISCOMFORT + DISTRESS TOLERANCE

I conclude this chapter by highlighting stories of moving through the discomfort of racial exhaustion as articulated by the Resistance through Resilience group of Interrupting Privilege participants, a diverse group of almost all people of color from both inside and outside the university. The group spent a year together practicing DBT skills such as mindfulness in order to combat racial exhaustion. It embraced a pedagogy of discomfort and learned the skills of distress tolerance as strategies to support naming, validating, and moving through racial exhaustion. Participants held each other's pain and did not try to solve it. At the heart of their discussions of suffering was one word that structured our year—*resilience*, or the ability to "bounce back" after stress. Our participants either embraced resilience as a way to hear and hold their racial exhaustion or rejected resilience as a way that outsiders blame individuals for their racial exhaustion instead of understanding the role of structural factors. In either case, our group understood "resistance as a form of resilience, i.e., an exercise of agency in adverse social contexts."[82]

Two community participants who named and validated each other's experiences as a key to their moving through discomfort were Ellen and Ada. These two Black women in their seventies were both doting grandmothers and retired professionals. They met through the Interrupting Privilege program and developed a friendship that grew beyond their paired conversations to their taking regular walks together. Both women commiserated about the discomfort that arose for them when people told them to always "be strong." Ellen tells Ada, "After my husband passed away people would tell me, 'You're so strong.' And it's like, I'm just coping. I'm not strong. I'm just coping, just putting one foot in front of the other, doing what I have to do." Ellen described how she combats her discomfort by resisting this stereotype—refusing to be named as a superwoman. Ada agrees, naming her own frustration that the word "strong" has been used with regard to Black women to denote "being heroic."

As Michele Wallace wrote half a century ago, the myth of the Black superwoman strips Black women of the opportunity to be fallible, to be protected, or to feel vulnerable. This is a type of what Helen Rosenboom and I describe as the "grueling management of self," which in more recent Black feminist communication scholarship is deemed "the Strong Black Woman (SBW) phenomenon."[83] The antidote to the SBW schema, writes Sharde Davis, is the SBW collective: social support of Black women, for Black women.[84] Exemplifying just this, Ada says that she likes the word "resilient" since to her it means "redefining [this term] for myself. It's not being heroic. It's just paying attention to those small things . . . on a day-to-day basis. . . . I'm not heroic." Paying attention is part of Ada's mindfulness practice; it is the tool that recenters her attention on being kind to herself, acknowledging that she doesn't need to be a superwoman always fighting racism to the point of exhaustion. Instead, she notes, "one moment I can identify a microaggression and address it. Another moment I might just revert to stuffing it." Ada checks in with her own levels of energy and discomfort to assess whether she is ready to tax herself emotionally by intervening. "Is it worth it?"—emotionally, spiritually, intellectually—is what she asks herself.

As with empathy, resilience was once understood as an innate quality but has been shown to be a skill that people can practice and learn. Or as

Ada puts it, "Over time it's just building and building and building." After moving through many moments of discomfort throughout her lifetime, Ada notes that now she has "a growing resistance [that enables me to be] . . . armored against the impact of systemic structures that oppress, interpersonal relationships that might oppress." After feeling years of discomfort with casual microaggressions from white women friends, Ada had enough and decided that she needed to cut ties with them. That distancing was hard in itself, but Ada sees this work of moving through interpersonal discomfort as part of the changemaking that she creates on a daily basis: "As I become older I can see whereas years ago I would say I have to be out there on the front lines doing something. Not so much now. It's my interpersonal relationships, it's a quieter resistance." Ada returns to the metaphor Ellen used earlier in their conversation, noting that her ability to move through this discomfort of her racial exhaustion is like surfing where "some days you fall off and some days you don't."[85] Embracing this metaphor reduces the pressure of always having to effectively intervene when experiencing racism. She doesn't have to teach her racist friends how to be anti-racist. Instead, she can walk away from these virulent friendships. Ada and Ellen's conversation reflects research that older Black women reported the highest levels of resilience (followed by Latinas, white women, and Asian/Pacific Islander women) because they have marshaled a variety of psychological resources such as "experiencing a sense of purpose" and having "control of [their] beliefs, energy, [and] personal growth."[86] Resilience, for them, is sometimes choosing to walk away.

Two other participants both named and validated each other's feelings about the concept of resilience. Devan, a Pacific Islander university staff member, and Solis, a Latina health researcher, reject the word "resilience," which in their definition lacks the "surfing" quality Ellen and Ada like. Devan says that this word actually stokes her racial exhaustion because it ignores disproportionate racialized expectations of holding racism and other forms of discrimination. She exclaims, "Why is it that communities of color have to put their heads down all the time?" Like Ada and Ellen, Devan is balking at the expectations that communities of color always having to be strong as they experience racial discomfort. Devan asserts, "There's nothing innate or natural about the fact that you have to take certain things [like racism, sexism, homophobia, transphobia] every certain day." Solis agrees: "I hate it, I hate that word [resilience]! Because I just feel like it gets used against us so often." Solis's problem with resilience—that "[Latinas] shouldn't have to be resilient, but [we] are"— is related to her critique that white heteropatriarchal culture portrays racism as an individual problem, an individual lack of fortitude, instead of a structural problem, a multitiered system of discrimination. Devan agrees, stressing that uplifting resilience does not actually combat the uncomfortable realities of racial exhaustion: "We're tired of taking white supremacy, anti-Blackness, poverty. These are not good things!" Solis builds on Devan's sentiment, exclaiming in frustration, "Why is this a strength? This should not be our problem to begin with. Like we're so strong for tolerating racism?" Devan agrees, adding that part of the harm in trying to be strong all the time is that "it doesn't allow us to feel vulnerable."[87] Pushing back on the individual expectations of fighting racism means refusing to place blame on the victims and instead redirects the focus onto structural forces—centering the problem on its root. Devan and Solis ease their racial exhaustion by refusing the discomfort of structural racism.

Finally, by naming and validating each other's embodied practices of sitting with discomfort, two other Resistance through Resilience participants connected. Thirty-year-old graduate student Latrice and forty-year-old community activist Sheree, both Black women, discussed how they create ways to move through their racial exhaustion. Latrice shares the breathing techniques she practices in order to process the discomfort that arises with racial exhaustion.[88] Sheree says that in her own moments of racial exhaustion, "I am learning to extend grace to myself and just breathe through it. And forgive myself when I need to. When it's the best thing for me to do. And just keep moving, keep moving forward. . . . Self-compassion, grace for self will just keep us moving forward to that future vision that we have."[89]

This peek into these three Resistance through Resilience conversations illustrate everyday, supportive ways to move through discomfort by naming and validating each other's experiences. As with these connecting moments, uncomfortable racialized interactions might be most easily identified when they are between individuals—for example, between Jean and her father as she confronted his bias, Jean and her husband as they strategized about how to talk race, Jean and her children as she explained their grandfather's comments, Jean and me as I inquired about her assumptions. Repeated, habitual individual actions (part of the very definition of microaggressions) highlight the systemic nature of racism. Sitting with discomfort—in a validating or more probing fashion—provides us with the opportunity to see racism in a systemic, not simply individual, fashion, and to combat racism not just through changing the actions of individuals, but the system of racism.

Changing systems comes about by altering an assumed way of doing things. And again, we return to the vital role of individuals. Systems theory scholars Erin R. Watson and Charles R. Collins argue that the key component in dismantling racist structures is shifting mindsets, or "collectively held beliefs, values, ideologies, and attitudes that create a way of viewing the world for those who share them."[90] Dwelling in the discomfort of vulnerable and honest conversations about race enables us to dismantle inequalities not just interpersonally, but structurally. Put another way: it's very possible to enact structural changes through individual dialogic work. For example, when Janelle pushed through her own discomfort (experiencing daily microaggressions) to take action (mentoring and advocating for young Black women), she provided a blueprint for her organization's Employee Resource Group to improve their company-wide mentorship-to-sponsorship program. Jean's discomfort helped push her to recruit some lawyers of color for the peer mentorship group of mother attorneys she represented, who had been all white. Emerging from individuals' work to move through discomfort and racial exhaustion, such formal mentoring programs make a tremendous difference for minoritized employees' future success.[91] Staying silent in the face of racial exhaustion creates additional racial exhaustion and worsens racial trauma for people of color, while moving through racial exhaustion creates structural change that can make this better for all.

As the stories in this chapter attest, the discomfort of being called on racism—a hallmark of white racial exhaustion—is markedly different from the discomfort of experiencing racism—what marks POC racial exhaustion. But what remains true in both cases is that we need to take care of ourselves through naming our moments of discomfort and conscientiously practicing moving through them.[92] This is apparent in a dialogue between Sonya, a Black teacher in her forties, and Annette, an Indigenous teacher in her fifties. While Sonya notes that her experience of racial discomfort enables her to cultivate compassion for the individual while allowing herself anger at the structure, Annette describes compassion—for self and others—as key to changing systems of oppression. She notes, "I have compassion for the people who are causing" such pain. One of the challenges in accessing the type of compassion that Annette promotes is the urge to "focus . . . primarily on an individual's behavior and overlook . . . or discount . . . the structural factors that shape and influence the person's lived experience."[93] This challenge is one of the ways in which the individual and structural are always intertwined. Structural—and historical and institutional—positionalities inform individual actions. Individuals play a vital role in critically communicating race in such a way that produces structural reverberations.[94] From radical listening to sitting with discomfort, we now move through the circuit of critically communicating race to radical speaking.

3

RADICAL SPEAKING

The assembled room of fifty participants—university students and community members alike—holds its collective breath in rapt silence as a female voice comes across the speakers. Sounding young and excited, Fana, a social work graduate student, exclaims, "Let's talk about the Angry Black Woman [stereotype]. You always say the person who created that was a *genius*."[1] The stereotype—quick-to-lash out, illogically furious, scolding, and racially exhausted—needs no explanation in Fana's dialogue with Tenneh, an undergraduate communication major, Interrupting Privilege participant, and Fana's good friend. Tenneh echoes Fana's affirmation, saying, "genius." The two women quickly reveal an easy rapport: they laugh often, speak over each other, and mirror each other with language and tone, an interpersonal mimicry psychologists deem the "chameleon effect."[2]

Fana adds that the stereotype of the Angry Black Woman constrains her speech. She says, "I feel like in situations where I'm being attacked or when someone's just being racist I can't fully express my feelings because I don't want to look like an Angry Black Woman." Sometimes this means staying silent in the face of uninvited but everyday commentary "about me eating fried chicken and drinking Kool Aid." The young women laugh incredulously after Fana says this, baffled by the baseness, the pure ridiculousness of someone iterating such a stereotype in this very day and age. She continues, sharing more benign racialized assumptions such as "I know every Black person on campus." To this, Fana states, "I wish I did, but I don't." These daily comments fall into the category of what she describes, with a spark of hope in her voice, as, "just little teeny things, right?"

Then Fana describes "the big boom, like the big drop where I was really shook." This time was not a "teeny" brush off moment for the young woman. Her manager at her waitressing job told her "to go clean [the tables] like your ancestors did." Immediately after recounting this line,

87

both women laugh again in shock and rage. Fana continues, clarifying that the manager's ignorance prevented him from seeing that she was Ethiopian, from people who were not enslaved on this continent. But, Tenneh, who, like Fana, is a first-generation African immigrant, points out that those who stereotype her also flatten all forms of Blackness and cannot begin to understand the diaspora. And indeed, the remark would be racist even if she were descended from people enslaved in the United States. Fana continues, speaking more quickly and angrily as she says that she told him, "Don't ever disrespect me like that again. Don't ever say anything like that again. You just crossed the line. You crossed the line."

After a beat, they laugh again in frustrated acknowledgment of the unfairness of the daily racism they endure and then comment on the laughter, noting that they return to it when experiencing the misogynoir of anti-Black woman sentiment. Laughter eases their pain. It is a protective buffer against not only racialized sexism itself, but also the stultifying expectations of the Angry Black Woman stereotype, those expectations that deny Black women the human experience of expressing true rage when they experience biased treatment. Fana explains that after hearing the "ancestors" comment, her first thought was to corral, to enclose, to hide her anger, saying, "I don't want to look like that [Angry Black] woman so I had to be calm and collect[ed]." And ultimately, Fana notes that calling out racism is a fraught proposition for Black women because "when you try to tell someone what they just said is racist, they fly off the wall" and act as if, and Tenneh inserts here, as if "you killed a dog." In pet-loving Seattle, this might be the cruelest crime imaginable. The conclusion the two come to is, Tenneh sighs, that "sometimes . . . [calling out something as racist] aren't worth it." She continues, "I'm not even going to bother because I know how [white people are] going to react." The clip ends with Tenneh's and Fana's assertion that while they regularly interrupt incidents of everyday racism, what truly soothes their racial exhaustion is their sisterhood, sharing and laughing together, seeing and hearing each other's stories of enduring microaggressions, supportively emoting and confirming for each other that yes, microaggressions are real, and indeed, they are unrelenting. Having each other combats the heaviness and brings the laughter.

After the clips ended the room fell silent while participants collectively held their breath. This was our very first Interrupting Privilege Radical

Listening Party themed the "First Time Experiencing Racism" project. The room was set up in listening pairs of university alumni and students who were instructed to share out one at a time what they heard in the clips in the radical speaking exercise I describe in chapter one, where each participant narrates what they heard without interruption, and while centering the speaker's words, not their own opinions, thoughts, and assessments. Fana and Tenneh took the mic to add some additional details of time, place, and space to the clips that had been recorded earlier that quarter and to update them with their most recent thoughts. They said they were eager to listen to what the room heard. As our pairs processed the clips, the room hummed with energy so that I had to announce two, three times that we needed to come together as a big group. People began speaking one at a time, both students and alumni, with many listeners nodding their heads in agreement: yes, they experienced racist microaggressions day in and day out, or as one student put it, "check, check, check." Some experienced the stereotype of the Angry Black Woman boxing them in; this is a racialized and gendered "controlling image," as sociologist Patricia Hill Collins notes, and, in the poet and scholar Bettina Judd's words, it "makes apparent the immediate threat that Black women experience by speaking and being."[3]

Other listeners—specifically, many of the community participants who were largely white, female, and over sixty—shook their heads in shock: they couldn't believe that this type of blatant racism still occurred today. They exclaimed, weren't we past this yet? Many of these respondents were also discomfited by Fana and Tenneh's laughter: they had a hard time understanding that the women were laughing not to make a joke of the situation, but to protect themselves from it. Other community participants couldn't believe that "in this day and age" Black women had to hold themselves back from responding to racism. They imagined that if they were in that same situation, they would be bolder in calling out inequality freely and openly. Such respondents didn't question their own privilege, their own safely encased bubbles, that would protect them in that imagined moment of interruption. They didn't imagine that racial exhaustion itself might dampen a response.

I begin this chapter on what I will soon define as "radical speaking" with a story that illustrates not just the pain of experiencing microaggressions, but the pleasurable moments of connection that can emerge from sharing such experiences both interpersonally and in larger groups. As this book has illustrated, moving through racial exhaustion is about changing the everyday flow, the common sense, the racialized communication structures that can compound inequality. Now, after examining the roles of listening and sitting with discomfort, we are three-quarters of the way through the critical communication of race circuit: it's time to speak. In the third step of the critical communication of difference circuit, the individual act of speaking helps individuals as well as communities move through experiences of racial exhaustion.

How do we intervene if, like Fana and Tenneh, we experience such microaggressions, or if, like the assembled group of allies, we are appalled to hear such a story? Sometimes we might ignore microaggressions. Sometimes we might respond quietly or combatively, immediately or months and months later, or sometimes not at all. Sometimes we experience the relief of receiving an apology or seeing someone change before our eyes; sometimes we never get that apology, as the process of interpersonal changemaking feels like it takes a lifetime. In this chapter I will explore how all of these options can help one move through racial exhaustion by learning more about radical speaking, as well as microaggressions and strategies to interrupt them.

RADICAL SPEAKING

My concept of radical speaking means naming race, racism, and its intersections in an uninhibited fashion. It is inspired by the great Audre Lorde's warning in *Sister Outsider*: "My silences had not protected me. Your silence will not protect you.... For we have been socialized to respect fear more than our own needs for language and definition, and while we wait in silence for that final luxury of fearlessness, the weight of that silence will choke us." Armed with strategies for radical listening and sitting with discomfort, we can "learn to work and speak when we are afraid in the same way we have learned to work and speak when we are tired."[4]

But radical speaking is not simply breaking the silence. Lorde's words push us toward speaking with a fortitude that extends beyond simply talking *about* race, which is what mainstream media outlets do. They stoke racial exhaustion by talking *about* race: in covering stories of racialized violence, they narrate racism through the lens of extraordinary, unusual acts of viciousness, failing to acknowledge their selective vision or the myriad other ways in which daily living is violent for people of color. It's also true that talking *about* race occurs only under extreme duress, which suggests that speaking forthrightly about—even noticing—race in everyday life is racist. Talking *about* race happens reluctantly, infrequently, and under coercion. Talking *about* race is about "them" not "us": talking about race configures people of color as the ones whose lives are shaped by race and racism and white people as those for whom race and racism are merely incidental. Talking *about* race doesn't acknowledge the fundamental ways in which racialized lives—Black, white, Latine, indigenous, Asian American, Southwest Asian and North African (SWANA)—are intertwined. Talking *about* race gives in to racial exhaustion and accepts silence as the answer.

In contrast, radical speaking means fluently and fluidly discussing the everyday ways in which race (and racism) infiltrates the world. Radical speaking might even be fear-based at times: it is terrifying to encounter and navigate racialized violence. Radical speaking through fear means a slow and steady version of "the talk"[5]—that conversation that Black and Brown families must repeatedly have with children and young adults about the non-engagement rules to follow if (and when) they are accosted by the police and told that they "fit the description." Radical speaking means preparing for the reality of racism, while critiquing and combatting it with everyday resistance. Radical speaking means disrupting class by questioning the wrong or absent perspective in a high school U.S. literature and history classes: "Why did you say that Melville's *Moby Dick* is a more significant American story than Jacobs' *Incidents in the Life of a Slave Girl*?" "Why does my U.S. history textbook say that William Lloyd Garrison was the most important abolitionist instead of Harriet Tubman?" "Why are there so few Black students like me in this honors class?"[6] Radical speaking names race and its many intersections alongside power, privilege, and the ways in which the fates of all racialized people—including white people (as white people have a race[7]) are intertwined. Radical speaking follows these additional words of Lorde: "I have come to believe over and over again that what is most important to me must be spoken, made verbal and shared, even at the risk of having it bruised or misunderstood. That the speaking benefits me, beyond any other effect."[8] Radical speaking is a means to combat and move through racial exhaustion. Radical speaking does not come easily. Radical speaking is not an inherited, natural trait. It's something that's learned and developed in community with thoughtful, consistent, challenging practice.

Radical speaking can disrupt conversation. The disruption can feel anything between uncomfortable to downright rude to the person who is interrupted. Imagine: your conversation partner is developing an idea out loud. In their inchoate thought you hear something that doesn't sit well with you. You can't wait, so you interrupt—maybe with "I'm going to stop you right there." Your impatience surprises them, throws them off guard, angers them. You have caused them to lose their train of thought, to halt their flow. And when they stop, emotions rise. Perhaps they even say, "How could you be so rude as to interrupt me?" Maybe they stop working out their thought completely; maybe they are so frustrated with you that they want to end the conversation entirely. Or maybe they attempt to talk over your interruption by getting their thought back on track. They might talk over you to rewind the conversation ("Wait, what was I saying?") and then barrel forward ("This is what I was trying to say"). The process of such a conversational rupture might feel especially wrong to the interrupted if they are on the upside of power. Imagine Jordan, the high school student who featured in the introduction, interrupting his teacher Mr. New in class when Mr. New failed to provide adequate instruction to Jordan or other Black members of the class. Not only might it not go well, but Mr. New might literally punish Jordan for the interruption.

But that's not the only way radical speaking can work. Radical speaking isn't necessarily about cutting people off mid-thought with a patriarchal "I'm going to stop you right there." It's also not always immediate. Radical speaking doesn't necessarily mean interrupting the same people who directly caused harm and during a singular time. Instead, as Jordan models, an intrepid person could radically speak to the person causing the harm immediately, with a potential ally a week later, and then with an entire community witnessing a month later. It might not mean interrupting a person at all. Even so, radical speaking can interrupt the dynamic, the silence, the workings of privilege.

In all cases, the process of radically speaking—the break in social norms, the potential moment of discomfort—is necessary for change.

Why? Because privilege feeds on stasis. Interruption is a way to alter a power dynamic from one that stands still to one that not just *can* move but *has to* move. Interrupting privilege is a multipronged, multi-peopled, multi-timed investment in forging justice.

Let's switch points of view to the person who is doing the interrupting, to Jordan. Why should Jordan fight so hard against his own racial exhaustion by speaking to his teacher, reaching out to his assistant principal, and finally, vulnerably sharing his experiences of casual racism to his whole high school? He's been in similarly stratified classrooms for years. He's felt white teachers underestimate him. He's heard Black administrators tell him the best way to succeed is by keeping his head down. And for the short term, not speaking is certainly easier. But his continuous efforts to fight this racial exhaustion include his investment in creating a more equitable classroom space not just for himself, but for fellow students like Kalia, the student who joined Jordan in dialogue and experienced her own exclusions.

Changemaking isn't a polite (and certainly not an easy) process. And yet, even when it is interpersonal, it doesn't have to be filled with rancor. Jordan's work to radically speak doesn't further cleave the relationships with his teacher and administrator but names the damage to those relationships and creates the possibility of rebuilding them in a more just manner. His bravery also creates the necessary change for others in his position to speak back to everyday oppression. We can even see radical speaking as an expression of love: if Jordan didn't love his school, his fellow Black students, and himself, he wouldn't put in the uncomfortable, exhausting efforts he did.

The radical speaker is one who might be experiencing racial exhaustion because the mic has been kept from them. Simply introducing conversation around race means fighting the "conspiracy of silence" surrounding "race talk," says psychologist Derald Wing Sue, who popularized the study of microaggressions.[9] In the Interrupting Privilege program we practice such fighting by coming together to radically listen to a recorded dialogue of radical speaking, such as Fana and Tenneh's, then radically speak together.[10] Splitting into groups of two to four, participants respond to a simple prompt: "What did you hear?" Each person speaks uninterrupted, for a set period of time (two minutes seems to be a sweet spot for most groups) to the others in the group, who radically listen. The radical speaker mindfully focuses on the prompt, attempting not to anticipate the listeners' agreement or disagreement. In speaking to what they heard, radical speakers might fight their impulse to solve a problem and instead speak fully to a problem. They articulate their complex individual, intersectional identities while consciously trying to free themselves of holding the listener's guilt. Radical speakers lay down the burden of what they imagine might be their listeners' expectations, including being a spokesperson for all "my people." For example, if there were only one Black woman in the radical speaking and listening group exercise I open this chapter with, she would fight against any urges to speak as the representative Black woman participant and explain Tenneh and Fana's comments. Instead, she speaks with her full voice to her own experience, without translation.

After the first radical speaker speaks, the next members have their turns. They have the tougher jobs, because they have to focus on what they heard in the dialogue clip, not the first group member's intermediating response. In this exercise, no one is allowed to skip a speaking turn. Rather, if the speaker draws a blank, they are instructed to speak about that—namely, about how they're feeling, or perhaps what it is about the topic that shuts them down. In listening and speaking in this manner, participants work to "embrace humility and to try to understand the truth of others even when those truths are at odds with our own ideological perspectives," as critical pedagogy scholars Christina Siry and colleagues write.[11]

I describe this form of communication as monologic; it is the type of communication Mikhail Bakhtin describes as speaking with a single voice.[12] It's not (yet) the reciprocal, community-building activity that dialogue is, as we'll explore in the next chapter. Monologic radical speaking lets each participant share their voice without debate. We can hear and hold difference when we are not assessing each statement and rehearsing a response but when we are radically listening, just trying to understand what the speaking partner says. After everyone in a group has radically spoken (and radically listened), we loosen up a bit. Participants often sigh in relief when switching from the monologic to dialogic forms of communication.

In our program, radical speaking can be a pedagogical exercise with clear boundaries defining speaking and listening for the purpose of developing both skills. Here and in everyday life it is also an important way for us to critically communicate race in order to move through racial exhaustion. Annette, the Indigenous teacher whom we met at the end of the last chapter, shows wisdom in her use of radical speaking to combat her racial exhaustion. When she "see[s] white supremacy in the moment," she responds unapologetically. Annette combats her own racial exhaustion by telling herself that "I'm doing them a big favor by speaking up. . . . I think speaking up is actually a gift to people." She continues:

> When I see people being racist and sexist and homophobic and agist and all those things, to be honest with you, compassion arises in me for them. Because you know that is a totally, a really unwholesome [way to live]. What that means in my spiritual tradition is that they have these big mental factors that are really in front of any interpretation of life that they have. So they're not seeing clearly whatsoever. And they're causing themselves a lot of pain. . . . I know that stuff is painful.

Of course their racism and sexism are also painful for Annette: "It hits me in the heart that's where it hits me."[13] Speaking up and back—radical speaking—helps Annette move through this pain.

Ruth King describes the type of radical speaking Annette exemplifies names as emerging from the Buddhist practice of Metta, or "kindness without exception"[14] (and Annette is in fact also a meditation teacher who draws from Buddhist traditions). King explains that

> Metta is the antidote to . . . [racial] distress . . . a feeling of well-being not dependent on external conditions, a quiet stream that is flowing at all times. . . . The practice of Metta supports us in priming the mind to embrace racial fear and distress in an atmosphere of nonresistance. The practice supports us in minimizing escalation and distortion by gathering the mind, focusing the mind, and steadying the mind in the present moment. . . . [W]e are not trying to change what we are facing. Rather, we are freeing ourselves in the moment by loving ourselves.[15]

Metta is the stance behind radical speaking. That is, radical speaking itself is a practice—just like radical listening and sitting with discomfort—that amounts to a way to free ourselves by loving ourselves.

Such a free space isn't created without careful practice of how to radically speak. The "how to" that the Interrupting Privilege program teaches is a set of strategies called "interrupting microaggressions."

HISTORICIZING MICROAGGRESSIONS RESEARCH (AND THE RESEARCHER)

The word "microaggressions" has entered the popular zeitgeist as the topic of internet listicles, MTV public service announcement videos, and social media projects.[16] In my work bringing the critical communication of race strategies to students, workers, and community members, some tell me that they feel a sense of attachment to this word that names the everyday experiences of identity-based animus they had intuited for years before learning this word. Others feel a sense of alienation from it in that they feel that it excludes the experiences of those who do not have minoritized identities. To explore both of these feelings—of identification and alienation—let's learn first about the person who coined the term, Chester Pierce (1927–2016), psychiatrist and professor of education, psychiatry, and public health at Harvard University. Honoring this history is key to understanding *why* we should strive toward critically communicating race.

Pierce broke barriers and experienced much everyday prejudice as "the first" across a variety of spheres in education, sports, the military, medicine, and academia. For example, when he was doing his medical residency, a white female patient threated that she would cry out that he had raped her because she didn't like that he had other patients to attend to and was too busy to check on her immediately.[17] In addition, in the same internship year, Pierce celebrated a Black female patient's naming her baby after him to honor his kindness and skill. His experiences of being the victim of racism who could never safely express the reality of the inequalities led him to "fear . . . his potential explosiveness," according to his biographer. Thus Pierce advocated that Black people should not argue in front of whites so to avoid exposing "potentially dangerous information [being] given freely to whites." Pierce worried that "whites automatically and instinctively use even minor discord by blacks to promote divisiveness, doubt, and strife [so that] blacks become trained to 'overexpose' themselves and their plans in the service of comforting whites.... This facilitates whites' efforts to manipulate blacks."[18]

Pierce saw Black people toggling between the experiences of being under the constant and contradictory forces of racist hyper- and hypo-surveillance; of always being under scrutiny because of racism (i.e., posing a threat) and simultaneously of being invisible also because of racism (i.e., registering as less than human).[19] For Pierce, part of the way to deal with this evident contradiction was to be "selectively silent in front of whites," which included strategies of dissemblance such as not laughing or arguing in front of whites.[20] In one example of such a performance, his biographer notes that "Chet warns against doing things that 'verify your inferiority' and that confirm whites' expectations that blacks be 'compatible, accepting, and of good cheer.'"[21] In other words, Pierce was concerned about validating whites' stereotypes and so sought to uphold a level of constantly performed control in front of them. Enacting such a level of constant control can cause constant racial exhaustion.

Pierce published over 180 books, articles, and reviews on a tremendous breadth of topics including the relationship between race, gender, class, age, weight, and suppressed anger and hypertension (a precursor to so much later work that documents physiological impacts of racism);[22] the "super-stress" of long journeys as experienced by Tarahumara Natives on a 250-mile-long foot in a thousand mile plus Alaska dog sled race;[23] race and drug use in the United States;[24] prejudice against children, or "childism";[25] and race and television commercials,[26] to cite just a few. One of his studies on television advertisements critiqued, for example, the ways in which white people were portrayed as connected to their families while Black fathers and mothers were rarely shown on screen with their own children, much less shown in moments of genuine connection.[27] In line with this critique, he was a senior advisor to *Sesame Street*, which launched in 1969, and he penned a "hidden curriculum" for mass media on the principle that children of color need to see themselves on television and that white children and children of color need to see diverse groups of children playing together and diverse groups of adults supporting them.[28] He argued that media itself could serve as an effective anti-racist tool, with television having a positive (to counter the negative) "pedagogical function."[29]

Pierce was deeply influenced by the extreme racialized violence of the time including the 1969 assassination of Martin Luther King Jr., which he called a "macroaggression."[30] But such acts of extreme violence did not emerge from a vacuum. Pierce wrote that we need to pay attention to the ways in which everyday racism, which he called the "most offensive actions," are not "gross and crippling," but are rather "subtle and stunning."[31] As the co-founder of the National Association of Black Psychiatrists, Pierce made the case that racism registered in everyday spaces including on our televisions, inside our bodies, and in hallowed institutions such as Harvard. Beginning in the 1960s Pierce first named acts of everyday prejudice "offensive mechanisms."[32] These everyday discriminatory actions emerge "from feelings of superiority [whereby] one group of people proceeds to brutalize, degrade, abuse, and humiliate another group of individuals." Writing specifically about whites' "superiority feelings" and "contemptuous condescension" toward Black people, Pierce argued that these emotions overshadow all Black–white interracial and interpersonal interactions.

The offensive mechanism, according to Pierce, is not the racialized violence of assassinations and lynchings, but another harmful form of casual racism, which he began calling a "microaggression."[33] Pierce described microaggressions as "black-white racial interactions . . . characterized by white put-downs, done in an automatic, preconscious, or unconscious fashion."[34] Microaggressions are the "subtle blows" that are "delivered incessantly" to Black people. These knocks might not feel like much at first, but they quickly add up. Pierce also argued that microaggressions deserved serious academic focus as "the study of microaggressions by whites and blacks is the essential ingredient to the understanding [how] . . . any program of action can succeed."[35]

Pierce described the impact of a microaggression: it "assure[s] that the person in the inferior status is ignored, tyrannized, terrorized, and minimized."[36] Here he lists verbs that might not always be seen together. Being "terrorized" and "tyrannized," two verbs that encapsulate the bloody viciousness of Dr. King's assassination, seem easy to pair and connect to racialized violence, while being "ignored" or "minimized" have far less heft. Put another way, whereas "terrorize" and "tyrannize" involve explicit articulations of prejudice, "ignore" and "minimize" are more implicit. When I've called attention to this distinction, audience members who regularly experience microaggressions rightly see a continuum, in that everyday microaggressions that "ignore" and "minimize" people of color accumulate into feelings of terror and tyranny. These words also capture the relationship between everyday and structural discrimination (we experience minimization, which cumulatively creates moments of racial terror). The relationship between everyday and structural discrimination is the very DNA of racial exhaustion.

MICROAGGRESSIONS TODAY: INTENTIONALITY AND DENIABILITY

In our post–Civil Rights moment, the landscape of race and racism has continued to shift so that the everyday racism of microaggressions can feel more coded, slippery, and subtle. Psychologist Derald Wing Sue, who became the scholar most associated with the study of microaggressions after Pierce's groundbreaking work, writes with his colleagues that racial microaggressions "communicate hostile, derogatory, or negative racial slights and insults toward people of color."[37] The build-up of adjectives and nouns echoes the similar build-up of Pierce's four verbs ("ignored, tyrannized, terrorized, and minimized"). Each of the nouns means something distinct—while a "slight" might be brushed off, an "insult" is downright harmful; all these effects also exist on a continuum. Likewise, microaggressions can be more or less overt.

Take, for example, Civil Rights leader James Lawson Jr.'s words to striking sanitation workers: "At the heart of racism is the idea that a man is not a man, that a person is not a person. . . . You are human beings. You are men. You deserve dignity."[38] Lawson's words refuted the daily indignity of white people calling grown Black men "boys" and inspired protest signs declaring, "I Am a Man," in face of the daily violence of Jim Crow. Speaking to a current day microaggression on this continuum, during an Interrupting Privilege session Annabelle, a Black administrative assistant in her forties, described a more subtle daily slight, which was that her coworkers and bosses regularly greeted each other in the office but failed to share a simple "good morning" with her. This kind of everyday slight echoes the "brief, everyday verbal behavioral or environmental indignities"[39] that cause humiliation and shame. It also illustrates a desire to erase people of color from the space, to expunge our presence. Such erasure not only feels bad and adds to daily stress, but also correlates with the fact that women of color employees experience more harassment, receive less support from managers, have fewer networking opportunities with mentors and sponsors, and tend not to be promoted at the same levels.[40] Interpersonal animus reflects and furthers structural discrimination.

Microaggressions can be more or less subtle, as the above examples illustrate. In other words, they can be more coded and restrained—so much so that they can be difficult to name—much less interrupt. They can even lead the target of the microaggression to question whether it even occurred: "Did that really just happen? Am I being oversensitive? Is that person being racist towards me? Was that intentional or unintentional?" The person experiencing the microaggression might also spend time wondering "whether or not the [perpetrator] . . . is a generally racist person or whether they were just curious and unaware," as communication scholar Alexandra To and colleagues put it.[41] This moment of questioning "ambiguously negative experiences" is hard to move on from; microaggressions "tend to linger longer and weigh heavier in a person's mind. In fact, cardiovascular responses are notably elevated in response to ambiguously racist events compared to overtly racist ones and subtle racism erodes heart health over time through psychological stress."[42]

A telling example of working through the subtlety of a microaggression comes from Leslie, a Black Interrupting Privilege participant in her early fifties, who is a stay-at-home mother of middle schoolers and a nonpracticing attorney. Raising her hand during one of our sessions, she tries to puzzle out what a microaggression looks like. "When I was younger," she says, "it was clear when I was being followed in a store, and it's still clear to me when I'm being ignored. But is it a microaggression if I'm always being asked if I need help?" Paula, a white woman, who is about a decade older, laughs off her question, saying, "No, that just sounds like good customer service." Here I stop and ask Leslie to tell me a bit more about the situation and whether she gets asked if she wants help in all stores. She clarifies, saying no, just in the fancy ones. When I then ask about the tone of the person asking to help her, she says, "If I were to identify it, I would describe it as passive aggressive. Not genuinely helpful. But letting me know that I'm being watched. And I'm not wanted there." While one type of indignity in a store might be registering as invisible in front of a salesperson, another might be hypervisibility, or being only and always seen in a store as a criminal, being followed around or relentlessly (perhaps passive aggressively) asked if you need help. This illustrates the slippery nature of microaggressions, which change with context.

Perhaps most important about the interaction between Leslie and me was her audible and visible relief—a laying down of her racial exhaustion—when I simply validated her feelings. Asking her to tell me more enabled her to articulate and identify that what she was feeling was not help, but surveillance. My radical listening to Leslie was in front of the Interrupting Privilege session, for all to hear, including Paula, which perhaps enabled her to stretch her understandings of microaggressions. Paula had not experienced such a microaggression, and so I reminded the class that *white* racial exhaustion might prevent a Black person's experience of a microaggression from registering as such. Paula listened as I returned the group to our circuit of critically communicating race: remember to radically listen and sit with your discomfort before entering into dialogue.

Leslie's simply having her experience of a microaggression being validated helps combat racial exhaustion. To put this another way, microaggressions lead to racial exhaustion, and radical listening, sitting with discomfort, and equitable dialoguing help those experiencing distress move through it. Alexandra To and colleagues write:

> When selecting a potential listener or supporter, the top priority for a target [of a microaggression] is that the supporter gets it. This concept of "getting it" or "not getting it" was core to every participant's conception of communicating about racism. "Getting it" usually implies that the supporter has a high degree of empathy for the target, either because they shared similar lived experiences or because they have in some way demonstrated that they are a legitimate ally (i.e., a person who has already said or done something in front of me that proves that they will legitimize and understand my lived experiences).[43]

Such validation helps one move through the indignity, the frustration, and the anger that comes with experiencing microaggressions. It also helps address the befuddlement that some microaggressions can cause—as when Leslie questioned whether she was reading the interaction "right." This is often a question of intention: Did that person mean to tail me in the store or was she just trying to help?

Questions of intentionality encase questions of microaggressions. A guiding principle in many diversity, equity, and inclusion (DEI) sessions is the adage "impact over intent."[44] This adage directs our focus away from what we imagine might be in someone's heart (intent) to how words land actions and (impact). In other words, good intentions are not an escape hatch for bad behaviors. And, of course, we want to assume a positive intent for almost everyone. But in the Interrupting Privilege program one of the things we've discovered is that when people are honest about their past experiences committing microaggressions, most understand when they do and do not abuse power. In other words, they do understand their intentions, even if they are partially hidden in a sideways comment. For those who might indeed casually commit a microaggression, learning how to critically communicate difference by practicing radical listening, sitting with discomfort, and equitably dialoguing provides a way to move away from automatic, immediate responses. It's through this process that one can understand how even (or especially) unintentional microaggressions have power.

Scholars waffle on the issue of intentionality when it comes to microaggressions. Wing Sue and colleagues describes microaggressions as "intentional or unintentional" with intentional microaggressions being "microassaults" and unintentional microaggressions being "microinsults" and "microinvalidations."[45] Monnica Williams notes that her definition of microaggressions as "*deniable* acts of racism that reinforce pathological stereotypes and inequitable social norms" are not always about "conscious intent of the offender."[46] Instead, illustrating how individual actions reflect structural practices, Williams notes that "microaggressions are part of an ideological social system that confers benefits to the dominant group at the expense of the subordinate group." Thus, microaggressions are particularly harmful in their unintentionality, as they are "the manifestation of the aggressive goals of the dominant group, taught to unwitting actors through observational learning or other social mechanisms."[47]

Microaggressions are often encoded with double messages, which make them difficult for their targets to decode and hence to radically speak back to. For example, at just about every Interrupting Microaggressions workshop that I have facilitated, Black participants working, studying, and living in predominantly white spaces say that they've heard some version of "you are the whitest Black person I know" (or its siblings: "You are so smart for a Black person," "I forget that you're Black," "You're so pretty for a Black girl," and so on). Such a microaggression ostensibly works as a "complement" (i.e., when a white person says a Black person is "close to white," that's supposed to be a good thing), or a joke (i.e., don't take this so seriously), and overall, a denial of a Black person's identity (how I'm being seen in my Black identity is being negated by the person racializing me).[48]

Microaggressions cause the person who is experiencing such questioning to remain off-kilter while they attempt to decode the meaning as well as the intent of the statement. As communication scholar Meshell Sturgis and I note, "Microaggressions . . . are linguistically complex: they don't say what they mean."[49] "You're so smart for a Black person," for example, means actually, "I want to let you know that I believe all Black people are dumb." The challenge emerges in the response: how does the listener respond when the speaker has ostensibly shared a compliment that actually couched in an insult to all of the speaker's people? They are also dependent upon context. Williams provides examples: "Telling a Black student that she is smart might not be a microaggression during office hours, but it might be if said during class with a look of surprise on the instructor's face. Asking an Asian American woman where she is from might not be a microaggression if the desire is to form a genuine connection over similar life experiences, but would be if the goal is to draw stereotypical conclusions on the basis of heritage and/or assumed immigrant status."[50] The context thus dictates how off-kilter the listener might feel.

The nature of racial microaggressions is that they are, as Wing Sue defines, "communicate hostile, derogatory, or negative racial slights and insults toward people of color."[51] In other words, white people cannot experience racial microaggressions. Extending to other identity categories, only the minoritized experience microaggressions: women experience gendered microaggressions, not men; trans folks experience transphobia, not cisgender people; and on. Although this might seem obvious to many, I've found this concept difficult for some people to grapple with because it lays power out in such a stark fashion. Hearing that microaggressions are individual expressions of structural discrimination immediately produces resistance and incredulity for members of many groups to which I've introduced this concept. Some of them ache to claim a microaggression while using the language of inclusion. They balk at not feeling included in Wing Sue's definition; they want to see microaggressions in terms of their own experiences of exclusion.

For example, in one senior group of tech workers, Michael, an affable fifty-ish white man who described himself as having strong relationships with diverse coworkers, was working hard to follow the first steps of the critical communication of difference circuit. He tried to radically listen to women of color colleagues at his organization sharing their daily experiences of microaggressions, including one situation in which a Black woman colleague reported being systematically eliminated and eventually cut from a high-profile project because a project partner in India deemed her to be too dark.[52] But as his coworkers pushed him to hear the story as someone who could reflect on his own privilege, he balked. Instead, after appreciating the story, in an effort to be included, Michael shared that he too experienced microaggressions and the one that came to mind was being excluded from a morning basketball game. I asked him to please tell us more. Michael said that the former white male head of the company famously hosted an early morning invitation-only basketball game that was *the* place for senior executives to network. Michael was just dying to be included and could never score an invitation. Years later, he was still lamenting his exclusion.

After listening to his story, I put the definition of a microaggression being directed toward those who are minoritized back on the screen and asked him if he could tell me about how this moment of exclusion—of a self-described white, cis, straight, middle-aged senior tech exec—illustrated marginalization. He shrugged but still looked hopeful until I shook my head, no. And I get it. It feels bad to be excluded. But while Michael did not intend to dismiss the experiences of his colleagues, especially that of his Black woman colleague, his desire for sameness fomented the racial exhaustion of the assembled group. Where Michael could have used his experience empathetically to understand how much worse racialized exclusion could feel compared to what he went through, instead he held onto the idea that all exclusion is the same and that racism (or more specifically, racialized sexism) really doesn't matter. In sharing his story, he almost seemed envious of his colleague's experience of racism.

Michael's example illustrates the need for those with identity-based power to understand how, and in which contexts, their power functions. This moment of understanding can lead to fully believing others' microaggressions and then working for changemaking. The circuit helps here: listening, pausing, dialoguing before intervening. But making sense of microaggressions if you haven't experienced them can be challenging. Michael needed to accept the fact that not all exclusion is the same; that racism can and should be named as such. The sometimes-subtle nature of microaggressions can make it harder for even well-meaning white people like Michael to believe people of color. Participants of color describe people not only articulating a variety of verbal slights, but also acting out nonverbal ones, from a white person choosing to move their purse to an opposite side of their body, or crossing the street when a Black or brown man approaches, or refusing to sit next to a Black or brown man on a crowded bus when the only free spot is one next to them. The subtlety of microaggressions is part of the reason why they are so insidious. The subtlety of microaggressions also fuels the skepticism of those whose tendency is to simply not believe that a moment was racist.

Sometimes skeptics tell me, "Ok, so you tell me there are these things called microaggressions. Prove it. Name them. Tell me ALL THE MICROAGGRESSIONS. I want them spelled out. It's not helpful to just hear about their impact on people." Such skepticism and demands fuels racial exhaustion in people of color; this suspicion and distrust render all charges of microaggressions expressions of bad faith, or "playing the race card."

Microaggressions are a daily reminder of the target's second-class status. They are intended to let the victim know that even if they have been allowed into this esteemed university, this prestigious job, this vaunted space, they are, as Eric Joy Denise and Bertin M. Louis Jr. note, only "conditionally accepted."[53] With sideways comments and nonverbal behaviors, the speaker puts the person on notice that they could be removed at any moment. In these moments, microaggressions do not register the progress that any particular individual or group has made, but rather function as history living in the present. They reveal the ways in which atrocities live concurrently: from enslavement and Jim Crow; to Native

American genocide; to anti-Asian immigration laws; to the abuse of Latine labor; to "ugly laws," which declared that people with disabilities couldn't be seen in public. Each of these historical atrocities leaves a contemporary mark on our skins through everyday, throwaway comments, behaviors, and actions. As Pierce wrote, "Our society does not stand in need of new laws or innovative plans as much as it stands in need of eliminating offensive maneuvers."[54]

We need scholarship not just on microaggressions, but how to interrupt them. That is, while researchers have analyzed different types of racial microaggressions, the contexts in which racial microaggressions occur, and the effects of racial microaggressions, they have for the most part not examined responses to racial microaggressions.[55] Moreover, as communication researcher Michelle Holling writes, intersectional microaggressions aren't captured in the calculus of microaggressions research as "there is general neglect of the ways in which individuals are the sum of their identities . . . [so that] even when scholars seek to examine race and gender, their results unintentionally manifest a gender binary of men experiencing racial microaggressions and womyn experiencing gendered microaggressions or fall short of fully unpacking the intersectional nature of microaggressions."[56]

We cannot change history. What we can do is work to change institutions and structures through individual and community struggle. Although we might feel as though we rarely see the impact of individual, interpersonal changes, our frustrations over historical inequities and structural stasis can be combatted everyday by our interpersonal acts of interrupting microaggressions through radical speaking.

THE POWER OF RADICAL SPEAKING TO INTERRUPT MICROAGGRESSIONS

Each moment of radical speaking ripples out in the process of change: "Through laughter, attention is brought to the tension caused by the injury."[57] As Meshell Sturgis and I write about interrupting a racist joke, interruption strategies enable one to "respond . . . to the microaggression rather than the ostensible joke." This response "interrupts the flow of communication; rather than proceeding forward through laughter, the attention and tension remain held on the moment of injury." A response creates a dialogic ethos, one that "brings both interlocutors into a shared present moment."[58] As we move from understanding microaggressions to understanding interruptions, racial exhaustion further complicates interruption. Interrupting microaggressions is a way to fight oppression in a small, everyday manner. Everyone can interrupt. No special skills are needed, outside of simply noticing more, listening more, and practicing more. Interruption is also a skill that all can choose.

For those who regularly experience microaggressions, one of the reasons that interrupting them can feel so exhausting is because the structure of microaggressions displaces the burden onto the target. In other words, the person who has already had to deal with discrimination also has to make sense of how to ameliorate, move on from, and sometimes even apologize for the racism/transphobia/sexism/ableism/homophobia that was slung at them. While an interruption should move the exhausting burden off the target and onto the perpetrator, the interruption itself can feel incredibly dangerous. As To and colleagues write, "Pushing back and saying no poses risks (e.g., further harassment, harm to professional relationships and opportunities, etc.)." Yet not responding "may incorrectly signal approval . . . and invite future microaggressive behavior."[59]

In addition, if the victim of a microaggression has not established a practice of critically communicating race, and especially radical speaking (and possibly even if they have), they won't feel comfortable attempting to clarify what happened. But interrupting can often feel worthwhile. Interrupting microaggressions is a tangible way of documenting discrimination and practicing anti-racism. It is a daily practice that can bolster our own mental health. Like every daily practice, such interruption will most likely feel difficult the first time that you do it. Like an exercise habit, a meditation practice, or a mindful eating regimen, getting into the mental discipline of changing daily behaviors to spring into action differently is challenging. For example, when you commit to an exercise routine, that first day, week, or month might feel brutal. However, at some point, your body takes over and not only does it feel good to move, but you feel incomplete without moving. This is akin to the daily practice of moving through racial exhaustion. Similarly, those who regularly experience microaggressions might go into training: they might think through past incomplete or unsatisfying responses and imagine how to safely, easily, and without nearly as much fear and trepidation, simply interrupt next time. Those who regularly witness others being on the receiving end of microaggressions might go into training to notice differently and then create similar scripts about how to use their privilege to interrupt. In such moments of using your privilege, you are activating allyship.

Jada, the Black social work student whom we met at the end of the introduction, says to Violet, a fellow Black graduate student, that allies need to be doing far more to interrupt racism. "Right now in society the people leading the [anti-racism] conversation are [Black] people who look like you and I," she says, "and I always try to speak up on it. And I feel like as a Black woman on this campus you feel [the pressure to speak up] even more." Agreeing, Violet adds, "It should be everyone's responsibility but that's not the reality. There are a lot of people who'd rather just go about their day and not think about racism but it's happening all around them." Witnesses need to fight the urge to ignore inequalities because they simply "don't affect them." And yet, as Jada and Violet's conversation illustrates, when a witness ignores a microaggression, that in itself shores up their privilege. Conversely, white racial exhaustion can be combatted by the practice of interrupting microaggressions. But such interruptions should be taken on with the utmost of care. As Violet puts it, "First you yourself get educated and then you can educate people. You don't want to be like spreading false information and just messing up the situation even more."[60]

In her advice to allies, Violet iterates her own racial exhaustion and her need to *not* have to always be the one interrupting microaggressions. Yet, minoritized people who are targeted by microaggressions should not feel as though it is their responsibility to respond; it is not. Amie Thurber and Robin DiAngelo make that point this way: "Targets of oppression do not *owe* a response to anyone." If you are a person experiencing a microaggression, you can decide how or when you act to speak back and whether it will exacerbate or alleviate your racial exhaustion to respond. However, as Thurber and DiAngelo also note, "To *not respond* when you are the victim is not the same as not responding when you are a witness or perpetrator; because of the difference in power positions, it is one of several *valid and strategic choices* in service of your mental health."[61]

If the ally has a relationship with the person who is experiencing a microaggression, they might discuss whether or to what extent the target would feel comfortable if the ally intervened. If they discuss permission in advance, they might be able to exchange a look through which the target communicates, "Yes, please interrupt now." Or perhaps a longer conversation takes place after the incident, with the ally asking, "I noticed something in there. Is it ok if I say something?" If the target says yes, then the ally can follow up with "Would you like to be present, or would you like for me to have this conversation without you in the room?" Those statements illustrate to the target that the ally not only has respect for them, but that they are willing to take the risks and put themselves on the line. Truthfully, the "on the line" risk that most of us face is the fear that someone else is going to be "mad at us" or that they will be uncomfortable when we speak up radically. This means, for example, that white women, who utilize "niceness, comfort, and neutrality as cover for racial harm," must practice radical speaking, according to higher education scholar Moira L. Ozias, in order to develop their stamina interrupt racial microaggressions.[62] They must risk their discomfort. To truly be an ally who practices moving through racial exhaustion, taking on risk is essential.

To ally oneself to people of color is to maintain an active state. It is not something achieved, a badge or a medal to be proudly displayed. Rather "to ally" is an active verb that people with privilege can be constantly practicing through the circuit of critically communicating difference. But it also takes a deep level of control to understand when not to jump in with a superhero cape and ostensibly save the day. I caution against what Thurber and DiAngelo exhort allies to do—namely, engage in a full-throated "speaking up," which they describe as something that "can be empowering for the witness to the microaggressions" even if the witness "do[es] it poorly." They continue, "There is much more to lose by not acting; integrity; alignment of your values with your behaviors; the trust of those targeted by the microaggression, passive collusion with oppression, and peace of mind."[63] Permission, however, is key. When a white person interrupts a microaggression on behalf of a person of color without that person's explicit permission, that white person is enacting their own privilege. The act might feel right to the witness, but the target might not concur. In that case, the interruption is not what Thurber and DiAngelo take it to be—namely, "acting in solidarity." In fact, "doing it poorly" might exacerbate the situation for the target of the microaggression by stripping them of the choice to speak up. Moreover, white people's managing of their white racial exhaustion entails shifting the focus from their own feelings (which might include wanting to save the day) to those of the target (which might include wanting to remain safe and even, perhaps for an initial moment, silent). Interrupting should never feel as though the ally is parachuting in to save the day. Allies need to consider if their interruption takes the voice of the target or interrupts the minoritized person in the name of doing "good work."

For allies to attempt to interrupt a microaggression without permission is to engage in a misguided form of radical speaking that can reproduce rather than interrupt a microaggression. To be more specific, the ally should not interrupt the target; the ally should interrupt the microaggression, which might mean the perpetrator. But for that to happen, a vital condition has to be satisfied, which is, again, permission. For example, a white ally might overhear a manager asking a fully bilingual Latina colleague who speaks clearly and in non-U.S. accented English if she needs help with presenting a project to a white English-speaking client. Before the ally jumps in to be the savior superhero, what he might do is say to his colleague, "I heard what our manger said to you yesterday and I haven't been able to stop thinking about it. I would love to help but I don't want to step on your toes." After pausing, listening, and hearing what might feel like an inroad to an affirmative, the ally might say, "I wanted to check in with you to see if it's ok if I follow up with them."

If the person who has experienced the microaggression declines the ally's help, the ally must respect their wishes even if they think that is the wrong decision. The target might be experiencing a whole array of emotions from wanting to be the one who interrupts (perhaps pointing out the unfair assumptions based in that question), to wanting to report it HR, to wanting to simply deal with it on her own terms. And there are other considerations. When someone intervenes "on your behalf," you, the target, are the one who must deal with the potential blowback. The manager, in this particular example, might come to her to process his feelings of racial exhaustion that have surfaced when it has been pointed out that he's "messing up." Then the target has an even greater burden placed on them of taking a "race confession" and thus having to smooth the way to the point that the target feels as though they must respond by saying "it really was nothing" (even if the incident was significant). The victim's racial exhaustion is exacerbated while the perpetrator's is soothed. Thus, permission is key.

Allyship is complicated because of the ways in which one's ego is wrapped up in it. But engaging in ostensibly positive action to fulfill your desire to be a good person simply recenters yourself. Essentially, my warning for allies in interrupting microaggressions is to carefully discern the critical communication of difference; in other words, before intervening, work through the circuit of understanding to hear the microaggression, to hold the target's feelings with discomfort, and to discuss an interruption through equitable dialogue. This circuit enables allies to better understand the ways in which power structures the how, where, when, and perhaps most importantly, why, to interrupt. And not interrupting in an individual way does not mean you're off the hook: instead the moment provides you with the opportunity to create other change within your sphere of influence.

In other words, the power for allies in radical speaking is not as simple as "using your privilege"—an aphorism that can incite those within the bubble of protection to speak up. Furthermore, not all power is the same. Interruptions between co-equals such as lateral colleagues, friends, or siblings differ from interruptions between a supervisor and someone they supervise, family members of different ages, and so on. Even co-equals or those in ostensibly similar positions of rank or hierarchy will likely feel the power-pull of race, gender, sexuality, disability, and other registers of difference.

In addition, not every microaggression is the same. When I conducted an interrupting microaggressions workshop for a leadership team at a multinational corporation, Kate, a thirty-something, thin, blonde executive who spoke English with a British accent raised her hand in front of the sixty-person group of diverse co-workers to say that the microaggression she experienced the most was people asking her where she was from. I pushed her to explain more, asking her to share the specific comments she received. Kate readily expounded that she was often complimented, told that in workplace settings her accent was "cute" or "charming," and asked to repeat words that sounded different in American- versus British-accented English. This disturbed her at times, she explained, because the "compliments" were sometimes a precursor to men hitting on her.

After a pause, Ahmed, a forty-something executive from Beirut, raised his hand and said that he experienced a similar microaggression when people asked, "Where are you from?" when they heard him speak. However, he said, most people did not find his accented English "cute" but rather, in his estimation, "threatening." Ahmed explained that sometimes people would follow up with "jokes" about him having a bomb or being a terrorist, while others would make awkward conversation before simply find a way to take their leave. Ahmed felt that his accent prevented him from opportunities at his workplace and that outside of his workplace he had to physically protect himself once people heard his accent and learned his country of origin. At no point did Kate talk about her accent getting in the way of her being seen as effective or competent in the workplace; in fact, she noted that in her experience male executives appeared to be drawn to her because of it. This indeed is the paradoxical power of whiteness, and in particular, white womanhood. While for many "cute" and "charming" would appear to be at odds with "effective" or "competent," this was not what she experienced. Instead, the extra attention opened doors for her in the workplace.

I share these two stories not to place one in a hierarchy above the other or to downplay one person's pain by uplifting another's. Both microaggressions reflect processes of minoritization: the white British woman was experiencing a form of gendered and sexualized microaggression in the workplace that would be encapsulated by the sexual harassment phrase #metoo in the year after I conducted that particular workshop. The Lebanese man was experiencing a form of Islamophobia in the workplace that spiked after 9/11 and then again after the election of Donald Trump, whose first presidency saw an epic rise in hate crimes.[64] Both microaggressions did not equally impact these corporate employees when it came to subsequent workplace opportunities (or a lack thereof). Thus, while both microaggressions were significant to the participants and reflect larger patterns of inequality, they are not equivalent. And both needed to be interrupted.

HOW TO USE RADICAL SPEAKING TO INTERRUPT MICROAGGRESSIONS

Radical speaking is time-, space-, and context-dependent. The context—and how race/ethnicity, gender, and religion (as the above context was laden with unspoken Islamaphobia as well) dictate the power inscribed in the context—is clear in the accent-targeting microaggressions I describe above. Time and space also dictate whether or how to interrupt. For example, if someone commits a microaggression publicly and I don't respond publicly (when I am the one experiencing the microaggression or if I have permission to respond), I am giving those around me a pass to act in the same biased way. Thurber and DiAngelo put it this way: "A private conversation is not guaranteed to be more caring than a public one, and a public intervention is not necessarily without care.... A public harm often calls for a public response."[65] That is, my public intervention is not only for myself (if I am the target or witness), but for all those around me who are vicariously experiencing the microaggression. But the interruption is also for me: if I ignore the microaggression, I ignore my pain, and I exacerbate my own racial exhaustion.

The practice of interrupting microaggressions creates a way to move through such moments of exhaustion. Interrupting microaggressions is also the final step on the circuit of critically communicating difference. For those who experience microaggressions, this circuit provides a blueprint of social support, which, as To and colleagues note, "is an incredibly useful tool in reducing and mitigating uncertainty and other negative impacts of dealing with racism." But as they also note, "Seeking support can be burdensome, present unique risks, and entail competing priorities," so that "just deciding whether or not to seek support is a difficult process in and of itself."[66] Thus, many of us need training for radical speaking.

Practitioners around the country have been conducting workshops that help people garner such support in order to respond to microaggressions. For example, educational psychologist Ishu Ishiyama's Anti-racism Response Training (ART) highlights "disagreeing/assertive interjection, asking the perpetrator to clarify/repeat his or her comments, expressing personal emotional reactions, empathic confrontation (i.e. helping the perpetrator to reflect on his or her feelings/behavior), noting the damage and offense caused, questioning the validity of the action, naming the action as racism, supporting the target, and mobilizing support from other bystanders/authorities."[67] Other trainings are targeted at those who are witnessing but not experiencing microaggressions and thus have the opportunity "to speak out about or to seek to engage others in responding (either directly or indirectly, immediately or at a later time) against interpersonal or systemic racism."[68] As psychologists Jacqueline Nelson and colleagues explain, "The most effective bystander action is that which communicates a message of disapproval or discomfort without damaging interpersonal relations."[69] Student affairs practitioner Greta Kenney's insightful work provides the model of utilizing three strategies to interrupt: questioning, declaring, or punting.[70] In the stressful moment that a microaggression arises, having three clear strategies on hand enables either a target or a witness to respond when without practice a response can feel impossible to conjure. Each strategy can be combined with the other, and also makes sense as a stand-alone approach.

Questioning is perhaps the easiest strategy for interrupting microaggressions because the emotion we are most immediately hit with as targets or witnesses is one of surprise and sometimes bewilderment. We ask questions of ourselves, and so it makes sense that we then respond back with questions of our own. Kenney lists different types of questions one can use to interrupt. One is neutral question, as in "Can you say more about that?," "Can you elaborate on that point?," and "What is it about this that concerns you the most?" For example, a so-called racially ambiguous person might often be asked "What are you?," a seemingly innocuous question that nonetheless illustrates the questioner's belief that the target's look is somehow unplaceable and hence foreign. The target might experience what Jay Smooth jokingly calls the "philosophical conundrum" that emerges for mixed people when they hear this question: he quips, "I'm not a philosophy major; my father is black and my mother is white, and what are we . . . ?"[71] In addition, another interruption strategy for this microaggression might be to simply refuse to answer the question and turn the question back on the questioner, saying "How did you arrive at that question?"

In Interrupting Privilege workshops, we practice the moments of response. After learning the history of and scholarship about microaggressions, participants connect with partners to script both the essence of the

Figure 3.1. Interrupting microaggressions in practice. Photo courtesy of Gina Aaftaab

microaggression they experience the most (represented on the left-hand side of the page in the illustrations below) and the interruption they can imagine utilizing (represented on the right side).

For example, consider a situation in which two Asian American women in the workplace are confused with each other. Questioning can be an effective strategy here, instead of clarifying who is who (i.e., dryly joking, "I'm the other one," which is also a valid response, but is neither radical speaking, nor earnestly sharing your name). Sandy, an Interrupting Privilege participant modeled this scenario, providing the radical speaking question, "What about us makes it hard to tell us apart?" (figure 3.1). This question creates a pause in the conversation, a moment to think about an answer. That may lead to a realization that mixing up two people of the same race is racist and produce an apology. But it may not, so the interrupter needs to be prepared for the very real possibility that the person who committed the microaggression is more likely not going to respond with "thank you" or "I apologize." Instead, caught up in embarrassment, guilt, or shame on being called on bad behavior, the perpetrator might make excuses, double down, or deflect. Sandy named all of these responses, ranging from the embarrassed excuse—"Oh, I think I got confused because both of you wear glasses"—to a doubling down of the racist remark—"Well I guess we shouldn't have hired two of you"—to a sly deflection—"That's not what I meant, stop being oversensitive"—to an angry dismissal—"You people need to learn how to laugh at yourselves." Having multiple interrupting strategies at your fingertips means you can meet these kinds of responses (which are also microaggressions). To these responses, Sandy said that she needed to preserve her peace by simply walking away. To quote Malcolm X, "Racism is like a new Cadillac; they make a new model every year."[72] Thus, we constantly need new models, like the one Sandy gives us, to combat racism.

One way to do this is to reframe questions in such a way as to encourage the person who committed the microaggression to engage in self-reflection and confront their own assumptions. For example, if Sandy decided a week later to bring up the microaggression only to be met with a "Why are you bringing up old news?" she could ask, "Could there be another way to look at my response?" thus providing a gentle way to shift a space. Or her questions might be more direct, leading with "Could you imagine a different outcome if you engaged in conversation with me instead of shutting me down?" or "How could considering the impact of your words on me help you to see where I'm coming from?" These interrupting microaggressions questions offer everyone a path toward radical speaking.

Another strategy for interrupting microaggressions is making a declarative statement. I find these to be harder to come up with on the spot, which means that they require more practice during times that do not feel stressful. One way to declare is to repeat back what the person has just said or to paraphrase the microaggression. Such reflecting and paraphrasing might begin with "It sounds like you think . . ." or "I'm hearing you say . . ." Keeping a neutral tone is a constant challenge in this work, when you are still reacting to the verbal assault and feeling somewhere on the spectrum between incredulous to angry. But in order to break through to the individual (especially in a workplace), in order to get them to truly hear you, you most likely need to do the very difficult work of controlling your tone. For example, if a colleague misgenders your coworker's spouse (in other words, if your colleague assumes that your female coworker is married to

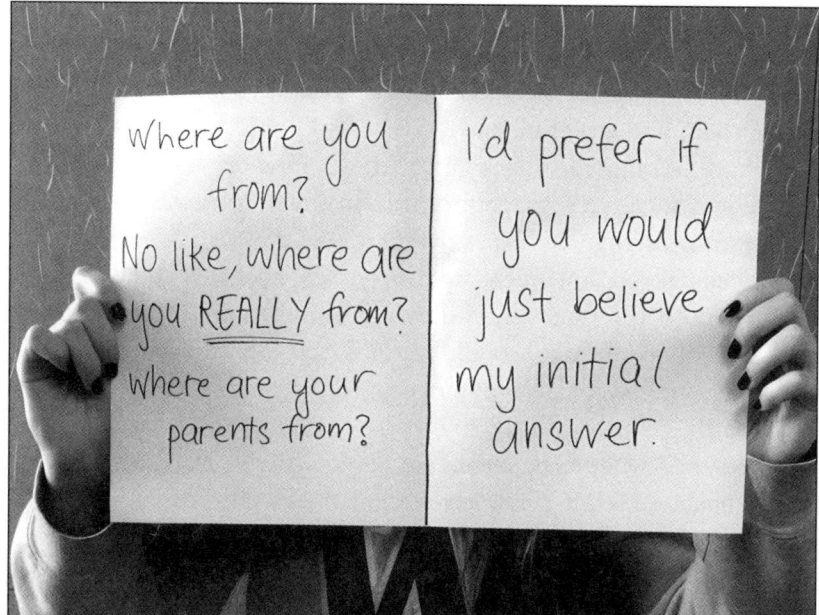

Figure 3.2. Workshop participant showing microaggression and interruption. Photo courtesy of Gina Aaftaab

a man), an ally might paraphrase the remark, with a neutral tone: "It sounds like you may have forgotten that our colleague is married to a woman and not a man." This might be enough to get the person to identify what they've done, correct themselves, apologize to their colleague, and work to change their behavior. Here you are assuming the best of an individual, and doing so leaves shame and guilt out of the picture. In another example of how to respond to the "What are you?" microaggression, one Interrupting Privilege participant who talked about relentlessly being asked "Where are you from?" because, she believed, of her racially ambiguous looks chose a declaratory response that refused to accept the legitimacy of the continuing questions: "I'd prefer if you would just believe my initial answer" (figure 3.2).

In an interrupting privilege dialogue, Darius and Ibrahim, two Black undergraduates at a predominantly white university, described the declarative interrupting microaggressions work they conducted with the white members of their fraternities. Both young men were the only Black members of their respective, predominantly white frats. Darius appreciated the fact that while he was the only Black member, he was not the first, and so there was an opening to have conversations about racism.[73] On the other hand, Ibrahim shared that he has to intervene in crudely vulgar misogynoir such as "The first thing most guys in my PC [pledge class] would ask me is have you fucked a Black girl?" To this, Ibrahim said that he "[sat] them down" for a "very straightforward and direct" conversation in which he began by saying, "It always baffles me when you ask me that." He continued, "If you don't speak up for yourself, no one is going to speak up for you."[74] Ibrahim's anger didn't stop him from engaging in the conversation—indeed it brought him in. And Ibrahim's approach was one model for how to interrupt microaggressions by not taking the racist, sexist bait.

However, I want to be clear that responding to microaggressions doesn't mean swallowing one's anger. Sometimes a situation is so maddening that it's impossible to strike a neutral tone. There is a place for anger, including an angry tone, in interrupting microaggressions. While this emotion can burn us up, it can also be powerful and productive. In "Uses of Anger," an address to white progressive women, Audre Lorde does not apologize that her "response to racism is anger" and that anger grows to "fury when the actions arising from those attitudes do not change."[75] But she is quick to explain that she uses her anger "for corrective surgery, not guilt."[76] Guilt, Lorde explains, is not useful in changemaking as it "is only another way of avoiding informed action, of buying time out of the pressing need to make clear choices." Instead, anger denotes engagement: "If I speak to you in anger, at least I have spoken to you." Lorde continues, "Anger expressed and translated into action in the service of our vision and our future is a liberating and strengthening act of clarification."[77] She ends the piece with an injunction for white women to hear women of color's needs and concerns and not to stop at fear of anger: "We welcome all women who can meet us, face to face, beyond objectification and beyond guilt."[78] Anger, then, is another strategy for interrupting microaggressions.

Amplification, which involves repeating something that someone has said, is another addition interrupting microaggressions strategy. One Interrupting Privilege participant described wishing for an amplifying ally when she said something in a meeting that didn't register with the person running the meeting. A beat later, a man in the meeting restated what

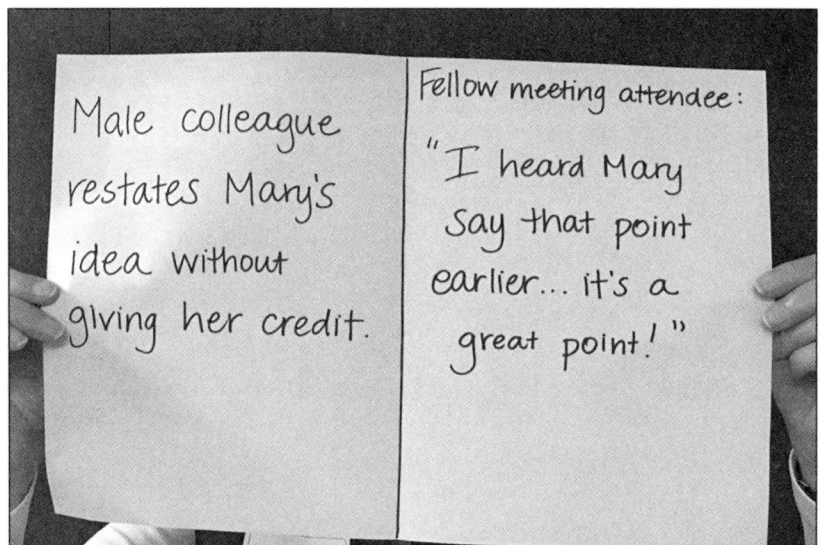

Figure 3.3. More interruptions. Photo courtesy of Gina Aaftaab

she had just shared without attributing the good idea to Mary; the boss then praised the man. In that situation, an ally might have stepped in to say, "I heard Mary say that point earlier . . . it's a great point!" (figure 3.3).

An additional strategy for interrupting microaggressions with declarative statements is using both "I" statements and "impact" statements. "I" statements take accountability for our feelings, highlight our own vulnerability, and remove guilt from the person to whom we are speaking. They work with a number of other interrupting sentences. For example, when she is mistaken for another Asian American woman, Sandy might say, "I felt frustrated when you called me by Ellen's name, the only other Asian American woman in the office, for the third time this month. You might have noticed that I stopped speaking in the meeting after you did that. Your comment had the impact of silencing me in our staff meeting as I felt like I could not be seen for the individual I am." This calm and clear statement explains Sandy's silence and the impact of her colleague's comments; she is not accusing anyone of racism or sexism but is rather reporting how she felt. She might deliver this comment in person or via email or perhaps both, in which case she would follow up on her initial in-person comment with an email saying, "I wanted to reiterate to you

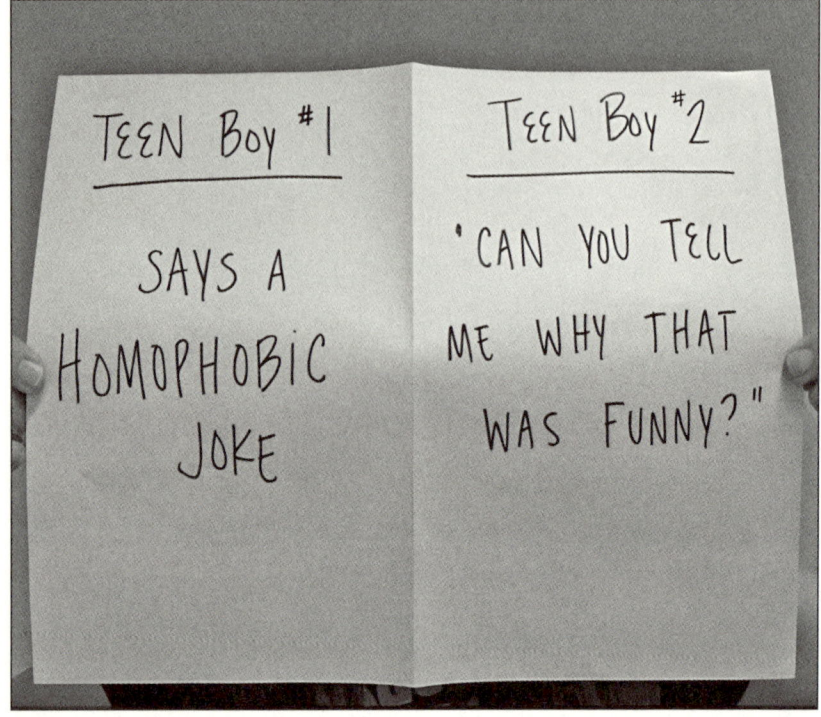

Figure 3.4. Interruption. Photo courtesy of Gina Aaftaab

what I shared with you in person"—here she would do so, and add, "It was hard to say, and I can imagine hard to hear." This also serves the purpose of documenting the incident.

Preference statements can also be used to guide the perpetrator of a microaggression even more directly. Some examples of preference statement sentence starters include "It would be helpful to me if . . ." or "How about if you say . . . ?" For example, a librarian participant in an Interrupting Privilege session recalled overhearing a teenage boy making a homophobic comment to a group of other teen boys (figure 3.4). One of the other teens first responded with a question, "Can you tell me why that was funny?" While this approach can feel necessary, it can lead to pushback because of its directness. In this case, the homophobic jokes escalated with that interruption so the radical speaker pivoted to an I statement: "I didn't think that was funny. I would like for you to stop." He didn't launch into a lecture or explanation. He expressed his intolerance for his friends'

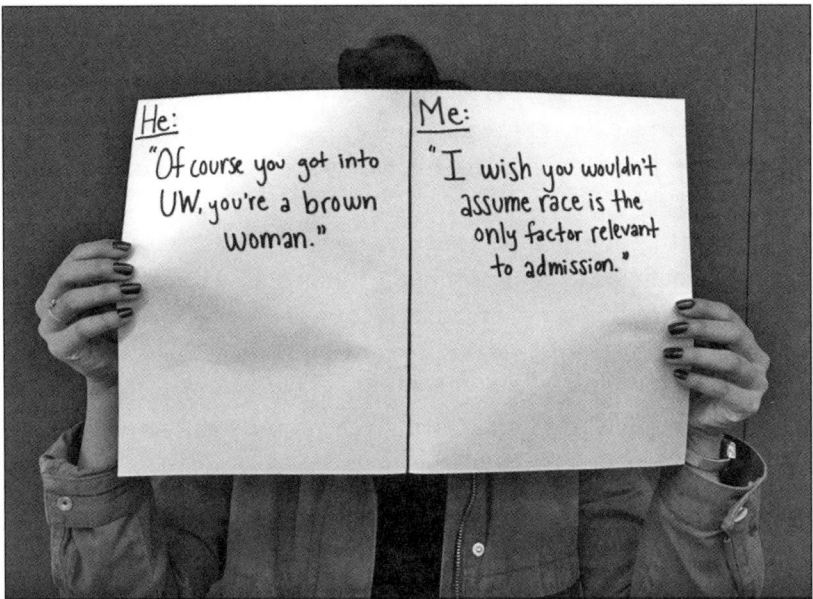

Figure 3.5. Interruption. Photo courtesy of Gina Aaftaab

casual homophobia. Such a statement does not invite dialogue. Instead, it asks people to cease their abhorrent behavior and illustrates that besides being hurtful to the target of the joke, it is also disrespectful to the audience hearing the joke. In a second example, a Latina Interrupting Privilege student participant recalled that in her first-year dorm, a fellow student made jokes about how she only got into the university because she was a "brown woman." To this she shared her preference: "I wish you wouldn't assume race is the only factor relevant to [college] admission" (figure 3.5).

Putting off a response, or punting, is another strategy for interrupting microaggressions, especially when it might not feel like the right moment to go head to head with someone or when you know that you may not be able to speak in the careful or measured way you usually do and drop the armor you might have worked so hard to put into place. Under the circumstances, you might instead choose to first redirect and then revisit the situation in a couple of minutes, days, months, or even years later. (I am an advocate of the "it's never too late if it's still bothering you" school of thought, as not addressing a microaggression can negatively impact you as much as the microaggression itself.) As Alexandra To and colleagues note, "communication needs for support for racism evolve over time . . . and may be triggered by proximity to the aggressor, the physical or metaphorical space where the aggression took place, etc. weeks, months, and even years later."[79]

Another way of punting if a microaggression comes your way and you don't feel equipped to address it in the moment is to redirect. In such a situation, you might say, "Let's shift the conversation." Or, if you are in a meeting or a classroom, you could call on others in the room, saying something like "What do others think about that comment?" For example, suppose someone says to Chris, "When I see you, I never see your race. I only see Chris!," what Chris might say in response is "I hear you telling me that when you see me you don't see a Black man. I'm wondering what other folks in the room think about that comment?" This is a potentially risky strategy as it relies on one or more people in the room stepping up. You might be met with silence, you might be met with the support you are seeking, or you might be met with a pushback equivalent to or greater than the first microaggression.

When I share the punting strategy with groups, they often balk at the thought of using it because it seems to give the perpetrator of the microaggression a pass or even permission to say such an egregious thing. I hear that. But I also believe that punting is a temporary strategy of pausing a moment of racialized violence. It doesn't have to be giving up on responding. It can simply be realizing that you don't have the bandwidth *at that exact moment* to respond, buying yourself time to respond later. Then when you are ready to have the conversation, you might begin to revisit the situation by saying something like "Let's rewind," or "I want to go back to something that was brought up at our last conversation." Then you can deploy any of the questioning or declaring strategies that you've learned.

Sometimes if I know that I can't respond at that particular moment but I want to keep myself accountable, I will mentally click through my critical communication of difference circuit, take a deep breath, pause, and say, "What you just said really resonated with me. I would like to make an appointment with you to talk about it. I can't talk right now, but I know that I need to. I will send you an email later today to set up a time." Not only will that statement commit me to follow-up with that individual, but it will let the person know that they did indeed do something worthy of a pause and a conversation. This statement might in itself nudge them to move into the critical communication of difference circuit. Of course, the person might not be satisfied with waiting and might insist on hearing what you want to say at that precise minute.

In an Interrupting Privilege dialogue Alina, a Black high school student, describes a situation that helped her understand when to punt and ask for help to interrupt, and when to interrupt by yourself. Alina heard a white student, Erica, balking at being corrected about writing the wrong last name for an Asian American classmate. Erica says, "I thought all Asian people's last name was Chang!" In response, Alina says, "I didn't exactly interrupt their conversation but I went and got an adult who could address it because it was a group of [white students] and if I all of a sudden went and said [goody goody voice] 'Oh guys, you can't do that!' they would be like [in a goofy, nasal voice] 'Oh well she's just annoying and she's just mad because I insulted her friend.'" Not wanting to be dismissed, Alina "went and got someone who could interrupt the problem." Alina contrasts this moment of punting with another immediate interruption, when she and Erica were at the board together and Erica said, "'I thought all Asians are smart'.... That's like saying all white people are successful.... So I called her out. I didn't exactly educate her, but did I called her out to say just think before you speak."[80]

Radical speaking to interrupt microaggressions is hard work for those who experience microaggressions and for allies. It bears repeating that if you are the one who has been experiencing microaggressions you *never* have to respond. Indeed, it might feel impossible to have the presence of mind to do so. This is where allies (heeding the early advice about permission) can come in to do the hard work of asking the questions that need to be asked and remove some of the burden of the asking. And this hard work helps all of us move through racial exhaustion.

THE ANGRY WHITE WOMAN, RADICAL SPEAKING, AND THE ESCAPE HATCH OF DENIAL

I began this chapter with the "Angry Black Woman" story, where virulent stereotypes prevent two young women from interrupting microaggressions. I want to tell you here that the story did not end neatly. As the facilitator for the evening in which we shared these clips, I echoed back the words of our students and community members who weighed in with appreciation for the authentic, brave, critical voices of Fana and Tenneh speaking their truth to power. I mirrored those who expressed experiencing the same and provided strategies for those who struggled to hear. And as I looked over the faces of the approximately sixty people in the multigenerational, multiracial room, I saw people wiping away tears, jotting down notes, squeezing partners' shoulders, looking plaintive and drawn. As some people struggled to fully grasp the how or what or why, all appeared to be listening. In the two-and-a-half-hour event no one expressed any verbal or visible discontent with the content, the speakers, or the format of the evening. Further, all participants—people of color and white—appeared to be fighting against their own racial exhaustion. They were staying in the work. At least that's what I thought as I left the event.

The next morning, I opened my email to find a note from Barbara, a white woman participant in her seventies who attended that session of Interrupting Privilege:

> I would like to talk with you about my reaction to the stories that [the Angry Black Women story] related. I found myself very angry at their condemnation of Seattle and the [university] without mentioning any sort of redeeming features. Perhaps they couldn't find any, in which case my question would be something about "if it's all so horrible, a) what are you doing to try to make it better; or, alternatively, b) why are you still here if you dislike it so much." We need to talk!!!

Reading these words, my heart and my stomach sank. My eyes prickled with frustrated tears. I had failed. This email exemplified Barbara's white racial exhaustion through which I hadn't helped her move at all. After feeling so proud of the young women for sharing their stories and of our room of listeners for what I thought was respectfully taking in this vulnerable experience of telling, I ended up feeling the same exhaustion the young women expressed to at the end of their story: "I'm not even going to bother because I know how you're going to react." And this indeed is the tack I took for several days (probably weeks if I'm being honest) as I ignored the email and let it eat away at me. I just didn't want to deal with this Angry White Woman. Then, at some point, I realized that I had radically listened, sat in my discomfort, and that I needed to radically talk this out. I couldn't preach to folks that they needed to be brave while failing to take those emotional risks myself.

So, I responded to her email and invited Barbara out for coffee. Even though her email to me had ended with "we need to talk" (with three emphatic exclamation points) about the "Angry Black Woman" clips, Barbara dove into some serious chitchatting, studiously avoiding the serious topic that had brought us together. With a latte in hand, I steered the conversation to her email topic and asked her if I could read it back to her. I flipped open my computer and did so. She looked down, uncomfortable, nodding. I didn't comment on her email, and she didn't provide any explanation. We sat in silence, with only the din of the coffeeshop audible. Then, after a pause, I asked if we could listen to the clips together again. The coffeeshop was noisy so we had to crane our heads together toward my laptop. My face was a few inches from hers as she heard, again, the two young women's words. After the clip ended, she looked up at me, blank-faced, and said flatly, "Well, I don't really know what I was talking about. Maybe I was thinking about another clip." I took this as her out, and said, "Maybe so."

There felt like no point in pushing the matter any further. I had done what I had come to do: confront her with her own words. We had tried to work through the first stages of our critical communication of difference circuit by listening and sitting with discomfort together. What emerged was Barbara's shame and her resistance to that shame; those two emotions exposed the wall between the two of us that I knew right away was impenetrable to radical speaking. So instead of pushing further, I smiled half-heartedly and following her lead, returned reluctantly to chitchatting my way through our coffee date. I vacillate between thinking my attempt at interruption was, on the one hand, as the kids (used to) say, an epic fail, and on the other hand, just part of the sometimes maddeningly slow process of interruption.

Maybe it just took my coffee date a little longer, maybe days, maybe weeks, maybe months, maybe even years. Or maybe Barbara got it right away and the shame was simply too much for her to admit to me. Either way, I try to reassure myself that I did the right thing in forcing myself to critically communicate race in the service of interrupting privilege. And here is the moment of hope: Barbara has continued attending Interrupting Privilege events after our coffee date, greeting me every time with a hug, a big smile, and enthusiastic questions about the event's agenda. Although she has yet to address what happened, she still participates with curiosity and engagement and, I do believe, is still learning. She listens alongside students and community members and dives earnestly into dialoguing. I think she is working through the white racial exhaustion that emerged in her email to me by simply showing up. As for me, while our coffeeshop meeting initially stoked my racial exhaustion, seeing that Barbara is still showing up has helped me move through my own racial exhaustion. Barbara is a part of my community, and I have to have faith that she is working her way toward dialogue.

4

REPARATIVE DIALOGUING

We have come to the final step in the critical communication of difference, community building through reparative dialoguing, which communication scholar Joel Allen and I define as "often difficult, truth-seeking conversations about social realities that uplift minoritized voices."[1] I begin this chapter with a story about the failure to make this final, essential step toward changemaking. Paralyzing exhaustion can short-circuit any of the steps from radical listening, to sitting with discomfort, to radical speaking to reparative dialoguing, especially when an incident rings in your brain with an incredulous "Did that really happen?" This happened to me on Halloween. Before you jump to conclusions, this isn't a story of Halloween-costume blackface or a more "socially acceptable" cultural appropriation such as drunken frat bros wearing sombreros and sarapes. This is a story about preschoolers, race, and gentrification in one of my former neighborhoods in Seattle. Let me set the scene.

My old neighborhood, which we moved to with a naïve and misplaced enthusiasm, was state-gentrified through a program called Hope 6, which urban planner Rachel Kleit describes as creating "New Urbanist, mixed-income developments in place of troubled public housing throughout the USA."[2] It appears perpetually ready for its photo shoot: a tastefully muted rainbow of Northwest Craftsman and Craftsman-inspired townhouses interspersed with single-family homes hug a gentle slope of a hillside. But spaces of gentrification are spaces of contradiction. If you squint you won't notice that the Housing Authority houses are always more than a bit shabbier, the moss on their roofs is never removed, the fading paint is rarely spruced up. Black public school kids with hijabs and white home-schooled kids with bare feet run down the sidewalk together, chasing a ball; their sweet peals of laughter can make you forget that you never see interracial/interclass/interreligious groups of teenagers or adults in conversation in the neighborhood. Lush waterfalls of lavender and garden trellises groaning with wisteria vines soften the neighborhood; if you focus on all that foliage, you might just forget the drive-by shootings on the corners.

We loved Halloween in this neighborhood of contradictions. In the weeks that lead up to the big day, many of the homes in the neighborhood begin sprouting comically oversized cobwebs, skeletons of all colors (ours, Mr. Bones, adorned cheekily with orange glitter), and intricately carved pumpkins, sometimes representing each child or household member, furbabies included. The neighborhood listserv—the main mode of community conversation—lights up the days before Halloween. New neighbors ask how much and what type of candy they should purchase to fill treat bags throughout the night. Are raisins appropriate, or am I going to get my house egged? More experienced neighbors try to troubleshoot the "problem" of "children who trick-or-treat without costumes." These children are never named by race although listserv users understand that the costume-less are the immigrant children, primarily African, sometimes Southeast Asian or Latine.

The whole neighborhood comes out to celebrate. Doorbells start ringing early, when excited Somali American kids as young as kindergarten—without costumes or parent chaperones—run directly off the school bus to trick or treat. White homeowners purse their lips and shut their doors, because it's just not done that way. They need time to prepare; the children need proper costumes and proper chaperones. Some children manage to snag an early afternoon fun-size bar; they eat it quickly, and shed the wrapper on the sidewalk, not yet knowing that the true American way is to hoard all the candy you collect until you get back home at the end of the night, then count it, trade disliked candy, strew wrappers around your own house, and gorge.

In some years (white) community members anxious over lack of costumes have created positive community activities, setting up a booth to paint faces, making masks, or providing and decorating treat bags. Were these experiences for the children, thinly veiling an injunction to acculturate to Halloween? Did they manage to generate moments of neighborhood inclusion and belonging for all? Or, as they were devoid of any actual dialoguing about Halloween, were they for adults who could now, in good conscience, give their candy to children who "looked like" they "deserved" treats?

On Halloween night in 2016, the neighborhood performed the Halloween gentrification shuffle. This was less than a week before Trump was elected and the quarter I launched my first Interrupting Privilege program. The inclusion and exclusion rituals of the season swirled around my head as I escorted my then-ten-year-old, along with neighborhood best friend at the time, who was also ten, and best friend's four-year-old sister. The older children were clad in coordinated angel/devil costumes, while the little sister was a tiny cop. Both best friend and sister were white and blonde, and almost white-blonde at that, with mid-back-length, cascading locks of thin, nearly translucent, wavy hair. We found ourselves keeping pace with a Somali mom and daughter, the little girl about the size of the blonde preschooler I was escorting. I stayed at the curb; the other mom stayed close behind her daughter. We smiled at each other and complimented the cute trick-or-treaters.

At one home, owned by a new-to-the-neighborhood straight white couple with a couple of younger kids and luxury SUVs that seemed out of place for this earnest neighborhood, the big girls received their fun-size bars, and the little ones approached. The blonde girl whisper-spoke her tentative "trick or treat" first as she had for the past few houses. The homeowner dad, a tall white man, oohed and ahhed, delighting in her adorable police girl fierceness. He gave her a choice of candy bars (not choosing for her as he had for the bigger girls—what a treat!). Then, he reached behind the door, to where none of us could see. "Wait," he said, "I have something special just for you." He proceeded to pull out a malleable fluorescent glow stick, the kind that can be shaped into an oversized bracelet for some, or for a tiny person, a necklace. The blonde girl was thrilled and turned around to wave it at me on the curb. I saw and smiled: she was going to look like a miniature raver.

The second tiny trick or treater stepped up. In a festive celebration of the holiday, she had a star painted on one cheek. But she wasn't wearing a costume; she wore what she did every day—a hijab. She had a plastic grocery bag instead of the blonde girl's bright orange felt tote emblazoned with a witch. The white male homeowner looked at her tiny self, greeted her with a closed-mouth smile, reached into his candy bowl, gave her a fun-sized bar, and shut the door. He wasn't violent. He wasn't even rude. He didn't spit out (or, to my ears, mumble) any anti-Black or Islamophobic slurs. But his whole affect had changed. Clearly, he did not think the second tiny girl was delightful. She wasn't special. She didn't deserve a glowstick. The older kids had already run to the next house, but both little girls watched the interaction, as did the little girl's mother and I. The white, blonde girl saw how she was prized. How she was special. How her specialness literally produced an additional reward. Her whiteness brought her greater bounty. The Somali American girl saw how she was tolerated but not embraced. How her Blackness, her religion, her signifiers of foreignness, her perceived poverty, prevented her from accruing the privileges of Halloween.

As I've told this story to groups, the first question they inevitably ask is: What did you do? I think people expect me to answer that I jumped in like an Interrupting Privilege superhero, cape and all. But that's not what happened. I was stunned into silence. Microaggressions, as Meshell Sturgis and I describe, can render the victim and witness "frozen" while "the perpetrator is free to move on without accountability."[3] I remember the mother and daughter not freezing like me, but fleeing quickly after this exchange to continue their trick-or-treating, and I remember them continuing a different way from us, perhaps crossing the street, perhaps going down another. I remember pausing too long on the sidewalk. I remember being immediately hit with exhaustion, with the overwhelming feeling that there is no escape from racism, not even on festive commercial holidays, not with the youngest of children. And I remember confusion, the sentence "Did that really just happen?" circling around in my brain as we finished our trick or treating loop. As I wrote about the incident later in field notes fashion, I chastised myself for my inaction. I did not say a word. Shouldn't I have said *something* to the homeowner? To the fellow mother? To the little girls? But what? There wasn't one form of an intervention that I could imagine would re-center power where it should be: with the young trick-or-treater. There wasn't one way I could imagine utilizing the power of, as we'll explore in this chapter, equitable dialoguing, or calling someone into a restorative conversation to create racial repair. Instead, my racial exhaustion took over. I simply couldn't summon the strength to respond.

In the years that have passed I've learned how to be easier on myself and to understand that immediate dialogue is not always possible. But this incident sticks with me as an example of how everyday racial exhaustion functions. It confounds. It befuddles. It stuns us into silence. And it infects all of us—those who are the beneficiaries, those who are the victims, those who are the perpetrators, and those who are the observers. The Halloween story is not simply a one-off, a case of bad luck for a young trick-or-treater or of me happening to observe a mean, stingy, or bad-tempered person. And, for the record, while I think what that that white homeowner did was indefensibly mean, stingy, and bad-tempered, and yes, gave out treats in a racialized manner, I don't know him, so I don't know if he is a mean, stingy, or bad-tempered person to all, or to put a finer point on it, if that man is racist. The interpersonal racism that the little girl experienced of simply not receiving the same form of a Halloween treat is a part of a larger system of structural inequality that is concomitant with race, gender, religion, class, and other identity categories. And we can choose to speak out or remain silent; we can choose to dismiss a community as racist or work toward changing it; we can learn to engage in reparative dialogue together to move through our racial exhaustion.

What was missing in my former Hope 6 neighborhood wasn't racial, ethnic, religious, or class diversity. Missing was a community that embraced a key part of the critical communication of race: reparative dialoguing in community. I open this chapter on speaking about, with, and through race and racism with a story about the incredible challenge of doing so in order to emphasize just how common it is for witnesses or allies to remain silenced by racial exhaustion at the very moments when racism arises. In this chapter I bring the critical communication of race circuit forward to the final step of reparative dialoguing. We follow this calculus: radical listening plus managing discomfort plus radical speaking enable the healing that can happen through reparative dialoguing in community. The reciprocal exchange of reparative dialoguing means inter- and intra-racial community movement through racial exhaustion. Speaking together, in community, through reparative dialoguing—the moment when radical listening, sitting with discomfort, and radical speaking converge for changemaking—is the focus of this chapter.

BUILDING CRITICAL COMMUNITIES TO FOSTER REPARATIVE DIALOGUE

Reparative dialogues happen best through community. And not just any communities, but critical ones. Building critical community means naming and working through power differentials. To get to critical community building, let's first consider community. Its dictionary definition, "a group of people living in the same place or having a particular characteristic in common,"[4] stresses an almost-accidental association stemming from mere geographical proximity. And yet, where people settle—and hence where they engage in dialogue—is far from random. Geographic communities are and have been racialized over centuries, with groups systematically included and excluded by law and by custom. Connection through a "particular characteristic" bears the imprint of identity and thus may also reflect the stamp of racialized and power-laden history, institutions, and structures. The second definition of "community" is "a feeling of fellowship with others, as a result of sharing common attitudes, interests, and goals." Here connection creates community through sameness of positions.[5] In the first definition, shared space fosters sameness. In the second version, feeling fosters sameness. In these definitions, community excludes differences—differences that are not encouraged to be held, but rather, as media studies scholar Samira Rajibi writes, "demand to be cured."[6]

A community's explicit or implicit desires or expectations for a sameness—sometimes expressed as cohesion—can silence difference. Such silence refuses to name or acknowledge intersectional differences even though these can be the very means of connection. Should we even strive to form "community" then? The concept of community is "dangerous" because it "creates enemies," writes education scholar Lynn Fendler, who cautions that "community building" cannot "counteract the divisive effects of racism, sexism, and other prejudices." In Fendler's estimation, articulating the idea—and ideal—of community actually creates antagonism rather than healing it; it forces people to coalesce "on the basis of what they oppose."[7]

It's not that scholars don't believe in the benefits of people identifying with one another and making connections that way. Instead, the critique is directed to the demand for sameness in communities. Consider the Halloween story. The white, blonde preschooler dressed as a cop shared a visible whiteness with the homeowner and a visible difference from the Black, Muslim, hijab-wearing preschooler. Neither party had to mention their racial similarity in order to solidify a bond of whiteness. Further, neighborhood declarations of (an undifferentiated) "multicultural community" did not provide a way for minoritized members of the community to experience belonging. But bringing community members together in dialogue to reciprocally exchange ideas about American Halloween and its traditions alongside conversations of Eid, for example, could have opened up the possibilities for connection.

So we can't throw out the possibly of community altogether. An alternative is the process education scholar Silva Bettez calls "critical community building." The descriptor "critical" in this context and throughout this book means *with attention to power*. Power challenges the creation of equitable communities.[8] And attending to power fosters community. This could happen, for example, by the neighborhood house launching a Fall community dinner (the first in a series of intentional conversations) in which all neighbors joined in dialogue around moments of inclusion, like the young children playing together, and exclusion, like the incident at Halloween, as a way to repair harm. Critical communities ask all members to embrace their vulnerability, to take risks—not just those on the downside of power, but also (or perhaps especially) those with the most privilege. This means first acknowledging inherent (and, for some, invisible) advantage and then consciously committing to leveraging one's privilege for good.

After public intellectual Brene Brown promoted exposing one's vulnerability as an asset at work, many high-profile leaders across fields from higher education to the tech world took note and articulated it as a strength and not a weakness.[9] And yet, in the business world, for example, valuing vulnerability can serve to "distort the value of being vulnerable in the first place [as] the point of being vulnerable is to share the authentic parts of yourself that you may have otherwise chosen to hide or keep private," writes mentorship guru Janice Omakdeke. Moreover, making our private selves public is easiest for those who have the most privilege. So not everyone can easily risk vulnerability: for LGBTQ+ folks in the workplace, disclosures about home life, for example, can prompt a microaggression from a homophobe.[10] Critics have noted that Brown fails to acknowledge that public vulnerability is racialized, gendered, and classed in ways that escape her along with the upper-middle-class white women who make up a good portion of her readership.[11] Those who are minoritized put on armor to get through the day, layer on layer of steel precisely to make themselves less vulnerable to everyday expressions of prejudice. Taking off that armor leaves them open to attack; asking them to take it off anyway, or refusing to recognize why it's there, is a racially exhausting act of cruelty. Critical communities must attend to this dynamic by building in vulnerability in safe and reciprocal ways.

Therefore, to invite vulnerability into a community, all members must see their power and acknowledge the inequitable experience of sharing their vulnerability. The community co-construction of vulnerability creates conditions for a positive interdependence, a "relational connectedness... to promote others' goals and value relational collaboration,"[12] write human communication scholars Stella Ting-Toomey and Atusko Kurogi. In contrast, communities that don't consider power function as a group of independent individuals who are motivated by "their own personal attributes and abilities" as opposed to "the thoughts and feelings of others." Critical communities don't spring up by happenstance. As Beth and Lydia, two white undergraduates who engaged in an Interrupting Privilege dialogue put it, "You can pretend to be on your own all you want [but] . . . you really are only as strong as your . . . support links." Lydia further explained, "Living in community always is a very intentional choice to make."[13] When community members "have a sense of their own agency as well as a sense of social responsibility toward and with others and the society as a whole,"[14] education scholar L.A. Bell writes, they—regardless or identity or power—seek each other out to foster diverse and inclusive communities.

Interdependence and social responsibility are two qualities that entwine in egalitarian communities. For those who are minoritized and often used to being "the only," seeking such communities is key. For example, in a recorded Interrupting Privilege dialogue Corey and Addis, who were the only two Black men in their graduate student cohort, talked about the incredible need to be in community with each other.[15] These two men are different in a variety of ways including ethnicity—Corey grew up in the Southwest with a Black American father and white mother, while Addis is an Ethiopian student who first came to the United States to attend college. But their similar experiences of being Black and male at a PWI helped fuse their connection. Community, in Addis's words, provides him with a "lightness" of not having to "second guess yourself." He notes that for those whose intelligence is constantly questioned, being in community means that "you don't have to worry that people are going to think you're not intelligent or . . . how you're approved of in that space." Community means that you can lay down the exhaustion that arises from having to ask, "Do I belong here?"

This question is at the heart of much scholarship on college students' success and well-being. Belonging is a sometimes inexplicable "feeling of being accepted, included, respected in, and contributing to a setting," psychologists Gregory M. Walton and Shannon T. Brady write. It is "a general inference, drawn from cues, events, experiences, and relationships, about the quality of fit or potential fit between oneself and a setting." Further, they say, feelings of belonging don't always come at once; they can emerge from "anticipating the likelihood of developing this feeling."[16] Individuals infer such a feeling by "assess[ing] their fit with the social world with an array of implicit worries and questions in mind, such as, 'Do I have anything in common with people here?'; 'Are people like me valued here, or devalued?'; and 'Can I be like me here?'" One can't answer these questions in isolation. In other words, belonging happens in community.

john a. powell, a law professor and founding director of the University of California-Berkeley's Othering & Belonging Institute, explains that belonging

> is . . . how you feel. I feel like this is my place, I feel like this is my home, I feel like I can exhale and be safe. But it goes further than that. We're talking about at the group level, at the institutional level. So what that looks like is that I get to co-create the thing I belong to. It's not something at someone else's school or someone else's house. It's our house. It's our nation. And we get to co-create. And those conditions of co-creating create a sense of belonging. So that requires agency that requires voice, that requires power, love, responsibility. And we co-create for everyone.

What we need to be conscious of, powell continues, is not constructing our "group by attacking some other group." This is the common pitfall where "my belonging is predicated on another group not belonging. . . . My belonging is predicated on my othering some other group. So we talk about belonging without othering, we talk about belonging where everyone belongs."[17] Community fosters this type of belonging.

Belonging can simply mean having a supportive community to turn just to talk. Renee, a South Asian therapist, and Adelle, a white teacher, discuss the importance of cultivating a space where, in Adelle's words, we "hold each other in a group or a collective." In such a space, Renee says, "We think about hopefulness, we think about willingness, and we have people in our lives that we turn to in moments of distress." Renee adds, "It's been really important to me to have a couple of really core people to turn to in moments of distress and not let that fester and recognize what these relationships mean to me in the sense of I'm valued and also . . . how I take care of myself affects other people."[18] This is a way of knitting together individual change and structural action in community.

One of the practices of belonging is bridging. Psychologist and bridging practitioner Allison Briscoe-Smith defines bridging "in the simplest of terms as connecting across our differences and seeing the 'other' as human." Bridging, Briscoe-Smith notes, "is not persuasion, it is not convincing, and it does not require us to give up our own convictions or beliefs. The skills involved in bridging differences are the foundations of much more complex skills involved in dialogue, conflict transformation and even peace." She adds, "but again, bridging differences is smaller than that or underneath those skills."[19] Bridging, in other words, is a way to work through the circuit of critically communicating race. In a connected vein, journalist Monica Guzmán notes that bridging conversations "help us understand each other by letting us explore the spaces between our perspectives."[20] But she also notes that "the most important thing about a bridge isn't that it's crossed but that it's *there*. That it exists and is maintained so that one day, when someone who's been nervous is ready, it can hold their weight, carry their truth, and expand their world."[21]

Critical community building requires making invisible rules of engagement visible. In formal spaces such as classrooms or work meetings, facilitators create transparency by providing a list of community norms. Norms help establish an "ethical praxis," in the words of Elizabeth Parks, which set the preconditions of radical listening, sitting with discomfort, and radical speaking within critical communities.[22] You can see that my community norms, which I have added to over the years with input from many students, also includes instructions for online spaces, including, for example, keeping cameras on while talking with each other (figure 4.1). My norms reflect the lessons I learned in developing my circuit of critically communicating race.

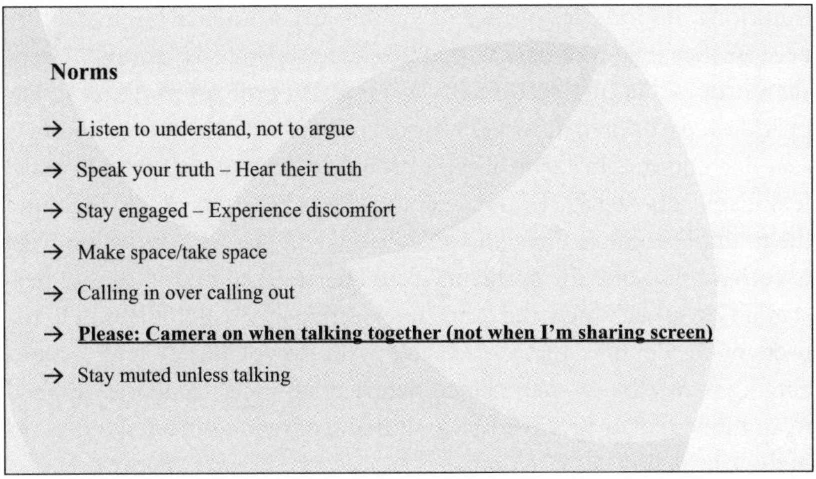

Norms

→ Listen to understand, not to argue

→ Speak your truth – Hear their truth

→ Stay engaged – Experience discomfort

→ Make space/take space

→ Calling in over calling out

→ <u>Please: Camera on when talking together (not when I'm sharing screen)</u>

→ Stay muted unless talking

Figure 4.1. My community norms slide

INTERSECTIONAL COMMUNITY BUILDING: SPACES OF RADICAL SPEAKING

Intersectionality is a key component in creating critical communities and setting the table for reparative dialoguing. Communities that place the most oppressed at the center create the conditions for radical speaking through community. The Combahee River Collective, a group of Black lesbian feminists who met together in the 1970s, famously produced a groundbreaking statement on intersectionality that argued that in order to address the needs of Black women forgotten by the sexism of the Civil Rights movement and the racism of white feminism, communities must center Black women. Such centering ensures the liberation of all: "If Black women were free, it would mean that everyone else would have to be free since our freedom would necessitate the destruction of all the systems of oppression."[23]

The term "intersectionality" was coined by Black feminist critical race and legal scholar Kimberlé Williams Crenshaw in 1989. Although today people often use it colloquially (and often incorrectly) to mean the mixture of all forms of identity, she was naming something very specific: the multilayered forms of discrimination that Black women face and that the traditional boundaries of race or gender jurisprudence fail to capture because they treat race/gender boundaries as separate dynamics.[24] Crenshaw argues that intersectionality is a framing problem: without it, law provides a partial and distorted view or an alternative narrative. Crenshaw said that coining the term "intersectionality" was her "attempt to make feminism, anti-racist activism, and anti-discrimination law . . . highlight the multiple avenues through which racial and gender oppression were experienced so that the problems would be easier to discuss and understand."[25] In other words, the term "intersectionality" calls attention to the overlapping identities that are invisible in the eyes of the law. Intersectionality identifies the interconnected nature of all social categories applied to an individual or group and the subsequent interconnected moments of discrimination.

Since the advent of the Black Lives Matter movement that grew in anguished response to the 2012 murder of teenager Trayvon Martin, the public has heard many dramatic stories of racialized violence, of police shootings. Names echo in protests: Michael Brown (2014), Tamir Rice (2014), Walter Scott (2015), Philando Castile (2016), Alton Sterling (2016), and so many more.[26] Although Black cis-men receive perhaps the most media attention, the Say Her Name movement has illustrated the ways in which such state sanctioned violence also disproportionately kills Black women, cis and trans. Protesters call out the names of Rekia Boyd (2012), Kayla Moore (2013), Michelle Cusseaux (2014), Sandra Bland (2015), Ataina Jefferson (2019), Breonna Taylor (2020). But such moments are not equitably upheld in the public consciousness. Many are unfamiliar with the names I've listed above, as well as that of Mya Hall, a Black transgender woman who was murdered in 2015 by officers after mistakenly turning onto National Security Agency property.

Crenshaw leads audiences through an exercise in which she illustrates just how invisible Black women's deaths are.[27] She begins by slowly reading the names of Black people murdered by the police, beginning with those who have been featured most heavily in media coverage. She instructs the audience to stand before she begins reading and to sit down when they hear an unfamiliar name.[28] When I saw Crenshaw give a version of this talk to a packed, diverse audience at Seattle's Town Hall, no one was standing up when she got just halfway through her list. She made her point: we did not know enough about the individuals behind the hashtag. Crenshaw also argued that because of the power of Black participatory social media, and especially Black Twitter, we have the ability to see the links between everyday discrimination and Black death, as well as the impact of what social media has deemed "living while Black"—the police being called on Black people having a barbeque, Airbnb vacationers, and graduate students dozing in a dormitory lounge.[29] Such actions make equitable dialoguing not just exhausting but dangerous for Black folks. Living while Black speaks to the ways police are daily pulled toward interpersonal racism. At the same time, we rarely hear about the steps that happen before the police are called. The scores of shady neighborhood listserv comments that continue unchecked. The offhand comments that go unchallenged. The years of simply not giving the little Black girl the same Halloween treats. The racism that happens in community. And we rarely hear how those who experience such intersectional discrimination create intersectional community to radically listen to each other, move through discomfort together, and radically speak.

In a recorded Interrupting Privilege dialogue, two queer Black women graduate students, April and Amanda, articulate how hard it is to create reparative dialogues in community when their multiple identities are ignored and erased.[30] April says that community is "one of those really big factors . . . that's missing for a lot of students of color." She explains that in addition to a community needing to embrace her because of her race, it needs to see her gender and sexuality. Communities that are oriented towards singular instead of multiple identities are unable to see her truth. This includes her family. April notes, "I'm Black, but my Black family doesn't like gay people. Ok . . . well I'm this Black queer person. And then you go into the queer space and you're like wow did you just tell me that you're into race play!?! Umm. Like this isn't, this is not a friendly place for me." Such anti-intersectional experiences force those who are multiply minoritized to choose singular aspects of their identities so that, in April's words, "you can either be Black or you can be queer" but you can't be both. This is what the Combahee Collective was talking about.

Amanda adds that the two of them deliberately combatted these moments of exclusion by creating a Black *and* LGBT+ graduate student community. Amanda explains, "The whole point of [our Black LGBT+] space was for us to not have to pick and choose which identity we wanted to try to relate to [and not] sacrifice of other parts of ourselves." A community embracing all of their identities means that all members can "really find . . . affinity with one another through our queerness [and] through our racialized identities." This intentionally inclusive space, Amanda notes, doesn't congratulate itself on achieving inclusivity, but rather, continually works to embrace "difference within that space as well" as not everyone who is Black and LGBT+ will have the same experiences. The creation of truly inclusive spaces, Amanda says, is a reparative endeavor: it's "work! It's work to sustain communities. It's work to educate people." This work, April agrees, is about regularly showing up to build intersectional community with each other.

Critical community is contingent on the co-creation of trust and connection. For many, connection has to come through validation, being truly and fully seen. Many people—especially those who are minoritized—are used to being unseen. As a result, they don't request the space, they don't require the community to stop and see them. The entire community loses as a result. In contrast, non-minoritized people are used to being constantly centered. They find ways to demand space, even (or especially) when communities are re-centered on those with minoritized identities. Ting-Toomey and Kurogi note that if community members "do not trust each other, they tend to move away (cognitively, affectively and physically) from each other rather than struggle-along with each other."[31] And creating trust takes concerted, intentional work. Communities that foster opportunities for reparative dialogue constantly build community as a matter of process, not as a singular end. Supporting the dynamic nature of groups means embracing uncomfortable moments of difference and power. It means, for those with outsized power, embracing silence in moments of dialogue or what Tanja Dreher calls "eavesdropping with permission."[32] This means that not everyone will feel like they are part of the inner circle all the time, and, in fact, those who have felt a part of the inner circle will experience what it's like to (if only temporarily) be a part of the periphery. Trust is key for the critical communication of race because "when we do not trust someone's words or actions, we automatically turn off."[33] How do we build and rebuild trust in order to arrive at reparative dialoguing?

DIALOGUING (WITHOUT ATTENDING TO POWER)

As we saw in the last chapter, in critically communicating race, radical speaking provides the speaker with a moment of truth-telling that creates necessary change in the world and helps the speaker move through racial exhaustion. But what about the listener's response? What role does reparative dialoguing—"an act of discovery where interlocutors and listeners learn more about themselves, social dynamics, and their positionality through the reflexive action and exercise of having frank conversations about topics such as race, racism, and harm"[34]—play in the critical communication of race? To move there, let's explore the difference between dialoguing and equitable dialoguing.

The word "dialogue" comes from the Greek words *dia* (or "through") and *logos* (or "word"). Dia-logos thus means "a word that moves" or a "multidirectional exchange of speech."[35] Thus, those engaged in dialogue construct meaning together—new meaning that they didn't have before the moment of coming together—through the movement of words. Humans forge themselves through dialogue. In a series of 1923 canonical essays philosopher Martin Buber describes the ways in which dialogue constitutes change from "I-It relationships" between speaker and listener (a relationship between self and object) to "I-Thou relationships" (a relationship between self and other selves). Whereas an I-It relationship is a monologic, interior form of communication, an I-Thou formulation is a dialogic, reciprocal one. Dialogue is thus the process of connecting humans.[36] And dialogue happens through relationality, or put another way, through community.[37] Dialogue needs listeners to carefully and actively listen.[38] Further, dialogue constructs shared meanings alongside community, as Mikhail Bakhtin wrote sixty years after Buber.[39]

The construction of meaning through dialogue is not a combative, oppositional process. Dialogue, notably, is not debate. While debaters argue for a singular, correct answer, dialoguers embrace the idea that many people have pieces of the answer and together can craft a solution. While debate is combative in its attempt to prove the other side wrong, dialogue is collaborative in its desire to work toward common understandings. While debate is about winning, dialogue is about exploring a common good together. While debaters engage in listening in order to hunt down flaws and create counter arguments, dialoguers engage in listening in order to foster understanding, find shared meaning, and craft moments of agreement. While debate defends assumptions as truth while critiquing all other positions, dialogue reveals assumptions as limited and up for evaluation. While debaters search for weakness in others' positions, dialoguers humbly admit that others' thinking can improve its own. While a debate seeks a conclusion or a vote to ratify its own position, a dialogue searches for strength and value in others' positions. While debate recycles the same ideas, dialogue searches for new opinions. While debaters disrespect others' opinions, and often other people in the process, dialoguers respect both people and their opinions.[40] Dialoguers neither cling stubbornly to their initial positions, nor do they abandon them. Rather, dialogue cultivates an openness that enables a focus "on what is going on in the co-created between rather than within the minds of individuals."[41]

And yet, dialogue alone can fall short of *reparative* dialogue if it does not explicitly consider power and difference. Simply bringing two parties together to speak without setting the preconditions to hear historical harms, intervene in interpersonal silences, cease structural discrimination, can exacerbate power differentials and inequalities. While a good starting point might be "display[ing] a genuine, inquiring attitude," as Guzmán writes, inquiry without critical consideration of difference can cause harm. Guzmán and other proponents of neutral dialogue strive to "uncover deep-level, common ground and common interests on the identity level."[42] This process of uncovering, if not done with careful attention to power, exacerbates the racial exhaustion of the minoritized.[43]

Such a power-evasive approach to dialogue is one that fits the label of being "equal" but not "equitable." While both words are colloquially used interchangeably, diversity, equity, and inclusion practitioners and scholars have pointed out that they differ. Equality means that everyone gets the same resources, opportunities, or access. But this same might be too much for some and not enough for others. Equity means that everyone gets what they need. One metaphor I often share is about eating pie. Let's say you cut a pie into eight slices. To equally distribute the pie, eight people must each be given a slice of pie. But what if four of those eight have just come from eating a huge meal and couldn't eat another bite? And one of those eight hasn't eaten in days? Equality holds onto the rule that each person should still receive their one piece of pie. Equity would give the

Figure 4.2. Inequality. Tony Ruth, "Business Town Tumblr," Creative Commons

hungry person more pie, perhaps five pieces to account for those who couldn't eat pie and are full, and the people who are full would get no pie.

There are a wide variety of visuals and metaphors that illustrate the differences between equality and equity, including the work of illustrator Tony Ruth. Riffing off the visuals of Shel Silverstein's classic 1964 children's book *The Giving Tree*, Ruth provides a sequence of four images to illustrate the language of power and inequality. In the first image, which showcases "Inequality," or what Ruth defines as "unequal access to opportunities," the giving tree drops an apple straight into the arms of one child positioned underneath the tree on the ground, while the other child waits with open arms but never receives an apple (figure 4.2). In the second panel titled "Equality?," which Ruth defines as "evenly distributed tools and assistance," both children now have equal-length ladders and bags to hold their apples, but one child has positioned himself on the side of the tree that bends toward him with laden fruit, while the other is perplexed by how to reach apples that are still out of reach even with his ladder (figure 4.3). In the third panel on "Equity," in which Ruth points to "custom tools that identify and address inequality," a taller ladder is provided for the child with the fruit on the harder-to-reach end (figure 4.4). And on the fourth panel, "Justice," which reads "fixing the system to offer equal access to both tools and opportunities," the ladders are the same, as

Figure 4.3. Equality. Tony Ruth, "Business Town Tumblr," Creative Commons

Figure 4.4. Equity. Tony Ruth, "Business Town Tumblr," Creative Commons

in the equality picture, but the tree itself has been adjusted so that both sides have fruit positioned at equal heights (figure 4.5).

Ruth's cartoons illustrate that moving from inequality to justice means carefully investigating systems of inequality and constructing new structures to combat them. Applied to dialoguing, striving for just dialogues—those that critically communicate race—means constructing critical

Figure 4.5. Justice. Tony Ruth, "Business Town Tumblr," Creative Commons

community to usher in such moments. Reparative dialogues provide what intergroup dialogue scholars describe as "a critical opportunity for participants to closely examine the socially constructed norms and ideologies that guide their (often unconscious) beliefs."[44]

INTERGROUP DIALOGUE: ATTENDING TO POWER

One way to repair power in the dialogic process is through intergroup dialogue, which emerged in the Civil Rights movement, in the context of interracial conversations on school desegregation.[45] Intergroup dialogue by definition is "face to face contact between people from social identity groups with a history of tension between them (i.e., people of color and white people)."[46] Psychologist Gordon Allport's 1954 contact hypothesis argued that creating positive conditions for such interracial interactions such as sharing goals, cooperating, having an external facilitator, and sharing status, can reduce racial bias.[47] In his words, "Prejudgments become prejudices only if they are not reversible when exposed to new knowledge."[48] However, Allport's study, and the vast majority of studies stemming from his (similarly authored with a white gaze), focus exclusively on reducing the role of prejudice in the "in-group" or white member and not the impact of intergroup dialogues on the member of the "out-group" of persons of color.

Conflict is often at the heart of such dialogues, as social work scholar Daphne Zuniga and co-authors have shown. Intergroup dialogues are not necessarily "feel-good types of cross-group encounters" in that they do not "attempt to promote understanding by avoiding, masking, or overcoming conflicts." Instead, "disagreements and conflicts" are key to intergroup dialogue encounters, which "can become valuable opportunities for participants to engage in significant conversations about different perspectives and tensions shaping their relationships."[49] Here people practice intergroup dialogue not to create "perfect" conditions for a singular one-off conversation, but rather to "sustain communication and involvement to bridge differences and move participants to deeper and more meaningful levels of engagement." This approach provides participants with a way to "critical[ly] examin[e] . . . the impact of power relations and social inequality on intergroup relations"[50] Reparative dialoguing takes up these elements of power that constitute the philosophy behind of intergroup dialogue. Intergroup dialogue thus includes both historical and current intergroup conflict, multiple flows of communication, noise and silence, intentionality, and emotional challenges and sustained tension.

Conflict is also central to connecting interpersonal dialogue to larger issues of interpersonal and historical power. Intercultural communication scholar Kate Willink and colleagues note that dialogue is a "mode of confrontation—where the marginalized other may dialogue with colonizing structures." For those on the downside of power, dialogue "becomes a technique of liberation—of decolonization—a method whereby one can 'speak back to power.'"[51] In the service of repair, when marginalized folks speak, those in power should consciously work against their urges to "consume" minoritized perspectives, in the words of Sara DeTurk; such consumption would stoke racial exhaustion during a dialogue.[52] The conditions of equitable dialogue include making space for listeners to remain silent. For those listeners, moving through racial exhaustion during a dialogue might mean "intentionally choosing restraint and knowing it directly," and thus to "do less harm to others and ourselves," as Ruth King writes. She also notes that "some of us impulsively speak when we feel racial discomfort. When this happens, we may instead set an intention to pay more attention to the impulse to speak. . . . Speaking wisely is a mindfulness practice."[53] And speaking wisely about race is a critical practice.[54]

The conditions for reparative dialoguing between minoritized and empowered groups must be intentionally created. They might indeed exist "only for that dialogic moment."[55] The animating impulse behind reparative dialogues should be love, writes education liberation scholar Paulo Friere: "Dialogue cannot exist . . . in the absence of a profound love for the world and for people. . . . Love is at the same time the foundation of dialogue and dialogue itself."[56] Dialogues based in methodologies of intergroup dialogue or critical intercultural communication might be successful for a moment, but without a conscientious coupling of community they often lack sustainability for changemaking, particularly for those on the downside of power. The way to get to love is through reparative dialoguing in critical, equitable communities.

Reparative dialogue "begins with radical listening [and] operates as both a process and an outcome of intentional conversations. It directly impacts interlocutors that are engaging in conversation, and has a secondary impact on the observers."[57] To engage in reparative dialogue, those who have experienced harm must join together with those who have caused harm in conversation. Both parties must create the communicative space (radically listening, sitting with discomfort, radically speaking) in order to advocate for and uplift historically neglected voices. This is not a one-off process; reparative dialogue must be committed to for as long as it takes the rupture to heal. Reparative dialogues create room for shared understanding to develop with time and work. But if, for example, "someone manipulates the process through disingenuous questioning or exaggerated recollection, reparative dialogue becomes ineffective."[58]

We can forge reparative dialogue in a variety of spaces, including the classroom. Education scholars Anna Steen-Utheim and Anne Line Wittek see what they call "dialogic feedback" as essential for students' learning.[59] In dialogic feedback, reciprocity defines the learning space, such that both students *and* teachers are not only willing to be challenged by each other but invite in critique. Providing emotional and relational support is another key element of dialogic feedback. Steen-Utheim and Wittek stress that feedback through dialogue should be regularly maintained. This means providing numerous opportunities for those being given feedback to express themselves. Finally, dialogic feedback isn't just about responding to a particular assignment; it's an opportunity to invest in the student's long- and short-term growth. To conclude this chapter I move to examples of reparative dialogue in action.

REPARATIVE DIALOGUING IN ACTION

How do you get to anything resembling love when someone offends you? Everything in your gut recoils in anger, and you are on the verge of clapping back and labeling that statement as the one-word offense that you know it to be. Imagine that instead you follow your critical communication of difference circuit: after radically listening you sit in your discomfort, breathing calmly as you radically ask a question, loop back to radically listening to the answer, and then asking another question that will bring your speaking partner into what you hope will be a reparative dialogue. The strategies in this book are all about engagement. In this spirit, radical listening, sitting in discomfort, and radical speaking set the table for reparative dialogue in community. Reparative dialogue starts with phrases such as "Tell me more," "What's that like?," and "Please help me understand." When you ask these questions, you find yourself speaking in a manner that allows you to unpack what you have heard (instead of blasting it as wrong) and begin a dialogue. Instead of shutting down, you have worked to build community.

As you begin to engage in reparative dialogue, you veer away from conversation-halting expressions such as "well," "but," or "what about?" Instead, you strive for conversation-fostering sentences such as, "I am hearing you say X. Is this what you mean?" Or "I'm not sure I understand. Could you tell me more about that?" Or "This sounds like [or reminds me of] X. Was that your intention? How did you come to that?"[60] This way of engaging is two-way and creates "varied and changing dialogic spaces."[61] In this two-way conversation you aren't trying to win (or debate). You are trying to exchange meaning and build community.

Reparative dialoguing is a "radically loving, radically hopeful dynamic," which "is sorely missing within contemporary conversations" about difficult issues such as race and other modes of difference, "which too often feel like static and defined battlefields."[62] To achieve such a "radically loving, radically hopeful dynamic,"[63] we need to fight the urge to "restore or save face," which can occur "when our social poise is attacked or teased," according to Ting-Toomey and Kurogi. Saving face "is a vulnerable identity-based resource because it can be enhanced or threatened in any uncertain social situation."[64] By being attentive to our own and others' needs to save face, we "suspend ... assumptions and refrain from imposing ... views on others."[65] Thus, reparative dialoguing is always conducted in tandem with radical listening and holding discomfort.

Incorporating reparative dialogue into any communication exchange is never easy, particularly in groups of strangers on whom we project all kinds of viewpoints that may or may not be true. Many folks who enter into dialogue feel anxious about being on the inside or on the outside. After attending one Interrupting Privilege session with an all-Black group, Roderick, a Black government worker and veteran in his fifties came to speak to me about his fear of entering into reparative dialoguing with the group. Wearing thin-framed glasses and a tailored button down shirt, Roderick focused his gaze squarely one me when he expressed his sincere concern that he felt uncomfortably judged during our last session when he disclosed that he was married to a white woman. After he spoke for a while, talking himself in and out of staying with the group because of his feelings of exclusion, I asked what someone had said to him. He said, "Well, nothing exactly, but I could tell they didn't approve so I didn't engage in conversation."

I paused and said, "You know, I think there are a lot of folks in the room who feel like they are on the outside of the circle too." In response to his puzzled expression, I listed not only those like him who were interracially partnered, but those who were mixed-race and feared being judged as inauthentic because of not being monoracial. Or African immigrants or children of African immigrants who expressed fears of inauthenticity as compared to those with a Black American identity defined by being ADOS (American Descendents of Slaves). I said, what about the LGBTQ folks in the space who didn't know if their own identities and areas of concern would be shared by others in the space? And what about the youth: Might they wonder if their voices were as central as those ten, twenty, thirty, forty, even fifty years their senior? To this Roderick grinned with utter and genuine surprise and said, "I had never thought of that. I had only thought that I felt uncomfortable." He stayed, and this first line—"I had never thought of that"—became his mantra as he boldly entered into reparative dialogues throughout the rest of the session. Not every dialogue was reparative. Roderick worked through his experiences of dissonance with the diverse group. He had much that he sought to repair. But by following the critical communication of difference circuit, he was able to find other folks who didn't feel "authentic" in this all-Black space, in order to redefine what Black authenticity really means.

And Roderick didn't come to his moments of reparative dialoguing alone, or even with me coaching him. He had the community of the Interrupting Privilege group. As this chapter has illustrated, creating a change is much more challenging—if not impossible—without a supportive community. You also need folks who can pick you up when you feel like your attempt at an intervention simply hasn't worked; people who can assure you that it *is* worth it to take the risk. April and Amanda, for example, play this role for each other within their LGBTQ+ BIPOC graduate student community, illustrating, once again, the link between the interpersonal and the structural. Individuals are a part of your change-making process, people who with whom you can share your racial exhaustion as you practice the difficult steps of the critical communication of difference including reparative dialoguing. One model for this is the critical pedagogy notion of cultivating a critical friend.[66]

Critical friends help us see the areas that we have difficulty seeing. They are true interlocutors who aren't scared to tell you when you're not being vulnerable, when you're not being truthful, when you are simply wrong. In other words, you need people who can lovingly push you in community, whether that means through radical speaking or reparative dialoguing. Feedback from critical friends can come in three different modes. The first mode is that of "warm" feedback: encouraging, enthusiastic statements, which the support that is necessary before any additional critique can happen. The second mode of feedback is "cool" and more impartial, and it might come in the form of questions. In the third mode a critical friend provides "hard" or challenging feedback with explicit concerns. Each of these forms of feedback builds on the previous mode. In order for people to hear a critique connected to power (something critical)—they must first understand that their efforts have been appreciated, even in some small way. Roderick, the interracially married man from the all-Black Interrupting Privilege session, became critical friends with Jordan, the high schooler in the introductory chapter who recorded his dialogue about discrimination in class, and taught his entire school about radical listening. When Jordan shared his experience with Rodrick, their dialogue

Figure 4.6. Multigenerational Dialogue between Roderick and Jordan. Courtesy of Darius Presley and Meshell Sturgis as part of an Interrupting Privilege Graphic Novel.

explored the repair that Jordan should expect in school. Roderick initially remained firmly in the camp that Jordan needed to stalwartly anticipate such discrimination and, as the Black vice principal also told Jordan, "keep it moving" (see figure 4.6). However, Roderick changed his position when he listened to how Jordan believed that his teachers could work toward change. They both experienced repair through the course of their ten weeks of dialogues.

Critical friends can aid each other in combatting racial exhaustion by working through the reparative dialogue process together. This is another form of critical community building. Laura and Lando, two of my women of color PhD advisees, shared in their Interrupting Privilege dialogue that they began playing the critical friend role for each other soon after they met. My colleagues and I intentionally admitted Laura and Lando into the graduate program as part of a cohort admission in which organizers invite a group of similarly minoritized people in order to strategically foster community where they are not "the only."[67] We know that our minoritized students are going to be immediately hit with racial exhaustion, and so our goal is to provide as many support structures to combat this exhaustion as possible. Creating critical communities for reparative dialoguing is key.

Following a critical communication of race circuit of radical listening/sitting with discomfort/radical listening/reparative dialoguing, Laura and Lando began by listening to each other's stories in our group advisee meeting in order to build their way to a relationship of accountability and support in their first, vital year of graduate school. I instructed them to simply text each other once a week to continue the conversation following the circuit all the way to reparative dialogue. In doing so, the two soon claimed each other as "accountabilibuddies."[68] Lando defines an accountabilibuddy as

> a friend who holds you accountable.... You're always with them every step of the way. And it's like someone you trust who's close, and you can tell them if they're doing something wrong, but [with] gentleness where it's like you are all allowed to speak your truth, and they won't take it personally, because they know it's coming from love and just concern.

Lando describes radical speaking in action: an unburdened, full-throated moment of "speak[ing] your truth." Laura agrees that her radical speaking with Lando entail pushing each other into reparative dialoguing about the hidden scripts of racialized sexism. This means, Laura, says, that she can ask Lando, "Hey, am I crazy, like you know what I mean? Am I crazy thinking that this is happening right now?" In response, Lando might say, "No, not at all crazy, or actually let's unpack it. Let me think through it with you." This is not an "echo-chamber" relationship where one critical friend tells the other what they want to hear. Instead, they have difficult conversations with "an unconditional support there." As they flush out racism, sexism, homophobia, classism, and more in their dialogues, they also heal in the process.

If racial exhaustion grows through experiences of discrimination remaining unspoken, unacknowledged, then Laura and Lando's dialoguing sessions offer rest and reparation. They take what they call "microaggression walks," during which they acknowledge the reality of racialized and gendered discrimination in their lives in order to work on their, in Laura's words, "unlearning." Unlearning is the process of combatting the exhausting script that "you take up too much space . . . you shouldn't be too loud, you shouldn't be too aggressive." Unlearning also means that they fight the urge to "put your voice in the footnotes, and . . . make old white men the center." For students used to feeling isolated and attacked, the critical communication of difference through reparative dialoguing reframes graduate school as an intentional, collaborative community where, in Lando's words, "Everything's a conversation. . . . It's not attack." Laura notes that their dialogues make her feel "lighter. We carry a lot by ourselves, [so to dialogue and realize] oh man, someone else is feeling the same things as I am, . . . [then] I feel less alone." Reparative dialogues like Laura and Lando's provide lifelines of support to combat racial exhaustion.[69]

EPILOGUE

THE WAKE OF DEI

Racial exhaustion is not a new phenomenon, nor are the skills one can apply to move through it. But there is something peculiar about the period of time when much of research I conducted for this book happened, a time when much of the world was waking up to the racism that has been surrounding us forever. There was an opening in that moment. And as I segue to a close I want to talk about the landscape that created the conditions for the Interrupting Privilege participants to share their stories, and what we can learn by historicizing this very recent moment that also created the conditions for the second election of Trump.

This book has examined racial exhaustion during the rapid rise and fall of the publicly proclaimed institutional investment (corporate, educational, media, and otherwise) in diversity, equity, and inclusion (DEI). DEI-as-institutional-investment exploded across sectors after the tragic and televised murder of George Floyd in the summer of 2020. This moment produced a "racial reckoning." After the solidarity statements, the expressions of care and concern, and the optimistic pledges for change, what did "racial reckoning" produce? Who faced this "settling of accounts," in Merriam-Webster's definition?[1] Whose race was accounted for? Where and when did power shift, and did it produce the conditions under which Black and brown scholars, teachers, tech workers, students and more can be heard, invited, promoted, and truly included? Or did power simply hide in plain sight behind the grandiloquent language of the newly woke organizations?

While the struggle for racial equity goes back centuries, I do believe the "DEI era"—the mainstream, representation-heavy interpretation of racial inclusion—lasted three short years that also match up with the Interrupting Privilege program that birthed the critical communication of race circuit. By the time Trump was elected for the second time, not only was the coffin was sealed, but it was being lowered into the ground. DEI began with the televised murder by police of George Floyd in 2020 and ended with the Supreme Court's ban on race-conscious college admissions in 2023. And yet, DEI did not emerge in a vacuum. DEI in those four short years was a continuation and an outcome of race-based movements and moments from the 1960s and 1970s Black Freedom Struggle (Civil Rights and Black Power movements demanding justice), through 1980s and 1990s multiculturalism (moments of celebrating inclusion through pluralism), through 2000s post-racialism (colorblindness confirming Barack Obama's hope and change moment), to the 2013 launch of Black Lives Matter (a movement surfacing anti-Blackness across areas). As beneficiary, DEI did not replicate each of these movements and moments but incorporated pieces of ideology.

Scholars of Black history use the phrase "Black Freedom Struggle" to eschew what historian Joy Williamson-Lott names as the "artificial split in the movement," which "position[s] [Civil Rights and Black Power] against each other as a way to turn difference into polar opposites."[2] The Black Freedom Struggle boasts grassroots beginnings, and a clearcut articulation of humanity and justice from the 1963 March on Washington to the federal demands for equal opportunity (and the beginning of affirmative action) in President Kenney's executive order 10925 in 1961, to the employment discrimination ban in Title VII of the Civil Rights Act of 1964, to the creation of the EEOC and the Voting Rights Act of 1965. The Black Freedom Struggle—and particularly the Civil Rights movement—forms a mythological starting point for DEI.

DEI was also a beneficiary of another movement for humanity and justice fifty years after the Black Freedom Struggle: *Black Lives Matter*. BLM illuminates and combats the continued existence of anti-Black violence, including state-sanctioned violence. Black Lives Matter emerged in 2013 after the murderer of seventeen-year-old Trayvon Martin was acquitted in Florida; the movement grew to worldwide prominence after the 2015 acquittal of the police officer murderers of Michael Brown in Ferguson, Missouri, and Eric Garner in New York City. BLM has succeeded in illustrating that anti-Black racism is not simply interpersonal animus or past grievance, but systemic, everyday oppression that reflects centuries of anti-Blackness in the U.S. and beyond.

DEI lacked these two movements' primary features—from their central ideologies skewering anti-Blackness to their organized protests from marching in the streets to mass boycotting, to their grassroots organizational beginnings, to their fighting for laws that systematically refute racism and create change. DEI, instead, promoted a diffuse belief system (not a justice-driven ideology), high profile representations of change (not marching in the streets), a leadership structure created from above including Chief Diversity Officer positions (not origins in grassroots), and a vague sense of corporate and institutional inclusion (not fighting for juridical justice).

Thus, DEI was a closer relative to a post-Civil Rights, 1980s and 1990s moment of *multiculturalism*, a polite pluralism that amounted to corrective expressions of more radical activism.[3] In the U.S., critical education scholars Christine Sleeter and Peter McLaren describe the multicultural moment as "the celebration of [minoritized people's] ethnic foods and festivals."[4] A "foods and festivals" multiculturalism celebrated differences through shining a light on the accomplishments of racially minoritized identities and high-achieving individuals within those groups. Racially minoritized groups gained visibility through month-based celebrations such as Black History Month. Where the Black Freedom Struggle movements pushed white America to grapple with anti-Blackness in the very foundations of this country, the multicultural and postracial moments gently provided an additive lens for white America. But larger demands for those in power to make structural, institutional, or juridical change, and to incorporate intersectional minoritized identities (i.e., LGBT+ and disabled identities) into a multicultural critique in addition to race remained missing.

Multiculturalism also laid the groundwork for the presidential election of Barack Obama in 2008, priming much of the nation for Obama's spirit-soaring messages of multicultural hope and change. In the Obama era, multiculturalism paved the way for postracialism, the colorblind declaration that the election of the U.S.'s first Black president marked the end of racism and the salience of race in this country. Postrace remains slippery, with its multiple meanings in various politicized spaces: elsewhere I describe how "postrace means after race, in an evolutionary, next-stage-of-humanity fashion, as well as behind race, in a hiding-in-plain-sight, out-of-sight-out-of-mind fashion." Further, postrace is "a term used by race commentators to sometimes describe, sometimes decry, and sometimes imagine another racialized world."[5] The postracialism of the Obama era congratulated itself on multiculturalism as well as *diversity*, organizations' high-profile featuring of not just racially different bodies, but bodies different in a variety of ways. Here intersectional diversity reigned. Thus, from multiculturalism, DEI gains a focus on celebratory and reparative representations in lieu of substantive and uncomfortable change.[6] From postracialism, DEI gains a focus on the high-profile inclusion of Black people in positions of power while not fundamentally changing the institutions themselves.

These two moments—and the movements that laid the groundwork for them—birthed DEI through televised tragedy. Much of the world was trapped inside, locked into televisions and phone screens during the early months of the COVID-19 quarantine. Many poured out of their houses to protest en masse, refuting the admonitions of scientists addressing the possible dangers of mass gatherings; racism, for many protesters, remained at least as big a public health crisis as COVID. The media captured protests around the globe which named Floyd alongside also other Black people murdered by police including Breonna Taylor in Louisville, Kentucky, and Ahmaud Arbery in Glynn County, Georgia. Protest rang out in both traditional and, in the words of Sarah J. Jackson, Moya Bailey, and Brooke Foucault Welles, "hashtag activism" ways where, "ordinary African Americans, women, transgender people, and others aligned with racial justice and feminist causes [who] have long been excluded from elite media . . . repurposed Twitter . . . to make identity-based cultural and political demands, [and] in doing so have forever changed national consciousness."[7] The groups Jackson, Bailey, and Welles name, who had been agitating for change, found a small and temporary opening for changemaking through the increasing ubiquity of what became known as DEI. Now, DEI was not this agitation, not activism or protests (boots on the ground or online), but rather an organizational gesturing towards the topics highlighted in the activism and protests.

One self-described white male business commentator in *Forbes* summed up white racial exhaustion with DEI this way: "The recent backlash against DEI suggests that the flurry of DEI activity of the past several years—and in particular the two years following the murder of George Floyd—has led to growing frustration among people, especially those who identify as white and male."[8] DEI became a convenient scapegoat, an easy focus for a particular brand of white male frustration about everything from still-sour grapes about Obama's presidency to the acknowledgment that white enfranchisement was the result of an uneven playing field. This is one form of white racial exhaustion. And in this moment, changemaking in policing—the arena most named in BLM protests—bore no sign of a reckoning. Journalist Wesley Lowery writes, "There was . . . no sweeping act of atonement. No radical reordering. Not even, at scale, the 'reimagining' championed by the moderates." Instead, Lowery continues, "Reactionary backlash has outpaced the changes that prompted it. Society's moral vacuum has been laid open before us. Rather than plug it, the most powerful among us watched as we were sucked further into the abyss."[9] And with this, Black racial exhaustion has grown.

Further, equity positions, or DEI jobs, illustrated companies' swift racial exhaustion. These positions peaked in the fall of 2020 with, by one measure, a 123 percent rise over previous years.[10] But when the economy turned and hit the tech sector particularly hard,[11] DEI jobs fell first, and by the beginning of 2022, they dropped to 19 percent *below* pre-2020 numbers.[12] That is, the DEI era began waning just a year after it began: by mid-2021, in Bradley's words, "Solidarity against anti-Blackness had begun to recede."[13] This was the moment when proclamations about DEI commitments had to reveal themselves as either markers of change or simply lip service. Those who sincerely sought change found that producing deliverables–a truly more diverse workforce throughout the ranks, an antiracist curriculum, a student body that looks like the community around them—was far harder than making a public statement. Inequalities were more intractable than the popular DEI approach of public proclamations and one-off training sessions. Perhaps the most compelling evidence the DEI era ended in the summer of 2023 is the recalling of affirmative action in *Students for Fair Admissions, Inc. v. President and Fellows of Harvard College/University of North Carolina et. al.* (SFFA for short), in which the Supreme Court ruled that race-conscious admissions policies violated the Fourteenth Amendment's Equal Protection Clause.

The increased demand from organizations wanting to flex their DEI commitments for those doing work for racial equity had always tapped into those particular workers' emotions without providing space or support for the emotional burden of this labor. The change that came with

DEI was that hope combated exhaustion. SFFA—along with the elimination of federal protections for abortion with the June 2022 ruling of *Dobbs v. Jackson Women's Health Organization* that overturned fifty years of federal constitutional abortion protection established with Roe v. Wade—replaced hope with exhaustion. All of this felt like too much to pretty much everyone. If, for those agitators for racial justice, a tempered hope marked the DEI era, then, for those tired of agitating or being agitated, exhaustion marks the post-DEI era.

The role of individual activists and communicators in racial equity work is critical, and one of the failures of DEI was not investing in their own health and wellbeing; the ongoing work of individuals in a vicious post-DEI world cannot take place without full institutional commitment. DEI was aspirational, handed down from above in statements of change but rarely with clearly delineated deliverables. And, as such, it was destined to unduly tax the individuals who had already been doing racial equity work to keep the institutions from emptily gesturing to the necessity of change. The DEI moment fell short of arriving at the point that critic Sarah Ahmed names as true "institutional diversity," a time "when [diversity] becomes part of what an institution is already doing."[14] This moment failed to, as education scholar Sonia Nieto writes, disrupt "the very center of power" but instead "tinker[ed] with the edges of the system [to] yield few positive results."[15]

Some of this failure lay in the inability of organizations to train their membership in the critical communication of race. While, alone, critical race communication is insufficient to create Ahmed's "institutional diversity," this book has argued that without critical race communication, we cannot arrive at Nieto's disruption of "the very center of power." DEI did not consider the role of the individual agitator long term how the critical communication of race builds the long-term stamina to create racial change. But while organizational DEI did not consider this strategy, smaller, grassroots programs did. This book has examined the wisdom of individuals sharing their strategies within one such program, Interrupting Privilege.

As I finish writing this book in the Autumn of 2024, days after the second election of Trump to the U.S. presidency, the acronym remains a lightning rod for both ends of electoral politics. It has been spat out by Republicans thinly veiling their racial animus by insisting that figures like

Figure C.1. Interrupting Privilege exhibit at the Northwest African American Museum. Photo credit: Tara Brown.

Democratic presidential nominee Kamala Harris are "Didn't Earn It" candidates. It has been quietly shuttered across higher education, governmental, and corporate spaces as a sullied term of entitlements. And this shuttering makes us tired. But just as so many of us fought our way out of the exhaustion that descended upon us with Trump's first presidency, we will find the space, the hope, and the grit to move through our racial exhaustion once again. My hope is that we can utilize some of the strategies in this book to regain energy for our long fight.

ACKNOWLEDGMENTS

This book is the culmination of twenty years of scholarly and community work in Seattle, Washington. I landed my first job in a communication department with a PhD in Ethnic Studies, with zero communication classes under my belt and a firm identity as a race and cultural studies scholar. The joy of learning the field and practicing the discipline of communication over the past two decades has expanded my way of seeing the world and transformed me into a race and communication scholar.

While my name is on the cover, this book has truly been a community and family effort. My family—at work, in the community, among friends, and immediate—is the reason Interrupting Privilege took off. Thank you to each of the hundreds of Interrupting Privilege participants who have generously shared their stories and dedicated themselves to (sometimes painstakingly) practicing critically communicating race. I am eternally grateful to all at the Center for Communication, Difference, and Equity (CCDE) for their partnership: assistant directors Gina Aaftaab and Josh Griffin; student researchers Shannon Advincula, Joel Allen, Chardonnay Beaver, Mercy Bertero, Anjuli Brekke, Jhasmine Cadiente, Jhanelle Cadiente, Jenny Cai, Julie Feng, Kaleb Germinaro, Laura Irwin, Marcus Johnson, Mia Lawrie, Thomas Locke, Fani Martinez, Jasmine Matchawate, jas l. moultrie, Darius Presley, Eve Rickenbaker, Grace Rogers, Helen Rosenboom, Meshell Sturgis, Victoria Thomas, Lando Tosaya, and Eli Wilson; faculty colleagues Amanda Friz, Carmen Gonzalez, LeiLani Nishime, Andrea Otáñez, Timeka Tounsel, and Savaughn Williams. Because of the hard work of each of these CCDE members, the Interrupting Privilege project has inspired graphic novels (Meshell Sturgis and Darius Presley), dissertations-transitioning-to-books (Anjuli Brekke), articles (Gina Aaftaab, Joel Allen, Anjuli Brekke, Laura Irwin, jas l. moultrie, Meshell Sturgis, Lando Tosaya), and podcasts (produced by too many to name!). Thank you to my research assistants, Julie Feng and Laura Irwin, for corralling scores of data and research for this book (and me).

All of the staff in the Graduate School, particularly Kima Cargill, Cheyenne Evans, Carolyn Jackson, and Maxine Wright, enlivened our sometimes-maddening equity and justice work. I thank our partners at the Northwest African American Museum, especially Leija Davis and LaNesha LeBardelaben, for hosting Interrupting Privilege sessions at NAAM and then for hosting a full-fledged exhibit. Witnessing the Interrupting Privilege exhibit come to life has truly been the highlight of this project. Thank you to our partners at the Resilience Lab, especially Sasha Duttchoudhury, Megan Kennedy, and Tyneshia Valdez. A special thanks to Laura Helper-Ferris, whose eagle eye has helped shepherd my writing over four books.

My own racial exhaustion is soothed daily by ridiculous shared memes, peptalks, and commiseration with my fierce UW posse, Janine Jones, Wadiya Udell, and Joy Williamson-Lott. I powered through the last year of writing this book thanks to morning, cross-time zone, Zoom catch ups and writing sessions with my dear friend and sister from another mister, Cherise Smith. One of my very oldest friends, Jennifer Neighbors, helped keep me laughing and grounded. My Brown buddies, Praveen Fernandes and Heather Reid, continue to be lights in my life, and although you are no longer with us on this earth, Jeffery Mingo, I feel you reading over my shoulder (and I miss you). Thank you to the best neighbors ever, Michael Lane and Paul McKee, who literally welcomed my family to the neighborhood with an enormous sign. Much love to my godfamily Allison Briscoe-Smith, Mike Smith, Alonzo Smith, Ava Marie Smith, Aria Smith, and Aggie Briscoe. I have unending appreciation for my very first advisees who are now homies in the field: Manoucheka Celeste, Jennifer McClearen, and Madhavi Murty. Gratitude to my SD crew, including my fitness role models Kristine Mandani and Fiona Mgharo, and BWBC sistas Alexia Brown, Maisha Cobb, Tanya Fields, Ronda Lewis, and Tiffany Thompson. Thank you to my Comm buddies including Andre Brock, Robin Means Coleman, Bryce Henson, Ron Jackson Jr., E. Patrick Johnson, Patrick Johnson, Raven Lloyd-Maragh, Al Martin, Isabel Molina-Guzman, Beretta Smith-Shomade, Angharad Valdivia, and Myra Washington. Thank you to Furqan Sayeed, Valerie Zaborski, Eric Zinner, the whole team at New York University Press, and the thoughtful anonymous reviewers of the manuscript.

My love and gratitude go to my parents, who instilled in me the desire to fight. Love also to Diane Sims and Grandpi, the Captains, Scanlans, and Whites.

Finally, to my first readers, to James, TJ, and Naima Joseph. This book is yours. And not just because you provided free research assistant and editing labor (but thank you for that). You animate every page. Thank you. I love you.

APPENDIX

SAMPLE DIALOGUE PROMPTS

This appendix shares a sample of the dialogic questions that the Interrupting Privilege research team of faculty, graduate, and undergraduate students provided for our participants. Dialogue participants choose to begin with, augment, or omit any of these questions and more. Each year of our project has a theme, which you can see below. Participants of any given group often attend subsequent radical listening sessions which happen anywhere between one and three times each academic year. The list of Interrupting Privilege researchers is at the end of the Appendix.

FIRST TIME EXPERIENCING DISCRIMINATION, 2017–2018

Interrupting Privilege partnered with National Public Radio's StoryCorps and Seattle's local NPR station KUOW for this first year of recording dialogues. We hosted conversations between university faculty, students, staff, and alumni. KUOW and campus radical listening sessions featured these dialogues.

1. Can you tell us about the first time you experienced discrimination?
2. How did you feel at that moment?
3. What coping mechanism do you use?
4. Do you think and talk about that experience now?
5. How do people react to you telling these stories?
6. How would you like them to react?
7. What have you learned from that experience?

GENERATION MIXED, 2018–2019

Interrupting Privilege partnered with local parenting groups including FOCS (Families of Color Seattle) for conversations between mixed-race children aged 5-19 and their siblings, parents, aunties, and more. Campus radical listening sessions featured these dialogues.

1. What advice would you give teachers for how they can best work with mixed-race kids?
2. What have your parents taught you about race and your racial identity?
3. What do you wish your teachers knew about what it's like to be your race/identity?
4. Can you describe a time when you saw people treated differently because of race at school?
5. What do you think other people think about your racial identity?

BLACK IN SEATTLE, 2019–2020

Interrupting Privilege partnered with the Northwest African American Museum (NAAM) and ACLS/Mellon to host dialogues between high school, community college, and university undergraduates, graduate students, and community members. NAAM hosted radical listening sessions on these dialogues.

1. What is it like being a Black student at your high school or university?
   Your workplace?
2. What is your advice for new Black students at your school or employees at your work?
3. What's it like being Black in Seattle and the Pacific Northwest?
4. When do you let microaggressions go and when do you interrupt them?
5. Whose responsibility is it to interrupt intersectional racism?

QUARANTINING WHILE BLACK, 2020–2021

With the COVID-19 quarantines in effect, the "Black in Seattle" Interrupting Privilege group transitioned into a "Quarantining While Black Group" also in partnership with NAAM. Interrupting Privilege hosted radical listening sessions online and, with COVID protocols in place, at the Othello Commons, a university space in South Seattle. We launched our Interrupting Privilege website, ip.ccde.uw.edu, at the Othello gathering.

1. Tell us a little bit about the stressors you have faced in the last year. Some examples could be loss of a job, childcare issues, family health, safety, food security, racism, media coverage of the police violence.
2. How have you been coping? Who do you go to for support and community?
3. What types of support are the most useful for you? Can you provide specific examples?
4. Who takes care of you?
5. Has this changed over the course of this year? In other words, if we were not in a pandemic, would you be doing things differently?
6. Tell us what resources, spaces, and/or programs would improve your quality of life. How could individuals and/or community members improve your quality of life?

RESISTANCE THROUGH RESILIENCE, 2021–2022

In an effort to provide additional strategies for participants to address their racial exhaustion, Interrupting Privilege partnered with the University of Washington's Resilience Lab. Interrupting Privilege and the Resilience Lab hosted radical listening sessions online this academic year.

1. When do you speak back? In other words, describe how you resist microaggressions, or everyday forms of racism, sexism, and homophobia, as well as other forms of identity-based oppression in your life?

2. Now shifting to resilience, is this a word that you use? What does resilience mean to you? Do you use any other words or phrases? Please explain.
3. How have you gotten to resistance through resilience? Resilience through resistance?
4. When it comes to resilience-based practices, who are your teachers/mentors? What spaces nurture your resilience?
5. Imagine a future when resilience through resistance is centered. What does that future look like? How do we get there?

BLACK CAPITALISM, 2022–2023

In partnership with the University of Washington's Foster School of Business and local Black business owners, Interrupting Privilege hosted conversations that were inspired by multi-year Interrupting Privilege participant and radical listening session host Alexandria Folino. Folino's Soul Collective Salon hosted our radical listening sessions.

1. What comes to mind when you hear the phrase "Black capitalism"?
2. What does it look like? Feel like? Sound like?
3. What do we (Black people) owe each other when it comes to making money?
4. Think through diasporic/immigrant differences when it comes to Black business in the United States. What does Black capitalism mean for those who are the descendants of the enslaved compared with more recent African immigrants and more recent immigrants from the Caribbean? How are these groups connected (or are they)?
5. Think about the location of Black business(es). Where should Black businesses be located? Why is this business located here?
6. How do Black people touch wealth?
7. What measures will you or do you take to protect your business(es)?
8. Is it possible to buy just Black?

DUAL PANDEMICS, 2023–2024

In order to remember the fine-grained experiences of living through the dual pandemics of (the racially disproportionate impacts of) COVID-19 and the "racial reckoning," Interrupting Privilege hosted dialogues inspired by Joy Williamson-Lott between university faculty, students, and staff. This project's radical listening session happened on campus.

1. In March of 2020 when UDub shut down, what was your connection to the university?
2. What job did you do and how did it change?
3. What changed in March of 2020? What did your life look like for you before March and after?
4. What happened after March 2020, when everything shut down? As the pandemics progressed, how did they shape your experience at UDub?
5. As we entered the 2020–2021 academic year, what did that look like for you? What changed and how did you adapt?
6. Where/with whom did you spend the most time at the height of the pandemic?
7. Where/from whom did you receive care or support during the pandemic?

GENPRIDE 2024–2025

Interrupting Privilege partnered with Seattle's GenPride, an advocacy organization for LGBTQ+ older adults to record dialogues of GenPride members of color through the work of Interrupting Privilege participant Naima Joseph. Our first radical listening session will be at GenPride.

1. How has your experience changed over the decades as a QTBIPOC (Queer, Trans, Black, Indigenous, Person of Color)? As an LGBTQ (Lesbian, Gay, Bisexual, Transgender, Queer) person? As a BIPOC?
2. If you had the chance to talk to your younger self, what would you tell them?
3. What do you wish your white LGBTQ community understood about being BIPOC and LGBTQ?

4. How have you strategically hidden or exposed your LGBTQ identity in different spaces? (Work, school, church, etc.) How did this feel?
5. What is it like being BIPOC in white LGBTQ spaces? What is it like being LGBTQ in BIPOC spaces?
6. How has being BIPOC and LGBTQ been different for you in different parts of the country? How has it been different in different countries around the world?

LIST OF INTERRUPTING PRIVILEGE RESEARCHERS:

Naheed Gina Aaftaab, 2016–2021 (staff), Carmen Gonzalez, 2016–present (faculty), Victoria Thomas, 2016–2017 (graduate student), Marcus Johnson, 2016–present (graduate student/faculty), Anjuli Brekke, 2016–present (graduate student/faculty), Meshell Sturgis, 2017–2024 (graduate student), Mia Lawrie, 2017–2018 (graduate student), Eve Rickenbaker, 2017–2021 (graduate student), Jhasmine Cadiente, 2018–2019 (undergraduate student), Jhanelle Cadiente, 2018–2019 (undergraduate student), Jenny Cai, 2018–2019 (undergraduate student), Thomas Locke, 2018–2020 (graduate student), Andrea Otañez, 2019–present (faculty), Chardonnay Beaver, 2019–2023 (undergraduate student), Darius Presley, 2019–2022 (undergraduate student), Laura Irwin, 2020–present, graduate student), Lando Tosaya, 2020–present (graduate student), jas moultrie, 2020–present (graduate student), Josh Griffin, 2021–present (staff), Kaleb Germinaro, 2021–22 (graduate student), Julie Feng, 2022–present (graduate student), Jasmine Matchawate, 2022–2023 (undergraduate student), Isabel Anderson, 2022–2023 (undergraduate student), Fani Martinez, 2022–2023 (undergraduate student), Joel Allen, 2023–present, (graduate student), Mercy Bertero, 2023–present (graduate student), Shannon Advincula, 2023–2024 (graduate student), Grace Rogers, 2023–present (graduate student), Helen Rosenboom, 2023–present (graduate student), Eli Wilson, 2024–present (graduate student).

NOTES

PREFACE

1 As DEI consultant and author Lily Zheng notes, "There is no shortage of acronyms in this space, from 'EDI' to "D&I' to 'DEIB,' 'IDEA,' and 'JEDI' (the 'B' is for 'belonging'; the 'A' is for 'accessibility'; the 'J' is for 'justice'" (*DEI Deconstructed: Your No-Nonsense Guide to Doing the Work and Doing It Right* [Oakland, CA: Berrett-Koehler Publishers, 2022], 6).

2 In a tribute to her mentor Shirley Chisolm, Donna Brazile shares that Chisolm told her, "If you wait for a man to give you a seat, you'll never have one! If they don't give you a seat at the table, bring in a folding chair" ("Tribute: Shirley Chisholm 1924–2005," *People*, January 17, 2005).

3 "Post-Loving" refers to the generation born after the landmark Supreme Court *Loving v. Virginia* (1967) decision, which invalidated all existing bans on interracial marriage.

4 See, for example, Sandra Tang, Vonnie C. McLoyd, and Samantha K. Hallman, "Racial Socialization, Racial Identity, and Academic Attitudes among African American Adolescents: Examining the Moderating Influence of Parent-Adolescent Communication," *Journal of Youth and Adolescence* 45, no. 6 (2016): 1141–55, 1142, https://doi-org.offcampus.lib.washington.edu/10.1007/s10964-015-0351-8.

5 As Steven L. Foy and Rayshawn Ray note, "Colorism is a key measure for assessing the broader social, cultural, and economic ramifications of living in a racialized society" ("Skin in the Game: Colorism and the Subtle Operation of Stereotypes in Men's College Basketball," *American Journal of Sociology* 125, no. 3 [2019]: 730). See also Cedric Herring, *Skin Deep: How Race and Complexion Matter in the "Color-Blind" Era* (Urbana: University of Illinois Press, 2004), xiv; Margaret Hunter, *Race, Gender and the Politics of Skin Tone* (New York: Routledge, 2005), 2; Evelyn Nakano Glenn, ed., *Shades of Difference: Why Skin Color Matters* (Palo Alto, CA: Stanford University Press, 2009).

6 Two well-publicized cases of racialized violence in the Seattle area are those of Charleena Lyles, a thirty-year-old pregnant mother killed by Seattle police in 2017, and Manuel "Manny" Ellis, a thirty-three-year-old killed by Tacoma police in 2020. See Kate Mettler and Mark Berman, "Seattle Police Fatally Shoot Pregnant Woman," *Washington Post*, June 19, 2017, www.washingtonpost.com/national/seattle-police-fatally-shoot-pregnant-woman/2017/06/19/628fc2c0-4fcf-11e7-be25-3a519335381c_story.html; Gene Johnson, "Officers Face Charges in Restraint

Death of Black man," Associated Press, May 27, 2021, https://apnews.com/article/george-floyd-7dbbc0146d17f4c26aeae1616d8d66cf.
7 In their classic book, *Racial Formation in the United States* (New York: Routledge, 2014), sociologists Michael Omi and Howard Winant define "racialization" as race lived not just interpersonally, but structurally and institutionally (2).
8 Daniel Solorzano, Miguel Ceja, and Tara Yosso "Critical Race Theory, Racial Microaggressions, and Campus Racial Climate: The Experiences of African American College Students," *Journal of Negro Education* 69, no. 1/2 (2000): 60–73, 70.

INTRODUCTION

1 Matthew Frey Jacobson, *Whiteness of a Different Color* (Cambridge, MA: Harvard University Press, 1999), 1–2.
2 Michael Omi and Howard Winant, *Racial Formation in the United States*, 3rd ed. (New York: Routledge, 2014).
3 Patricia Hill Collins writes, "Oppressions of race, class, gender, sexuality and nation mutually construct one another" and the other two parts of the matrix are disciplinary, or power enacted through punishment and control, and hegemonic, or power enacted through common-sense beliefs (*Black Feminist Thought: Knowledge, Consciousness, and the Politics of Empowerment*, 2nd ed. [New York: Routledge, 2009], 299).
4 In addition, as Ruth King writes, "Power is not inherently abusive. Whites with institutional power and racial consciousness can become morally responsible by using their power for good, if they are willing to be condemned by those who resent their attempts at greater equity" (*Mindful of Race: Transforming Racism from the Inside Out* [Boulder, CO: Sounds True, 2018], 203).
5 Again, this is a tenet of Omi and Winant's *Racial Formation in the United States*.
6 Centers for Disease Control, "Racism and Health," June 20, 2024, www.cdc.gov/minority-health/racism-health/index.html.
7 William A. Smith, Walter R. Allen, and Lynette L. Danley, "'Assume the Position . . . You Fit the Description': Psychosocial Experiences and Racial Battle Fatigue among African American Male College Students," *American Behavioral Scientist* 51, no. 4 (2007): 555.
8 Smith, Allen, and Danley, "'Assume the Position," 556. See also Larry Charleston, "Headache Disparities in African-Americans in the United States: A Narrative Review," *Journal of the National Medical Association* 113, no. 2 (2021): 224, doi: 10.1016/j.jnma.2020.09.148; Deanna R. Befus, Megan Bennet, Irby Remy R. Coeytaux, and Donald B. Penzien, "A Critical Exploration of Migraine as a Health Disparity: the Imperative of an Equity-Oriented, Intersectional Approach," *Current Pain and Headache Reports* 22, no. 79 (2018): 78, https://doi.org/10.1007/s11916-018-0731-3.
9 William Smith cites Chester Pierce in the development of his concept, noting that Pierce encourages researchers to "not look for the gross and obvious. The subtle, cumulative mini-assault is the substance of today's racism" (Chester Pierce, "Psychiat-

ric Problems of the Black Minority, in *American Handbook of Psychiatry*, ed. Silvano Arieti [New York: Basic Books, 1974], 516). Smith and his colleagues draw on scholarship on racism and health, which documents the many ways in which people of color experience physical and psychological harm due to racism. Smith writes that "RBF is the culmination of these racist micro-level and macro-level aggressions and the subsequent negative health sequelae on marginalized and oppressed people" ("Foreword," in *Racial Battle Fatigue in Faculty: Perspectives and Lessons from Higher Education*, ed. Nicholas D. Hartlep and Daisy Ball [New York: Routledge, 2020], xx).

10 See, for example, the work on racial battle fatigue including Smith, Allen, and Danley, "'Assume the Position,'" 556. See also Charleston, "Headache Disparities"; Robert T. Carter, "Racism and Psychological and Emotional Injury: Recognizing and Assessing Race-Based Traumatic Stress," *Counseling Psychologist* 35, no. 1 (2007): 37; Rodney Clark, Norman B. Anderson, Vernessa R. Clark, and David R. Williams, "Racism as a Stressor for African Americans: A Biopsychosocial Model," *American Psychologist* 54, no. 10 (1999): 811–12.

11 See, for example, Jennifer A. Richeson and Sophie Trawalter, "Why Do Interracial Interactions Impair Executive Function? A Resource Depletion Account," *Journal of Personality and Social Psychology* 88, no. 6 (2005): 934–47.

12 Darren Lenard Hutchinson, "Racial Exhaustion," *Washington University Law Review* 86, no. 4 (2009): 970.

13 Hutchinson, "Racial Exhaustion," 970.

14 See, for example, Andrew M. Jones and Anni Vanhatalo, "The 'Critical Power' Concept: Applications to Sports Performance with a Focus on Intermittent High-Intensity Exercise," *Sports Medicine* 47, no. 1 (2017): 65–78, https://doi-org.offcampus.lib.washington.edu/10.1007/s40279-017-0688-0.

15 See Tricia Hersey, *Rest Is Resistance: A Manifesto* (New York: Little, Brown Spark, 2022).

16 Jordan, Kalia, Davarius, and most of the participant names I use in this book are pseudonyms, most of which have been chosen by the participants themselves. A couple of participants did insist on my using their actual names. You can listen to a selection of this particular dialogue in Laura Irwin, "They Would Give Them All the Help They Needed, with Us It Would Be Two Words," Interrupting Privilege, July 1, 2021, http://ip.ccde.com.uw.edu/?p=774. All of the dialogues discussed in this book are on the Interrupting Privilege website, http://ip.ccde.com.uw.edu.

17 In the 2019–2020 academic year I was supported to do this work by the inaugural "Scholars and Society" fellowship funded by American Council of Learned Societies and Mellon Foundations. I spent that year in residence at the Northwest African American Museum.

18 Mr. Day also features in Ralina Joseph and Allison Briscoe-Smith, *Generation Mixed Goes to School* (New York: TC Press, 2021). One of our youth participants named Mr. Day as the teacher who made him feel included at school; we quote include Mr. Day's words to help explain how teachers can foster inclusion.

19 See the Interrupting Privilege archive at https://ip.ccde.com.uw.edu/.

20 A disclaimer: my observations are like those of communication scholars Matthew L. Sanders and Matthew A. Koschmann, whose "review and application of communication scholarship . . . is intended to be representative and demonstrative, not exhaustive" (*Understanding Nonprofit Work: A Communication Perspective* [United Kingdom: Wiley-Blackwell, 2020], ix.

21 Robin R. Means Coleman and Jennifer McGee Reyes, "Assessing Programmatic Mentoring: Requiem for Carmen," *Communication, Culture & Critique* 14, no. 4 (2021): 677. https://doi-org.offcampus.lib.washington.edu/10.1093/ccc/tcab051.

22 I created this circuit while teaching the Birmingham School's circuit of culture (production, representation, consumption, regulation, and identity), and the recirculating modes undoubtably influenced me. For more see Stuart Hall, *Representation: Cultural Representations and Signifying Practices* (London: Sage in association with the Open University, 1997).

23 My co-author Allison Briscoe-Smith and I first articulated a version of these in print in *Generation Mixed Goes to School*.

24 This is how critical pedagogy scholar Joe Kinchloe defines radical listening. See Melissa Winchell, Tricia Kress, and Ken Tobin, "Teaching/Learning Radical Listening: Joe's Legacy among Three Generations of Practitioners," in *Practicing Critical Pedagogy: The Influences of Joe L. Kincheloe*, ed. Mary Frances Agnello and William Martin Reynolds, 99–102 (Germany: Springer International Publishing, 2015).

25 Jennifer Eberhardt, "How Racial Bias Works—and How to Disrupt It," June 2020, TED Talk video, 14:08, www.ted.com/talks/jennifer_l_eberhardt_how_racial_bias_works_and_how_to_disrupt_it.

26 See Megan Boler, "A Pedagogy of Discomfort: Witnessing and the Politics of Anger and Fear," in *Feeling Power*, 175–202 (New York: Routledge, 1999), https://doi.org/10.4324/9780203009499-8; Marsha Linehan, *DBT Skills Training Handouts and Worksheets*, 2nd ed. (New York: The Guilford Press, 2015).

27 Kim Mills, Interview with Derald Wing Sue, *Speaking of Psychology*, podcast audio, August, 2023, https://www.apa.org/news/podcasts/speaking-of-psychology/microaggressions.

28 Understanding language and terminology that best reflect power—and lack thereof—is essential. See the index to Özlem Sensoy and Robin DiAngelo's *Is Everyone Really Equal? An Introduction to Key Concepts in Social Justice Education* (New York: TC Press, 2017), 245.

29 Dictionary.com, s.v. "interrupt," n.d., accessed August 22, 2024, www.dictionary.com/browse/interrupt.

30 Sanders and Koschmann, *Understanding Nonprofit Work*, 304.

31 See Stuart Hall, "Encoding/Decoding," in *Culture, Media, Language: Working Papers in Cultural Studies*, ed. Stuart Hall, Dorothy Hobson, Andrew Love, and Paul Willis (London: Hutchinson, 1980), 128–38.

32 In addition to Michael S. Kimmel and Abby L. Ferber, eds., *Privilege: A Reader* (New York: Routledge, 2017), there are many useful books on privilege. Some, like Frances Kendall, *Understanding White Privilege: Creating Pathways to Au-*

thentic Relationships across Race (New York: Routledge, 2013), home in on white perspectives. Others address the intersections of race and gender, including Jenna Arnold, *Raising Our Hands: How White Women Can Stop Avoiding Hard Conversations, Start Accepting Responsibility, and Find Our Place on the New Frontlines* (Dallas: BenBella Books, 2020), or sexuality, including Elizabeth Evans and Éléonore Lépinard, eds., *Intersectionality in Feminist and Queer Movements: Confronting Privileges* (New York: Taylor & Francis, 2020).

33 See Trip Gabriel and Dana Goldstein, "Disrupting Racism's Reach, Republicans Rattle American Schools," *New York Times*, June 1, 2021, www.nytimes.com/2021/06/01/us/politics/critical-race-theory.html.
34 King, *Mindful of Race*, 41.
35 King, *Mindful of Race*, 10, 61.
36 Jay Smooth, "How I Learned to Stop Worrying and Love Discussing Race," November 15, 2011, TEDx Talks, 11:56, www.youtube.com/watch?v=MbdxeFcQtaU.
37 Dictionary.com, s.v. "privilege," n.d., accessed August 22, 2024, www.dictionary.com/browse/privilege.
38 Brett Marsh, "Post Traumatic Slave Syndrome: DeGruy Talks to Oakland Audience about the Lingering Trauma of African Diaspora," *Oakland North*, September 17, 2019, https://oaklandnorth.net/2019/09/17/post-traumatic-slave-syndrome-degruy-talks-to-oakland-audience-about-the-lingering-trauma-of-african-diaspora/. The two examples reflect elements of what Joy DuGruy calls "post traumatic slave syndrome." In the second example, the Black parent's concerns harken back to enslavement, when Black parents couldn't publicly praise their children without fear of an enslaver hearing such praise and taking the children. See Joy DuGruy, *Post Traumatic Slave Syndrome: America's Legacy of Enduring Injury and Healing* (Portland, OR: Joy DeGruy Publications, 2017).
39 See National Partnership for Women & Families, "Black Women and the Wage Gap," October 2022, www.nationalpartnership.org/our-work/resources/economic-justice/fair-pay/african-american-women-wage-gap.pdf.
40 You can listen to an excerpt of Michele and Janelle's dialogue in Laura Irwin, "The Black Tax," Interrupting Privilege, July 1, 2021, http://ip.ccde.com.uw.edu/?p=788.
41 David Foster Wallace, "This Is Water: Some Thoughts, Delivered on a Significant Occasion, about Living a Compassionate Life" (Kenyon College Commencement, Gambier, OH, March 21, 2005) [Transcript], http://bulletin-archive.kenyon.edu/x4280.html.
42 Kimmel and Ferber, *Privilege*, 1.
43 Peggy McIntosh, "White Privilege: Unpacking the Invisible Knapsack," *Peace and Freedom*, July/August, 1989, 10–12, https://med.umn.edu/sites/med.umn.edu/files/2022-12/White-Privilege_McIntosh-1989.pdf.
44 Jose Luis Vilson, "The Need for More Teachers of Color," *American Educator* 39, no. 2 (2015): 27–31.
45 "The ADOS Advocacy Foundation," homepage, n.d., accessed August 14, 2022, https://adosfoundation.org.

46 Seattle Times Staff, "Here's How Seattle Voters' Support for Trump Compared to Other Cities," *Seattle Times*, November 17, 2016, www.seattletimes.com/seattle-news/politics/heres-how-seattle-voters-support-for-trump-stacks-up-to-other-u-s-cities/.
47 "An Examination of the 2016 Electorate, Based on Validated Voters," Pew Research Center, August 9, 2018. www.pewresearch.org/politics/2018/08/09/an-examination-of-the-2016-electorate-based-on-validated-voters/.
48 To read more about this project see Joseph and Briscoe-Smith, *Generation Mixed Goes to School*.
49 Sheryl Gay Stolberg, "Pandemic within a Pandemic': Coronavirus and Police Brutality Roil Black Communities, *New York Times*, June 7, 2020, www.nytimes.com/2020/06/07/us/politics/blacks-coronavirus-police-brutality.html.
50 CDOs increased 123 percent between 2015 and 2022. Drew Goldstein et al., "Unlocking the Potential of Chief Diversity Officers," McKinsey and Company, November 18, 2022, https://www.mckinsey.com/capabilities/people-and-organizational-performance/our-insights/unlocking-the-potential-of-chief-diversity-officers.
51 Rizvana Bradley, "Picturing Catastrophe: The Visual Politics of Racial Reckoning," *Yale Review* 109, no. 2 (2021): 159, doi:10.1353/tyr.2021.0044.
52 Wesley Lowery, "Why There Was No Racial Reckoning: Systemic Problems Will Not Be Solved by Representational Victory," *The Atlantic*, February 8, 2023, https://www.theatlantic.com/ideas/archive/2023/02/tyre-nichols-death-memphis-george-floyd-police-reform/672986/.
53 Sheena S. Williams, "Racial Reckoning: I Am Exhausted," *Nursing Management* 54, no. 4 (2023): 6, 10.1097/01.NUMA.0000921896.45611.ed.
54 Williams, "Racial Reckoning," 7.
55 Kimberly D. Manning, "A Reckoning of Racial Reckoning," *The Lancet* (British Ed.) 399, no. 10327 (2022): 784–85, doi:10.1016/S0140-6736(22)00317-8.
56 Aaron Morrison, "Racism of Rioters Takes Center Stage in Jan 6. Hearing," AP News, July 28, 2021, https://apnews.com/article/joe-biden-government-and-politics-riots-race-and-ethnicity-capitol-siege-b3eb4a7f1a0d183c9db89a08c84a70cb.
57 See https://www.flsenate.gov/Session/Bill/2022/148/BillText/Filed/HTML.
58 Francesca Sobande, Akane Kanai, and Natasha Zeng, "The Hypervisibility and Discourses of 'Wokeness' in Digital Culture," Media, Culture & Society 44, no. 8 (2022): 1579. doi:10.1177/01634437221117490.
59 Penny O'Donnell, Justine Lloyd and Tanja Dreher, "Listening, Pathbuilding and Continuations: A Research Analysis of Listening," *Continuum: Journal of Media & Cultural Studies* 23, no. 4 (2009): 426. We host dyadic conversations.
60 See, for example, Frank Dobbin and Alexandra Kalev, "Why Doesn't Diversity Training Work? The Challenge for Industry and Academia," *Anthropology Now* 10, no. 2 (2018): 48–85, https://doi.org/10.1080/19428200.2018.1493182; Patricia G.

Devine and Tory L. Ashy, "Diversity Training Goals, Limitations, and Promise: A Review of the Multidisciplinary Literature," *Annual Review of Psychology*, 73, no. 1 (2022): 403–49, doi:10.1146/annurev-psych-060221-122215; William Taylor Laimaka Cox, "Developing Scientifically Validated Bias and Diversity Trainings That Work: Empowering Agents of Change to Reduce Bias, Create Inclusion, and Promote Equity," *Management Decisions* 61, no. 4 (2023): 1038–61, doi:10.1108/MD-06-2021-0839.

61 Ralina L. Joseph, "What's the Difference with 'Difference'? Equity, Communication, and the Politics of Difference," *International Journal of Communication (Online)* 11 (2017): 3306.

62 He continues, "This is a biopolitics that flags phenotype as the final arbiter of hierarchical difference, categorizing and codifying bodies along a continuum of recognizable somatic privilege" (John L. Jackson Jr., "The Strange Immortalities of Race," *Soundings: An Interdisciplinary Journal* 96, no. 1 [2013]: 12, 15–16, https://doi.org/10.5325/soundings.96.1.00120.

63 King, *Mindful of Race*, 10–11.

64 The four guiding points of interrupting privilege—radical listening, sitting in discomfort, radical speaking/dialoguing race, and reparative dialogue—become actionable in the form of creating time-based, or short-term, mid-term, and long-term, goals. *Interrupting Privilege* provides not just critique but tools, so that readers can leave each chapter with a greater understanding of how to create their own individual change within their *sphere of influence*, and how their individual change can create the building blocks of a structural revolution. A sphere of influence simply illustrates that an individual has true power to enact change, or what Michelle Obama calls the "power of small." (Michelle Obama, *The Light We Carry: Overcoming in Uncertain Times*. [New York: Crown, 2022], 23. While the phrase *sphere of influence* has colonial and imperial roots, here it draws on Helen Jennings's 1937 study of individuals' power within networks; Jennings's subsequent work with co-author Jacob Moreno is the basis of network analysis. Jennings notes that one can assess an individual's sphere of influence through a "range of emotional expansiveness and the capacity of the individuals who make up the population to receive and respond to the particular feelings projected by the individual sender" ("Structure of leadership: Development and sphere of influence," *Sociometry* 1, no. 1/2 [July–October 1937]:, 99). While much of the research that stemming from Jennings's work focuses on the power of leaders, interrupting privilege as a concept and tool argues that each of us has a sphere of influence in which we can create change.

65 For more on white racialization, see Noel Ignatiev, *How The Irish Became White* (New York: Routledge, 1995); Jacobson, *Whiteness of a Different Color*; Steve Martinot, *The Machinery of Whiteness: Studies in the Structure of Racialization* (Philadelphia: Temple University Press, 2010); Nell Irvin Painter, *The History of White People* (New York: W.W. Norton & Company, 2011).

66 Listen to an excerpt from Jada's dialogue here in Laura Irwin, "When Should You Interrupt Privilege?" Interrupting Privilege, September 2, 2021, https://ip.ccde.com.uw.edu/?p=1338.

1. RADICAL LISTENING

1 See, for example, Nell Irvin Painter, *The History of White People* (New York: W.W. Norton & Company, 2011).
2 Scott Jaschik, "Quantifying the Advantage of Legacy Applicants," *Inside Higher Ed*, August 20, 2017, www.insidehighered.com/admissions/article/2017/08/21/data-provide-insights-advantages-and-qualifications-legacy-applicants.
3 Stella Ting-Toomey, "Identity Negotiation Theory: Crossing Cultural Boundaries," in *Theorizing about Intercultural Communication*, ed. William B. Gundykunst, (Thousand Oaks, CA: Sage, 2005), 227.
4 Michael Spencer, "Dialoguing across Difference: Listening with Ting," Zoom lecture, University of Washington's Graduate School, January 10, 2023.
5 For example, Clint Smith's *How the Word Is Passed: A Reckoning with the History of Slavery across America* (New York: Little, Brown and Company, 2021) traces the legacies of slavery through counter-histories of monuments and landmarks; Roxanne Dunbar-Ortiz's *An Indigenous Peoples' History of the United States* (Boston: Beacon Press, 2015) tells U.S. history from anticolonial Native perspectives; and Richard Rothstein's *The Color of Law: A Forgotten History of How Our Government Segregated America* (New York: Liveright, 2017) examines racist segregation policies such as redlining that have often been hidden.
6 Elizabeth Parks, Meara Few, and Laura Lane, *Listening: The Key Concepts* (New York: Routledge Press, 2024).
7 See Graham D. Bodie, "Listening as Positive Communication," in *The Positive Side of Interpersonal Communication*, ed. Thomas J. Socha and Margaret J. Pitts (New York: Peter Lang, 2012), 111.
8 As interpersonal communication scholar Elizabeth Parks tells us, listening "does not just function as a counterpart to speaking, but rather creates a unique communication practice of its own" ("Introduction," *Listening: Journal of Communication Ethics, Religion, and Culture* 56, no. 2 [2021]: 92). Parks also notes that "listening is often overshadowed by speaking in communication research and organizational research in particular. . . . When comparing a search of EbscoHost's CMM database there were three times as many articles for speaking as listening" ("Listening with Empathy in Organizational Communication," *Listening: Journal of Communication Ethics, Religion, and Culture* 56, no. 2 [2021]: 10).
9 Such "unknowing" enables listeners "to be strong enough to relinquish our perceived mastery, control, and foreknowledge while remaining attentive and aware" (Lisbeth Lipari, *Listening, Thinking, Being: Toward an Ethics of Attunement* [University Park: Pennsylvania State University Press, 2014], 99). At the same time, Lipari notes, listening does not happen in a vacuum as we are always engaged in "listening otherwise," an "interlistening" when the immediate moment of listening

"resonates with echoes of everything we have ever heard, thought, seen, touched, said, and read throughout our lives." (Lipari, *Listening, Thinking, Being*, 9).

10 Laurie Lewis, *The Power of Strategic Listening in Contemporary Organizations* (United Kingdom: Rowman & Littlefield, 2019): 70.

11 Alison Macadam, "Six Ways to Run a Listening Session," NPR Training, February 16, 2016, https://training.npr.org/2016/02/16/six-ways-to-run-a-listening-session/.

12 Lewis, *The Power of Strategic Listening*, xiv, xiii.

13 "Trump Holds Listening Session with Students on Mass Shootings," February 21, 2018, https://abcnews.go.com/Politics/trump-holds-listening-session-students-mass-shootings/story?id=53245367.

14 "Trump Holds Listening Session."

15 In passive listening, the sound might become meaning a beat after hearing. Teachers or parents might think of calling out instructions to a child, once, twice, maybe even three times without recognition only to have them parrot back what you said.

16 International Listening Association, "Definition of Listening," 2012, https://www.listen.org/listening-definition.

17 Andrew D. Wolvin and Carolyn Gwynn Coakley, "Appreciative Listening," in *Listening*, 2nd ed. (Dubuque, IA: Wm. C. Brown Company, 1996), 151. In addition to discriminative and comprehensive listening, Wolvin and Coakley name "critical listening," "appreciative listening," and "therapeutic listening" in their listening typology.

18 Paul J, Kaufmann, *Sensible Listening: The Key to Responsive Interaction*, 7th ed. (Dubuque, IA: Kendall Hunt, 2015), 223.

19 Lewis, *The Power of Strategic Listening*, 2.

20 Neurologists and psychologists note that we move when we listen more fully, but when we listen passively, we are still. See, for example, Victor C. Fung and Joyce Eastlund Gromko, "Effects of Active versus Passive Listening on the Quality of Children's Invented Notations and Preferences for Two Pieces from an Unfamiliar Culture," *Psychology of Music* 29, no. 2 (2001): 128–38, https://doi.org/10.1177/0305735601292003.

21 See for example, in medicine, Kathryn Robertson, "Active Listening: More Than Just Paying Attention," *Australian Family Physician* 34, no. 12 (2005): 1053–5; in education, Michael Rost and J. J. Wilson, *Active Listening: Research and Resources in Language Teaching* (New York: Routledge, 2013); in social work, Juan Enrique Huerta-Wong and Richard Schoech, "Experiential Learning and Learning Environments: The Case of Active Listening Skills," *Journal of Social Work Education*, 46, no. 1 (2010): 85–101, https://doi.org/10.5175/JSWE.2010.200800105; in journalism, Tony Harcup, *Listening to the Voiceless: The Practices and Ethics of Alternative Journalism* (New York: Routledge 2015).

22 Carl R. Rogers and Richard E. Farson, *Active Listening* (Mansfield Centre, CT: Martino Publishing 2015), 1.

23 To learn more about an extension of active listening called "active empathetic listening," see Tanya Drollinger, Lucette B. Comer, and Patricia T. Warrington,

"Development and Validation of the Active Empathetic Listening Scale," *Psychology & Marketing* vol. 23, no. 2 (2006): 161–80, https://doi.org/10.1002/mar.20105; Pamela Fitzgerald and Ivan Leudar, "On Active Listening in Person-Centered, Solution-Focused Psychotherapy," *Journal of Pragmatics* 42, no. 12 (2010): 3188–98, https://doi.org/10.1016/j.pragma.2010.07.007.

24 See, for example, Albert Mehrabian, *Silent Messages: Implicit Communication of Emotions and Attitudes*, 2nd ed. (Belmont, CA: Wadsworth, 1981); Albert Mehrabian, *Nonverbal Communication* (Chicago: Aldine-Atherton, 1972).

25 David Lapakko, "Communication Is 93% Nonverbal: An Urban Legend Proliferates," *Communication and Theater Association of Minnesota Journal* 34, no. 1 (2015): 13, https://doi.org/10.56816/2471-0032.1000.

26 Penny O'Donnell, Justine Lloyd, and Tanja Dreher, "Listening, Pathbuilding and Continuations: A Research Analysis of Listening," *Continuum: Journal of Media & Cultural Studies*, 23, no. 4, (2009): 436.

27 Lipari, *Listening, Thinking, Being*. 90.

28 Aki Myllyneva and Jari K. Hietanen, "The Dual Nature of eye Contact: To See and to Be Seen," *Social Cognitive and Affective Neuroscience*, 11, no. 7 (2016): 1089–90, https://doi.org/10.1093/scan/nsv075. They note that "faces with direct gaze are memorized more readily than faces with averted gaze" and that "faces with direct gaze can better hold attention, detracting from performance in concurrent cognitive tasks" (1089).

29 See, for example, the explanation of women's lowered eye gaze when interacting with men in Awatif Elnour and Khadar Bashir-Ali, "Teaching Muslim Girls in American Schools," *Social Education* 67, no. 1 (2003): n.p.

30 See, for example, Allie Khalulyan, Katie Byrd, Jonathan Tarbox, Alexandra Little, and Henrike Moll, "The Role of Eye Contact in Young Children's Judgments of Others' Visibility: A Comparison of Preschoolers with and without Autism Spectrum Disorder," *Journal of Communication Disorders* 89 (January–February 2021): 106075, https://doi.org/10.1016/j.jcomdis.2020.106075.

31 Elizabeth S. Parks, "Dialogic Listening: Moving Beyond Idealism to Intercultural Ethical Praxis," *Listening (River Forest)* 56, no. 2 (2021): 132, https://doi.org/10.5840/listening202156219.

32 Lipari, *Listening, Thinking, Being*, 90.

33 Elizabeth Molina-Markham, "Listening Faithfully with Friends: An Ethnography of Quaker Communication Practices" (PhD diss., University of Massachusetts, Amherst, 2011), vi; personal correspondence with Laura Helper, May 2023.

34 Poppy de Souza and Tanja Dreher, "Dwelling in Discomfort: On the Conditions of Listening in Settler Colonial Australia," *borderlands* 20, no. 2 (2021): 31, https://sciendo.com/article/10.21307/borderlands-2021-012.

35 Sara Ahmed, "Not in the Mood," *new formations: a journal of culture/theory/politics* 82 (2014): 17. Ahmed refers to Heidegger's concept of "a lack of attunement," which he defines by what it is not: a lack of attunement is not apathy or indifference, for example.

36 Ting-Toomey, "Identity Negotiation Theory," 227.
37 Lipari, *Listening, Thinking, Being*, 57.
38 Traditional listening scholarship, according to critical listening scholar Anjuli Brekke, tells us that meaning is created intersubjectively—in other words between two people—but this doesn't take power into account See Anjuli Joshi Brekke, "Radical Listening: Cultivating a Feminist Ethics of Reception through Collective Listening," *Listening (River Forest)* 56, no. 2 (2021): 96–107, https://www.doi.org/10.5840/listening202156216.
39 Carol Gilligan, Renée Spencer, M. Weinberg, and Tatiana Bertsch, "On the Listening Guide: A Voice-Centered Relational Method," in *Qualitative Research in Psychology: Expanding Perspectives in Methodology and Design*, ed. P. M. Camic, J. E. Rhodes, and L. Yardley, 157–72 (Washington, DC: American Psychological Association, 2003).
40 Sanja Petrovic, Daphne Lordly, Susan Brigham, and Mary Delaney, "Learning to Listen: An Analysis of Applying the Listening Guide to Reflection Papers," *International Journal of Qualitative Methods* 14, no. 5 (2015): p. 1.
41 Krista Ratcliffe, *Rhetorical Listening: Identification, Gender, Whiteness* (Carbondale Southern Illinois Press, 2005), 28.
42 Ratcliffe, *Rhetorical Listening*, 17. Like the LG, rhetorical listening has four nonlinear steps: "promoting an *understanding* of self and other," "locating identifications across *commonalities* and *differences*," "analyzing *claims* as well as the *cultural logics*," and utilizing "an *accountability* logic." (Ratcliffe, *Rhetorical Listening*, 26)
43 de Souza and Dreher, "Dwelling in Discomfort," 32.
44 Tanja Dreher, "Eavesdropping with Permission: The Politics of Listening for Safer Speaking Spaces," *Borderlands E—Journal: New Spaces in the Humanities* 8, no. 1 (2009): 1.
45 de Souza and Dreher, "Dwelling in Discomfort," 31.
46 de Souza and Dreher, "Dwelling in Discomfort," 30.
47 O'Donnell, Lloyd, and Dreher, "Listening, Pathbuilding, and Continuations," 423.
48 O'Donnell, Lloyd, and Dreher, "Listening, Pathbuilding, and Continuations," 429.
49 john a. powell's Othering and Belonging Institute discusses the importance of belonging without othering. See https://belonging.berkeley.edu/.
50 Wendy Hui Kyong Chun, "Unbearable Witness: Toward a Politics of Listening," *differences: A Journal of Feminist Cultural Studies*, 11, no. 1 (1999): 140.
51 Janeta F. Tansey, "Existential Listening as Ethical Distancing: The Meaningfulness of Imposterism, Fear and Shame in Relation," *Listening (River Forest)* 56, no. 2 (2021): 142. https://www.doi.org/10.5840/listening202156220.
52 Tansey, "Existential Listening," 145–46. She calls this step toward erasing inequality "intersubjective distance."
53 This is a type of pause that I will investigate in the next chapter on discomfort. Such of pausing creates "an orientation to difference that does not presume to know or seek to control" it, writes rhetorician Preston Carmack. By leaning into

it, the listener "does not make over the other in the listener's own image" ("Roots and Wings: Emergent Listening and Attentiveness to Narrative Ground as a Unity of Contraries," *Listening [River Forest]* 56, no. 2 [2021]: 149–50, https://www.doi.org/10.5840/listening202156221). Poststructural theorist Bronwyn Davies refers to a "moment of the pause" (*Listening to Children: Being and Becoming (Contesting Early Childhood* [New York: Routledge, 2014], 35).

54 Megan Laverty calls this "existential listening" in "Philosophy for Children and Listening Education: An Ear for Thinking," in *Listening to Teach: Beyond Didactic Pedagogy*, ed. Leonard J. Waks (Albany: State University of New York Press, 2015), 65.

55 Angela Y. Davis, *Women, Culture, and Politics* (New York: Random House, 1984), 14.

56 Brekke puts it this way: radical listening "highlight[s] how the interpersonal and public dimensions of listening are enmeshed and exist within systems of power" ("Radical Listening," 96).

57 Radical is thus a "critical attitude or ideology that promotes the idea that complete change is necessary to reduce social problems" (Della V. Mosley, Helen A. Neville, Nayeli Y. Chavez-Dueñas, Hector Y. Adames, Jioni A. Lewis, and Bryana H. French, "Radical Hope in Revolting Times: Proposing a Culturally Relevant Psychological Framework," *Social and Personality Psychology Compass* 14, no. 1 [2020]: e12512, 19).

58 Melissa Winchell, Tricia Kress, and Ken Tobin, "Teaching/Learning Radical Listening: Joe's Legacy among Three Generations of Practitioners," in *Practicing Critical Pedagogy: The Influences of Joe L. Kincheloe*, ed. Mary Frances Agnello and William Martin Reynolds (Germany: Springer International Publishing, 2015), 5.

59 Kenneth Tobin, "Tuning into Others' Voices: Radical Listening, Learning from Difference, and Escaping Oppression," *Cultural Studies of Education* 4, no. 3 (2009): 506.

60 Tobin, "Tuning into Others' Voices," 505.

61 Winchell, Kress, and Tobin, "Teaching/Learning," 13.

62 Winchell, Kress, and Tobin, "Teaching/Learning," 14.

63 Decades of interdisciplinary scholarship examine the uses of silence. See sociolinguist Adam Jaworski's *The Power of Silence: Social and Pragmatic Perspectives, Language and Language Behaviors* (Newbury Park, CA: Sage Publishing, 1992), xxii, for a thorough accounting of the literature.

64 Elizabeth Molina-Markham, "Finding the 'Sense of the Meeting': Decision-Making through Silence among Quakers, *Western Journal of Communication* 78, no. 2 (2014): 155, www.tandfonline.com/doi/abs/10.1080/10570314.2013.809474.

65 In radical listening, "new awarenesses and mutual culture [can] be collaboratively generated" (Winchell, Kress, and Tobin, "Teaching/Learning,"(6).

66 For more on radical listening, see Konstantinos Alexakos and Agnieska Pierwola, "Learning at the 'Boundaries': Radical Listening, Creationism, and Learning from the 'Other,'" *Cultural Studies of Science Education* 8, no. 8 (2013): 39–49; Shannon A. Moore, "Radical Listening: Transdisciplinarity, Restorative Justice and Change," *World Futures* 74, no. 74 (2018): 471–89.

67 Anjuli Joshi Brekke, "Listening across Difference: Mapping StoryCorps' Affective Archives" (PhD diss., University of Washington, 2020), 10.
68 We follow dialogic interviewing principles as articulated by Sara DeTurk and Elissa Foster, "Dialogue about Dialogue—Investigating Intersubjectivity in Interview Research," *Qualitative Research Journal* 8, no. 2 (2008): 24, https://doi.org/10.3316/qrj0802014; Steinar Kvale, "The Dominance of Dialogical Interview Research: A Critical View," *Barn—forskning om barn og barndom i Norden* 23, no. 3 (2021): 89, https://doi.org/10.5324/barn.v23i3.4438; Amy K. Way, Robin Kanak Zwier, and Sarah J. Tracy, "Dialogic Interviewing and Flickers of Transformation," *Qualitative Inquiry* 21, no. 8 (2015), https://doi.org/10.1177/1077800414566686.
69 Brekke, "Radical Listening," 100.
70 Ralina Joseph and Allison Briscoe-Smith, *Generation Mixed Goes to School: Radically Listening to Multiracial Kids*. (New York: TC Press, 2021), 10.
71 Brekke, "Radical Listening," 96.
72 Lilian Comas-Diaz, Gordon Nagayama Hall, and Helen A. Neville, "Racial Trauma: Theory, Research and Healing: Introduction to the Special Issue," *American Psychologist* 74, no. 1 (2019): 1.
73 Anjuli Brekke, Gina Aaftaab and Ralina L Joseph, "'I Address Race Because Race Addresses Me': Women of Color Show Receipts through Digital Storytelling," *Review of Communication* 21, no. 1 (2021): 47.
74 Ralina L. Joseph, *Postracial Resistance: Black Women, Media, and the Uses of Strategic Ambiguity* (New York: New York University Press, 2018), 3.
75 See, for example, John F. Dovidio, Susan Eggly, Terrance L. Albrecht, Nao Hagiwara, and Louis A. Penner., "Racial Biases in Medicine and Healthcare Disparities," *TPM* 23, no. 4, (2016): 489–510, www.tpmap.org/racial-biases-in-medicine-and-helathcare-disparities/.
76 See Lisa A. Cooper, Debra L. Roter, Rachel L. Johnson, Daniel E. Ford, Donald M. Steinwachs, and Neil R. Powe, "Patient-Centered Communication, Ratings of Care, and Concordance of Patient and Physician Race," *Annals of Internal Medicine* 139, no. 11, (2003): 907–15, doi: 10.7326/0003-4819-139-11-200312020-00009; Susan Eggly, Ellen Barton, Andrew Winckles, Louis A. Penner, and Terrance L. Albrecht, "A Disparity of Words: Racial Differences in Oncologist-Patient Communication about Clinical Trials," *Health Expectations, An International Journal of Public Participation in Health Care and Health Policy* 18, no. 5 (2015): 1316–1326, https://doi.org/10.1111/hex.12108; Rachel L. Johnson, Debra Roter, Neil R. Powe, and Lisa A. Cooper, "Patient Race/Ethnicity and Quality of Patient-Physician Communication during Medical Visits," *American Journal of Public Health* 94, no. 12 (1971): 2084–90, doi: 10.2105/AJPH.94.12.2084; Laura A. Siminoff, Gregory C. Graham, and Nahida H. Gordon, "Cancer Communication Patterns and the Influence of Patient Characteristics: Disparities in Information-Giving and Affective Behaviors," *Patient Education and Counseling* 62, no. 3 (2006): 355–60, doi: 10.1016/j.pec.2006.06.011.

77 See Tyler W. Buckner and Nigel S. Key, "Venous Thrombosis in Blacks," *Circulation* 125, no. 6 (2012): 837–9, doi: 10.1161.
78 Dona Schneider, David E. Lilienfeld, and Wansoon Im, "The Epidemiology of Pulmonary Embolism: Racial Contrasts in Incidence and In-Hospital Case Fatality," *Journal of the National Medical Association* 98, no. 12 (2006): 1967–72.
79 Ralina L. Joseph, "Opinion: Skirting Death by Implicit Bias at the Doctors Office," *South Seattle Emerald*, February 4, 2021, https://southseattleemerald.com/2021/02/04/opinion-skirting-death-by-implicit-bias-at-the-doctors-office/. To read more about the ways in which health care is considering the role of listening in health disparities, see work on narrative medicine, such as, Sayantani DasGupta, "Listening as Freedom: Narrative, Health, and Social Justice," in *Health Humanities Reader*, ed. Therese Jones, Delese Wear, and Lester D. Friedman (New Brunswick, NJ: Rutgers University Press, 2014), 251–260.
80 See Kaiser Permanente, "Equity, Inclusion, and Diversity," accessed April 16, 2025, https://about.kaiserpermanente.org/commitments-and-impact/equity-inclusion-and-diversity.

2. SITTING WITH DISCOMFORT

1 Jean's language here likely reflects that of Ibrahim X. Kendi in *How to Be an Antiracist* (London: Bodley Head, 2019), 15. This book, which was ubiquitous in progressive circles of white people the summer of 2020, was not the first to iterate such ideas, but it was certainly the most popular.
2 You can listen to a piece of this dialogue in Anjuli Brekke, "Talking to Your Family about Race," Interrupting Privilege, September 10, 2024, https://ip.ccde.com.uw.edu/?p=3385.
3 Here is the complete list of questions that we provided these participants in advance of their dialogue: 1. Please introduce yourself. Share a little bit about yourself and your family unit. 2. Does your family have an official or unofficial mission statement, i.e., words to live by? How might other folks describe your family? 3. How racially diverse is your immediate family? Extended family? Is this something you discuss with your family? 4. How racially diverse is your neighborhood? Was neighborhood diversity an issue when you chose your neighborhood? Do you talk about neighborhood diversity as a family? Please explain. 5. When you entertain socially, how diverse are your gatherings? Is this something you think about? Talk about as a family? Please explain. 6. How diverse are your children's schools? Was the school's diversity something you thought about prior to choosing their schools? Do you talk about your children's school's diversity with your kids? Please explain. 7. How diverse are your children's friend groups? How often do you host children of color at your house? How often do your children spend time at a friend of color's house? Do you talk about race and friendship with your children? 8. Do your children have Black, Indigenous or other people of color doctors, dentists, teachers, or other important caregivers in their lives? Is race

something you consider when you think about who will care for your children's well-being? Please explain. 9. Prior to the recent protests, how did you and your partner discuss race? Do you have any stories? 10. Prior to the recent protests, how did you and your partner, or perhaps you alone, discuss race with your children (there may or may not be a distinction from the question above)? Do you have any stories? 11. Have you discussed your children's white racial identity with them? Why or why not? (Note: this is different from discussing race.)

4   Megan Boler, "A Pedagogy of Discomfort: Witnessing and the Politics of Anger and Fear," in *Feeling Power* (New York: Routledge, 1999), 176–77, doi:10.4324/9780203009499-8; and Marsha M. Linehan, *DBT Skills Training Handouts and Worksheets*, 2nd ed. (New York: Guilford Press, 2015).
5   Merriam-Webster.com Dictionary, s.v. "discomfort," n.d., accessed August 29, 2024, www.merriam-webster.com/dictionary/discomfort.
6   Merriam-Webster.com Dictionary, s.v. "distress," n.d., accessed August 29, 2024, www.merriam-webster.com/dictionary/distress.
7   Ruth King, *Mindful of Race: Transforming Racism from the Inside Out* (Boulder, CO: Sounds True, Inc., 2018, 77.
8   King, *Mindful of Race*, 31.
9   See Eduardo Bonilla-Silva, "The Linguistics of Color Blind Racism: How to Talk Nasty about Blacks without Sounding 'Racist,' *Critical Sociology*, 28, nos. 1–2 (2002), https://doi.org/10.1177/08969205020280010501.
10 For more on listening on the upside and downside of power, see Dylan Robinson, *Hungry Listening: Resonant Theory for Indigenous Sound Studies* (Minneapolis: University of Minnesota Press, 2020).
11 Brigitte Vittrup, "Color Blind or Color Conscious? White American Mothers' Approaches to Racial Socialization," *Journal of Family Issues*, 39, no. 3 (2018): 668. https://doi.org/10.1177/0192513X16676858.
12 See Jennifer Eberhardt, *Biased: Uncovering the Hidden Prejudice That Shapes What We See, Think, and Do* (New York: Penguin Random House, 2019).
13 Quoted in Poppy de Souza and Tanja Dreher. "Dwelling in Discomfort: On the Conditions of Listening in Settler Colonial Australia." *borderlands* 20, no. 2 (2021), 49, doi:10.21307/borderlands-2021-012.
14 Shari Stenberg, "Cultivating Listening: Teaching from a Restored Logos," in *Silence and Listening as Rhetorical Arts*, ed. Cheryl Glenn and Krista Ratcliffe (Carbondale: Southern Illinois University Press, 2011), 258.
15 King, *Mindful of Race*, 31.
16 Laura Irwin, "Processing Microaggressions," Interrupting Privilege, September 7, 2021, https://ip.ccde.com.uw.edu/?p=1385.
17 Boler, "A Pedagogy of Discomfort," 186.
18 Boler, "A Pedagogy of Discomfort," 186.
19 See Moya Bailey, *Misogynoir Transformed: Black Women's Digital Resistance* (New York: New York University Press, 2021).

20 Boler, "A Pedagogy of Discomfort," 178.
21 Michalinos Zembylas and Megan Boler, "On the Spirit of Patriotism: Challenges of a 'Pedagogy of Discomfort,'" *Teachers College Record* 104, no. 5 (2022): 4.
22 Boler, "A Pedagogy of Discomfort," 186, 184.
23 Boler, "A Pedagogy of Discomfort," 178.
24 Boler, "A Pedagogy of Discomfort," 197.
25 Janice Omadeke, "What's the Difference between a Mentor and a Sponsor?" *Harvard Business Review*, October 20, 2021, https://hbr.org/2021/10/whats-the-difference-between-a-mentor-and-a-sponsor.
26 See work on pedagogies of discomfort plus trigger warnings in Michelle Bentley, "Trigger Warnings and the Student Experience," *Politics* 37, no. 4 (2017), https://doi.org/10.1177/0263395716684526; on teaching evaluations in Jill Blackmore, "Academic Pedagogies, Quality Logics and Performative Universities: Evaluating Teaching and What Students Want," *Studies in Higher Education* 34, no. 8 (2009), https://doi.org/10.1080/03075070902898664; on racialized emotions in Eduardo Bonilla-Silva, "Feeling Race: Theorizing the Racial Economy of Emotions," *American Sociological Review* 84, no. 1 (2019), https://doi.org/10.1177/0003122418816958; on community in Urmitapa Dutta, "Decolonizing 'Community' in Community Psychology," *American Journal of Community Psychology* 62, nos. 3–4 (2018), https://doi.org/10.1002/ajcp.12281; on peace education in Basma Hajir and Kevin Kester, "Toward a Decolonial Praxis in Critical Peace Education: Postcolonial Insights and Pedagogic Possibilities," *Studies in Philosophy and Education* 39, no. 5 (2020), https://doi.org/10.1007/s11217-020-09707-y; and on literacy in Antero Garcia, "Centering Analog Literacy in an Era of Digital Harm," *Research in the Teaching of English* 54, no. 2 (2019): 192–94. For critical pedagogy with a focus on race, gender, sexuality, and difference writ large, see Kristin Gregers Eriksen, "Discomforting Presence in the Classroom—The Affective Technologies of Race, Racism and Whiteness," *Whiteness and Education* 7, no. 1 (2022), https://doi.org/10.1080/23793406.2020.1812110; Mariona Massip Sabater and Edda Sant, "Gendering Citizenship Education: Feminist-Relational Approaches on Political Education," *Revista de investigación en didáctica de las ciencias sociales* no. 11 (2022), doi:10.17398/2531-0968.11.35; Maria do Mar Pereira, "Uncomfortable Classrooms: Rethinking the Role of Student Discomfort in Feminist Teaching," *European Journal of Women's Studies* 19, no. 1 (2012), https://doi.org/10.1177/1350506811426237c; Aideen Quilty, "Queer Provocations! Exploring Queerly Informed Disruptive Pedagogies within Feminist Community-Higher-Education Landscapes," *Irish Educational Studies* 36, no. 1 (2017), https://doi.org/10.1080/03323315.2017.1289704.
27 Peace education presents a particularly compelling application of a pedagogy of discomfort. Its scholars and practitioners, according to Hajir and Kester, "facilitate building a just and equitable world through increasing tolerance, reducing prejudice, and changing perception of the self and other" ("Toward a Decolonial Praxis," 517). Further, Hajir and Kester argue that without an explicit examination of power—and individual vis-à-vis structural, institutional, and

historical power—such goals are unattainable. Kester puts it this way: "To create real and lasting change for peace, we don't just need epistemological change (change in ways of thinking) but ontological change (change in ways of being). And ontological change requires a fundamental analysis of power" (Kevin Kester, "Global Citizenship Education and Peace Education: Toward a Postcritical Praxis," *Educational Philosophy and Theory* 55, no. 1 [2023]: 50, https://doi.org/10.1080/00131857.2022.2040483). Proponents of critical peace education (CPE) note that without attending to power, peace education itself can reproduce power inequities. Focusing on power through the lens of CPE "seeks to disrupt asymmetrical power relationships and unpack their political, economic, social, and historical roots.... It offers individuals a deeper understanding of the forces that affect their lives and stimulates them to respond at both a micro and macro level" (Hajir and Kester, "Toward a Decolonial Praxis," 518).

28 De Souza and Dreher, "Dwelling in Discomfort," 47.
29 Ralina Joseph and Allison Briscoe-Smith, *Generation Mixed Goes to School: Radically Listening to Multiracial Kids*. (New York: TC Press, 2021), 6–7.
30 Stenberg, "Cultivating Listening," 254.
31 King, *Mindful of Race*, 1.
32 King, *Mindful of Race*, 1.
33 King, *Mindful of Race*, 31.
34 Paul Gilbert, "Evolution, Social Roles, and the Differences in Shame and Guilt," *Social Research: An International Quarterly* 70 no. 4, (2003): 1205–30, https://doi.org/10.1353/sor.2003.0013.
35 Gilbert, "Evolution, Social Roles, and the Differences in Shame and Guilt," 1206.
36 Saiqua Naz, Romilly Gregory, and Meera Bahu, "Addressing Issues of Race, Ethnicity and Culture in CBT to Support Therapists and Service Managers to Deliver Culturally Competent Therapy and Reduce Inequalities in Mental Health Provision for BAME Service Users," *Cognitive Behavior Therapist* 12, no. e22 (2019): 8, doi:10.1017/S1754470X19000060.
37 Naz, Gregory, and Bahu, "Addressing Issues of Race," 6.
38 Naz, Gregory, and Bahu, "Addressing Issues of Race," 7.
39 Jeannie Gaines and John M. Jermier, "Emotional Exhaustion in a High Stress Organization," *Academy of Management Journal* 26, no. 4 (1983): 568, doi:10.5465/255907.
40 Gaines and Jermier, "Emotional Exhaustion," 570. Gaines and Jermier, who study the role of emotions at work, also notes that women report experiencing more emotional exhaustion than men, but they don't note differences in emotional exhaustion in white people and people of color (Gaines and Jermier, "Emotional Exhaustion," 581).
41 L. Dyrbye, J. Herrin, C. P. West, N. M. Wittlin, J. F. Dovidio, R. Hardeman, S. E. Burke, et al., "Association of Racial Bias with Burnout among Resident Physicians," *JAMA Network Open* 2, no. 7 (July 3, 2019):e197457, doi: 10.1001/jamanetworkopen.2019.7457.

42 Eberhardt, *Biased*, 285.
43 Some in health care have added to literature on burnout by describing the structural barriers to explain such emotions in terms they call "moral distress" and "moral injury." See, for example, Pedro Weisleder, "Moral Distress, Moral Injury, and Burnout: Clinicians' Resilience and Adaptability Are Not the Solution," *Annals of the Child Neurology Society* 1, no. 4 (2023): 262–66, doi: 10.1002/cns3.20048.
44 Sara Ahmed, *The Cultural Politics of Emotion* (New York: Routledge, 2004), 119.
45. *Merriam-Webster Dictionary*, "empathy," accessed April 16, 2025, https://www.merriam-webster.com/dictionary/empathy.
46 Susan Lanzoni, *Empathy: A History* (New Haven, CT: Yale University Press, 2018), 2.
47 Jakob Håkansson Eklund and Martina Summer Meranius, "Toward a Consensus on the Nature of Empathy: A Review of Reviews," *Patient Education and Counseling* 104, no, 2 (2021): 300–307, https://doi.org/10.1016/j.pec.2020.08.022.
48 Helen Reiss, "The Science of Empathy," *Journal of Patient Experience* 4, no. 2 (2017): 74, doi:10.1177/2374373517699267.
49 See Raymond A. Mar, "Stories and the Promotion of Social Cognition," *Current Directions in Psychological Science* 27, no. 4 (2018), https://doi.org/10.1177/0963721417749654.
50 Paul Bloom, *Against Empathy: The Case for Rational Compassion* (New York: Ecco, 2016), 5.
51 Stenberg notes that higher education teaches critique, or "reading against the grain," more than dwelling deeply with ideas, which is the step before critique. She also promotes the notion of "standing under" ideas as a first step. Standing under means not "impos[ing] one's own agenda" while listening ("Cultivating Listening, 253).
52 Stenberg, "Cultivating Listening," 258.
53 Boler, "A Pedagogy of Discomfort," 158.
54 Boler, "A Pedagogy of Discomfort," xx.
55 Boler, "A Pedagogy of Discomfort," 156. In a similar vein, political scientist Andrew Dobson writes of the need for "less empathy and more causal responsibility. . . . Those who cause harm are required as a matter of justice to rectify that harm" ("Thick Cosmopolitanism," *Political Studies* 54, no. 1 [2006]: 172, https://doi.org/10.1111/j.1467-9248.2006.00571.x.
56 Boler, "A Pedagogy of Discomfort," 155.
57 De Souza and Dreher, "Dwelling in Discomfort," 33.
58 Boler, "A Pedagogy of Discomfort," 164. Stella Ting-Toomey and Atsuko Kurogi write, "Analytical empathy leads to new insights and an alternative set of cultural experiences" ("Facework Competence in Intercultural Conflict: An Updated Face-Negotiation Theory," *International Journal of Intercultural Relations* 22, no. 2 [1998]: 203).
59 Naz, Gregory, and Bahu, "Addressing Issues of Race," 10.
60 Listen to Mele and Chelsea's dialogue here in Kaleb Germinaro, "Being Brave and Humble," Interrupting Privilege, May 14, 2022, http://ip.ccde.com.uw.edu/?p=1673.

61 Naz, Gregory, and Bahu, "Addressing Issues of Race," 9.
62 Marsha M. Linehan, *Building a Life Worth Living: A Memoir* (New York: Random House, 2020), 11.
63 Stacey B. Daughters, Stephanie M. Gorka, Jessica F. Magidson, Laura MacPherson, and C. J. Seitz-Brown, "The Role of Gender and Race in the Relation between Adolescent Distress Tolerance and Externalizing and Internalizing Psychopathology," *Journal of Adolescence (London, England)* 36, no. 6 (2013): 1054, doi:10.1016/j.adolescence.2013.08.008. These behaviors include "oppositional defiant, conduct, and somatic problems" (1061).
64 Linehan, *DBT Skills Training*, 1.
65 Marsha M. Linehan and Chelsey R. Wilks, "The Course and Evolution of Dialectical Behavior Therapy," *American Journal of Psychotherapy* 69, no. 2 (2015): 98.
66 Linehan and Wilks, "The Course and Evolution of Dialectical Behavior Therapy," 103.
67 Rhonda Magee, *The Inner Work of Racial Justice: Healing Ourselvs and Transforming Our Communities through Mindfulness* (New York: Penguin Random House, 2019), 7.
68 Linehan and Wilks, "The Course and Evolution of Dialectical Behavior Therapy," 98.
69 De Souza and Dreher, "Dwelling in Discomfort," 33.
70 Linehan, *DBT Skills Training*, 181.
71 Ashley M. Pierson, Vinushini Arunagiri, and Debra M. Bond, "'You Didn't Cause Racism, and You Have to Solve it Anyways': Antiracist Adaptation to Dialectical Behavior Therapy for White Therapists," *Cognitive and Behavioral Practice* 29, no. 4 (2022): 806.
72 Megan Kennedy, Pandemics Radical Listening Party, November 7, 2023.
73 King, *Mindful of Race*, 5.
74 Psychologists Ashley M. Pierson, Vinushini Arunagiri, and Debra M. Bond note that "when behaviors are not clearly described, or identified at all, it prohibits behavioral change" ("'You Didn't Cause Racism, 800).
75 Pierson, Arunagiri, and Bond, "You Didn't Cause Racism," 806.
76 Pierson, Arunagiri, and Bond, "You Didn't Cause Racism," 807.
77 Stacey B. Daughters, Stephanie M. Gorka, Jessica F. Magidson, Laura MacPherson, and C. J. Seitz-Brown, "The Role of Gender and Race in the Relation between Adolescent Distress Tolerance and Externalizing and Internalizing Psychopathology," 1054.
78 Christopher M. Perez, Bonnie C. Nicholson, Eric R. Dahlen, and Melanie E. Leuty, "Overparenting and Emerging Adults' Mental Health: The Mediating Role of Emotional Distress Tolerance," *Journal of Child and Family Studies* 29, no. 2 (2020): 374, doi:10.1007/s10826-019-01603-5.
79 Jennifer R. Dahne, Kelcey Stratton, Ruth Brown, Ananda Amstadter, Carl W. Lejuez, and Laura MacPherson, "Race as a Moderator of the Relationship between Distress Tolerance and Cigarette Smoking among Black and White Women," *Drug and Alcohol Dependence* 146 (2015): e256, doi:10.1016/j.drugalcdep.2014.09.162.
80 Linehan and Wilks, "The Course and Evolution of Dialectical Behavior Therapy," 106.

81 Andrada D. Neacsiu, Shireen L. Rizvi, and Marsha M. Linehan, "Dialectical Behavior Therapy Skills Use as a Mediator and Outcome of Treatment for Borderline Personality Disorder," *Behaviour Research and Therapy* 48, no. 9 (2010): 832–39, doi:10.1016/j.brat.2010.05.017.
82 Wendy Sims-Schouten and Patricia Gilbert, "Revisiting 'Resilience' in Light of Racism, 'Othering' and Resistance," *Race & Class* 64, no. 1 (2022): 90, doi:10.1177 /03063968221093882.
83 Helen Rosenboom and Ralina L. Joseph, "'What Makes You Think I'm African American?' Identity Performance, Code Switching and the Strong Black Woman on Love Is Blind," *Critical Studies in Media Communication* 41, no. 3 (2024): 276–81, doi:10.1080/15295036.2024.2385459.
84 See Shardé M. Davis, "The 'Strong Black Woman Collective': A Developing Theoretical Framework for Understanding Collective Communication Practices of Black Women," *Women's Studies in Communication* 38, no. 1 (2015): 20–35, doi: 10.1080/07491409.2014.953714.
85 Hear Ada and Ellen's dialogue in Kaleb Germinaro, "On the Meaning of Words Like Resilience," Interrupting Privilege, May 16, 2022, http://ip.ccde.com.uw.edu /?p=1679.
86 Sparkle Springfield, Feifei Qin, Haley Hedlin, Charles B. Eaton, Milagros C. Rosal, Herman Taylor, Ursula M. Staudinger, et al., "Modifiable Resources and Resilience in Racially and Ethnically Diverse Older Women: Implications for Health Outcomes and Interventions," *International Journal of Environmental Research and Public Health* 19, no. 12 (2022): 1, doi:10.3390/ijerph19127089.
87 Devan and Solis's dialogue can be heard in Kaleb Germinaro, "Stop Calling Us Resilient," Interrupting Privilege, May 16, 2022, http://ip.ccde.com.uw.edu/?p=1677.
88 Latrice shares her breathing techniques in Kaleb Germinaro, "Breathing for Resistance," Interrupting Privilege, May 11, 2022, https://ip.ccde.com.uw.edu/?p =1660.
89 Kaleb Germinaro, "Making Space for Self Compassion," Interrupting Privilege, May 11, 2022, http://ip.ccde.com.uw.edu/?p=1662.
90 Charles R. Collins and Erin Watson, "Subverting Whiteness: A Systems Theoretical Approach to Anti-Racist Praxis," *Global Journal of Community Psychology Practice* 12, no. 3 (2021): 3.
91 Kate Den Houter and Ellyn Maese, "Mentors and Sponsors Make the Difference," Gallup, April 13, 2023, www.gallup.com/workplace/473999/mentors-sponsors -difference.aspx.
92 Different parts of Sonya and Annette's dialogues can be heard in Laura Irwin, "Managing the Toll of Resistance on Our Bodies," Interrupting Privilege March 11, 2022, http://ip.ccde.com.uw.edu/?p=1539; Laura Irwin, "Changing the Systems," Interrupting Privilege, March 11, 2022, http://ip.ccde.com.uw.edu/?p=1536.
93 Pierson, Arunagiri, and Bond, "You Didn't Cause Racism," 807.
94 Peace studies scholars Kevin Kester and Hilary Cremin describe a "post-structural violence" that emerges from "well-intentioned actors in the field find[ing] them-

selves complicit in furthering the very violence that they seek to mitigate" ("Peace Education and Peace Education Research: Toward a Concept of Poststructural Violence and Second-Order Reflexivity," *Educational Philosophy and Theory* 49, no. 14 [2017]: 1418, doi:10.1080/00131857.2017.1313715).

3. RADICAL SPEAKING

1 Hear Fana and Teneh's conversation herein Anjuli Brekke, "Let's Talk About the Angry Black Woman," Interrupting Privilege, December 2, 2020, https://ip.ccde.com.uw.edu/?p=405.
2 See Tanya L. Chartrand and John A Bargh, "The Chameleon Effect: The Perception-Behavior Link and Social Interaction," *Journal of Personality and Social Psychology* 76, no. 6 (1999): 893, doi:10.1037/0022-3514.76.6.893.
3 Patricia Hill Collins, "Controlling Images and Black Women's Oppression." In *Black Feminist Thought: Knowledge, Consciousness, and the Politics of Empowerment*, 266–273. New York: Routledge, 1991; Bettina Judd, "Sapphire as Praxis: Toward a Methodology of Anger," *Feminist Studies* 45, no. 1 (2019): 178. https://dx.doi.org/10.1353/fem.2019.0003.
4 Audre Lorde, *Sister Outsider: Essays and Speeches* (Trumansburg, NY: Crossing Press, 1984), 44.
5 See, for example, Kelley Bouchard, "African-American Parents Say 'The Talk' Is a Life-and-Death Matter," *Portland Press Herald*, July 17, 2016, www.pressherald.com/2016/07/17/african-american-parents-say-the-talk-is-a-life-and-death-matter/; German Lopez, "Black Parents Describe "The Talk" They Give to Their Children about Police," *Vox*, August 8, 2016, www.vox.com/2016/8/8/12401792/police-black-parents-the-talk.
6 Questions from Naima Joseph.
7 For more on white racialization, see Noel Ignatiev, *How The Irish Became White* (New York: Routledge, 1995); Matthew Frye Jacobson, *Whiteness of a Different Color: European Immigrants and the Alchemy of Race* (Cambridge, MA: Harvard University Press, 1999); Steve Martinot, *The Machinery of Whiteness: Studies in the Structure of Racialization* (Philadelphia: Temple University Press, 2010); Nell Irvin Painter, *The History of White People* (New York: W.W. Norton & Company, 2011).
8 Lorde, *Sister Outsider*, 40.
9 See Derald Wing Sue, *Race Talk and the Conspiracy of Silence: Understanding and Facilitating Difficult Dialogues on Race* (New York: Wiley, 2015).
10 In the Interrupting Privilege program we practice radical speaking in a variation on an activity called "Serial testimony," which refers to the regular practice of sharing one's truth. See Peggy McIntosh, "Beyond the Knapsack," *Teaching Tolerance Magazine* 46 (Spring 2014), www.learningforjustice.org/magazine/spring-2014/toolkit-for-beyond-the-knapsack.
11 Christina Siry, Michelle Brendel, and Roger Frisch, "Radical Listening and Dialogue in Educational Research," *International Journal of Critical Pedagogy* 7, no. 20 (2016): 120.

12 This is not to say that radical speaking fulfills the second part of Bakhtin's definition of "monological," which involves not just speaking with a single voice, but speaking with a single voice that presumes an ultimate and singular truth. Mikhail Bakhtin, *Speech Genres and Other Late Essays*, trans. Vern W. McGee (Austin: University of Texas Press, 1986), 68.

13 Hear more from Annette in Laura Irwin, "Speaking Up Is a Gift for People," Interrupting Privilege, March 11, 2021, http://ip.ccde.com.uw.edu/?p=1532.

14 Ruth King, *Mindful of Race: Transforming Racism from the Inside Out* (Boulder, CO: Sounds True, 2018), 96.

15 King, *Mindful of Race*, 94. One strategy to arrive at Metta is to use the RAIN (recognize, allow, investigate, and nonidentification) technique developed by Vipassana meditation teacher Michele McDonald (King 109). RAIN practice is not problem solving but "examining our relationship to racial distress and learning how to bear witness to its nature—discovering directly that racial distress is not personal, permanent, or perfect" (King 110).

16 See, for example, assembled listicles on "Microaggressions," Buzzfeed, n.d., accessed August 14, 2024, www.buzzfeed.com/au/tag/microaggressions; the assembled videos on "You Look Different," MTV, n.d., accessed August 14, 2024, www.youtube.com/playlist?list=PLBPLVvU_jvGssvzwax_GijPAnZqbiQqyB; and social media posts on The Microaggressions Project, "Microaggressions: Power, Privilege, and Everyday Life," n.d., accessed August 14, 2024, www.microaggressions.com/.

17 Ezra H. Griffith, *Race & Excellence: My Dialogue with Chester Pierce* (Iowa City: University of Iowa Press, 1998), 48.

18 Griffith, *Race & Excellence*, 91, 134, 137.

19 Griffith, *Race & Excellence*, 148–49.

20 The historian Darlene Clark Hine uses the word "dissemblance" to describe the strategic, covering behaviors that protect Black lives from prying white eyes in "Rape and the Inner Lives of Black Women in the Middle West," *Signs: Journal of Women in Culture and Society* 14, no. 4 (1989): 912, doi:10.1086/494552. The historian Evelyn Brooks Higginbotham refers to such moments of dissemblance as creating a Black "politics of respectability" in *Righteous Discontent: The Women's Movement in the Black Baptist Church, 1880–1920* (Cambridge, MA: Harvard University Press, 1993), 185.

21 Griffith, *Race & Excellence*, 149.

22 Joel Dimsdale, Chester Pierce, D. Schoenfeld, A. Brown, R. Zusman, and R. Graham, "Suppressed Anger and Blood Pressure: The Effects of Race, Sex, Social Class, Obesity, and Age," *Psychosomatic Medicine* 48, no. 6 (1986): 430–36, https://doi.org/10.1097/00006842-198607000-00005.

23 Dimsdale et al., "Suppressed Anger and Blood Pressure."

24 Chester M. Pierce, "Race, Deprivation and Drug Abuse in the U.S.A.," *Proceedings of the Anglo-American Conference on Drug Abuse. London: Royal Society of Medicine*, 1973.

25 Chester M. Pierce and Gail B. Allen. "CHILDISM." *Psychiatric Annals* 5, no. 7 (1975), 15–24, https://doi.org/10.3928/0048-5713-19750701-04.
26 Chester M. Pierce, Jean V. Carew, Diane Pierce-Gonzalez, and Deborah Wills, "An Experiment in Racism: TV Commercials," *Education and Urban Society* 10, no. 1 (1977), https://doi.org/10.1177/001312457701000105.
27 Pierce et al., "An Experiment in Racism."
28 See Bryan Greene, "The Unmistakable Black Roots of Sesame Street," *Smithsonian Magazine*, November 7, 2019, www.smithsonianmag.com/history/unmistakable-black-roots-sesame-street-180973490/; David Beard, "How a Black Psychiatrist Shaped 'Sesame Street' as a Tool against Racism," *Mother Jones*, June 5, 2019, www.motherjones.com/media/2019/06/recharge-56-sesame-street-anniversary-inclusion-chester-pierce/.
29 "'The Forgotten Tale of How Black Psychiatrists Helped Make 'Sesame Street,'" *Daily Beast*, May 19, 2019, www.thedailybeast.com/chester-pierce-the-forgotten-tale-of-how-a-black-psychiatrist-helped-make-sesame-street.
30 Chester Pierce, "Offensive Mechanisms," in *The Black Seventies*, ed. F. B. Barbour, 265–82 (Boston: Porter Sargent, 1970). When I share work on microaggressions with students and community members, many balk at the term, saying it feels "too small." People comment that the prefix "micro" doesn't do justice to the experiences of everyday racism that infiltrate our lives, keep us off-kilter, and make us feel like our very existence isn't as valuable as that of others. And I hear that. But for Pierce it's not that "micro" means "small"; it's that microaggressions mean everyday aggressions, not extraordinary, racialized violence such as assassination.
31 Pierce, "Offensive Mechanisms," 265–66.
32 Psychologist Monnica Williams notes that Pierce's use of this phrase functions as "a type of analogue to the Freudian concept of defensive mechanisms, which, like microaggressions, often occur outside conscious awareness" ("Microaggressions: Clarification, Evidence, and Impact," *Perspectives on Psychological Science* 15, no. 1 [2020]: 5, https://doi.org/10.1177/1745691619827499). Further building on Pierce, sociologist William Smith writes that "offensive racist mechanisms are those 'racistly' microaggressive practices, policies, procedures, intuitional climates, symbols, expressions, language, and traditions that continue to render People of Color invisible, isolated, confined, tormented, overwhelmed, second-guessing, and physically, emotionally, and psychologically fatigued" ("Foreword," *Racial Battle Fatigue in Faculty: Perspectives and Lessons from Higher Education*, ed. Nicholas D. Hartlep and Daisy Ball [New York: Routledge, 2020], xx).
33 Griffith, *Race & Excellence*, 144.
34 Chester M. Pierce, "Psychiatric Problems of the Black Minority," in *American Handbook of Psychiatry*, ed. Silvano Arieti (New York: Basic Books, 1974), 515.
35 Pierce, "Offensive Mechanisms," 266.
36 Pierce, "Offensive Mechanisms," 267.
37 Derald Wing Sue, Christina M. Capodilupo, Gina C. Torino, Jennifer M. Bucceri, Aisha M. B. Holder, Kevin L. Nadal, and Marta Esquilen, "Racial Microaggressions

in Everyday Life: Implications for Clinical Practice," *American Psychologist* 62, no. 4 (2007): 271.
38 See "This Week's Profile: Rev. James Lawson," Memphis Public Libraries, n.d. accessed 20 March 2025, www.memphislibrary.org/diversity/sanitation-strike-exhibit/sanitation-strike-exhibit-march-17-to-23-edition/this-weeks-profile-rev-james-lawson/.
39 See Philomena Essed's notion of "everyday racism" in *Understanding Everyday Racism: An Interdisciplinary Theory* (Thousand Oaks, CA: SAGE Publications, 1991), 2:2, https://doi.org/10.4135/9781483345239. See also Kira Hudson Banks, Laura P Kohn-Wood, and Michael Spencer on "everyday discrimination in "An Examination of the African American Experience of Everyday Discrimination and Symptoms of Psychological Distress," *Community Mental Health Journal* 42, no. 6 (2006): 555–70, https://doi.org/10.1007/s10597-006-9052-9.
40 McKinsey & Company, "Women in the Workplace," 2023, https://sgff-media.s3.amazonaws.com/sgff_r1eHetbDYb/Women+in+the+Workplace+2023_+Designed+Report.pdf.
41 Alexandra To, Wenxia Sweeney, Jessica Hammer, and Geoff Kaufman, "'They Just Don't Get It': Towards Social Technologies for Coping with Interpersonal Racism," *Proceedings of the ACM on Human-Computer Interaction* 4, no. CSCW1 (2020): 4, https://doi.org/10.1145/3392828.
42 To et al., "'They Just Don't Get It,'" 4.
43 To et al., "'They Just Don't Get It,'" 16.
44 While this adage has been around in workshops for decades, the first time I saw it in print was in Wernie Reed, "Framing the Discussion of Racism," in *Africana Cultures and Policy Studies: Scholarship and the Transformation of Public Policy*, ed. Z. Williams (New York: Palgrave Macmillan, 2009), 56.
45 Wing Sue et al., "Racial Microaggressions in Everyday Life," 278.
46 Williams, "Microaggressions," 4, emphasis added.
47 Williams, "Microaggressions," 8.
48 We heard it so often that Meshell Sturgis and I wrote "'You're the Whitest Black Person I Know': Speaking Back to Microaggressions through the Poetics of Interruption," *Women's Studies in Communication* 45, no. 3 (2022): 358–77, doi:10.1080/07491409.2021.2020193.
49 Sturgis and Joseph, "You're the Whitest Black Person I Know," 366.
50 Williams, "Microaggressions," 7.
51 Wing Sue et al., "Racial Microaggressions in Everyday Life," 271.
52 Listen to this story in Laura Irwin, "Transnational Microaggressions," *Interrupting Privilege*, August 12, 2021, https://ip.ccde.com.uw.edu/?p=1144.
53 Bertin M. Louis and Eric Joy Denise, *Conditionally Accepted: Navigating Higher Education from the Margins* (Austin: University of Texas Press, 2024), 8, doi:10.7560/324882.
54 Pierce, "Offensive Mechanisms," 266.

55 This is a critique found in Lindsay Pérez Huber and Daniel G. Solórzano, "Racial Microaggressions: What They Are, What They Are Not, and Why They Matter," *Latino Policy & Issues Brief*, no. 30 (2015), 1–4.
56 Michelle A. Holling, "'You Intimidate Me' as a Microaggressive Controlling Image to Discipline Womyn of Color Faculty," *Southern Communication Journal* 84, no. 2 (2019): 100. doi:10.1080/1041794X.2018.1511748.
57 Michelle Obama, *The Light We Carry: Overcoming in Uncertain Times* (New York: Crown, 2022), 363.
58 Obama, *The Light We Carry*, 363.
59 To et al., "'They Just Don't Get It,'" 24:4.
60 Listen to Violet and Jada's conversation in Laura Irwin, "When Should You Interrupt Privilege," Interrupting Privilege, September 2, 2021, https://ip.ccde.com.uw.edu/?p=1338.
61 Amie Thurber and Robin DiAngelo, "Microaggressions: Intervening in Three Acts," *Journal of Ethnic & Cultural Diversity in Social Work* 27, no. 1 (2018): 25, emphases in the original, doi:10.1080/15313204.2017.1417941.
62 Moira L. Ozias, "White Women's Affect: Niceness, Comfort, and Neutrality as Cover for Racial Harm," *Journal of College Student Development* 64, no. 1 (2023): 31, doi:10.1353/csd.2023.0000.
63 Thurber and DiAngelo, "Microaggressions," 19.
64 See Kuang Keng Kuek Ser, "Data: Hate Crimes against Muslims Increased after 9/11," The World, September 8, 2016, https://theworld.org/stories/2016/09/08/hate-crime-against-muslim-never-same-after-911; Sam Petulla, Tammy Kupperman, and Jessica Schneider, "The Number of Hate Crimes Rose in 2016," CNN, November 13, 2017, www.cnn.com/2017/11/13/politics/hate-crimes-fbi-2016-rise/index.html.
65 Thurber and DiAngelo, "Microaggressions," 20.
66 To et al., "'They Just Don't Get It,'" 24:18.
67 Ishiyama's key points include "Don't remain silent," "Always use 'I' statements," and "Always be a co-witness." Brooke Adams, "Microaggression and Racial Battle Fatigue," @THEU, December 2, 2016 https://attheu.utah.edu/facultystaff/microaggression-and-racial-battle-fatigue/.
68 Jacqueline K. Nelson, Kevin M. Dunn, and Yin Paradies, "Bystander Anti-Racism: A Review of the Literature," *Society for the Psychological Study of Social Issues* 11, no. 11 (2011): 265. DOI: 10.1111/j.1530-2415.2011.01274.x.
69 Nelson, Dunn, and Paradies, "Bystander Anti-Racism," 272. Their review includes the Confronting Prejudiced Responses (CPR) model, a "classic social psychological research" model that is "an attempt to take the theory and research on bystander helping and apply it to antiprejudice action." In this model, the bystander should follow these five steps: "(1) An incident must be interpreted as racism or discrimination; (2) the bystander must decide whether the incident warrants confrontation; (3) the bystander needs to take responsibility for intervening or confronting the perpetrator; (4) once a bystander has taken responsibility, that

person is required to decide how to confront or intervene. This means a bystander has to make an assessment that he or she has the skills or ability to intervene; and (5) a bystander takes action, and this may involve a cost-benefit analysis" (276).
70 The Interrupting Privilege program combines elements of both Ishiyama's and Nelson and colleagues' approaches in the final, culminating session, which also draws from higher education administrator Greta Kenney's popular "Interrupting Microaggressions" (College of the Holy Cross, Diversity Leadership & Education, October 2014, https://www.uua.org/files/pdf/g/gretakenney-interrupting-microaggressions.pdf). See also Ron Kraybill "Cooperation Skills," in *Conflict Transformation and Restorative Justice Manual*, 5th ed., ed. M. E. Armster and L. S. Amstutz (Akron, PA: Office on Justice and Peacebuilding (OJP), 2008), 116–7; Michelle LeBaron, "The Open Question," in *Conflict Transformation and Restorative Justice Manual*, ed. M. Armster and L. Amstutz, 2008; F. Peavey, "Strategic Questions as a Tool for Rebellion," in *The Wisdom of Listening*, ed. M. Brady (Boston: Wisdom Publishers, 2003), 168–89.
71 Jay Smooth, "How I Learned to Stop Worrying and Love Discussing Race," November 15, 2011, TEDx Talks, 11:56, www.youtube.com/watch?v=MbdxeFcQtaU.
72 Malcolm X quoted in Julie Livingston and Andrew Ross, *Cars and Jails: Freedom Dreams, Debt, and Carcerality* (New York: OR Books, 2022), 129.
73 Listen to Darius and Ebrima's conversation in Laura Irwin, "Race and Gender in the Greek system," Interrupting Privilege, July 1, 2021, https://ip.ccde.com.uw.edu/?p=782; Laura Irwin, "Being Black in the Greek System," Interrupting Privilege, July 1, 2021, https://ip.ccde.com.uw.edu/?p=782.
74 Irwin, "Race and Gender in the Greek System."
75 Audre Lorde, "The Uses of Anger," *Women's Studies Quarterly* 9, no. 3 (1981): 9.
76 Lorde, "The Uses of Anger," 7.
77 Lorde, "The Uses of Anger," 9.
78 Lorde, "The Uses of Anger," 10.
79 To et al., "'They Just Don't Get It,'" 24:18.
80 Listen to the entire conversation in Laura Irwin, "I Went and Got Someone Who Could Interrupt the Problem," Interrupting Privilege, September 8, 2021, https://ip.ccde.com.uw.edu/?p=1425.

4. REPARATIVE DIALOGUING

1 Joel Allen and Ralina L. Joseph, "'This Space Works for Me': Fostering Reparative Dialogue in Institutions," in *Reconciliation: The Final Step in Achieving Nonviolent Social Change*, ed. Amy Aldridge Sanford, Kathryn B. Golsan, Kristina M. Scharp, and Stephen A. Spates, (Solana Beach, CA: Cognella Press, forthcoming).
2 Rachel Garshick Kleit, "HOPE VI New Communities: Neighborhood Relationships in Mixed-Income Housing," *Environment and Planning. A* 37, no. 8 (2005): 1413, https://doi.org/10.1068/a3796.
3 Meshell L. Sturgis and Ralina Joseph, "'You're the Whitest Black Person I Know': Speaking Back to Microaggressions through the Poetics of Interruption," *Women's*

Studies in Communication 45, no. 3 (2022): 358–77, https://doi.org/10.1080/07491409.2021.2020193.

4 Merriam-Webster.com Dictionary, s.v. "community," n.d., accessed September 9, 2024, www.merriam-webster.com/dictionary/community.

5 Political scientists and psychologists among other scholars have long disabused us of the notion that attitudes aren't racialized. Malte Friese, Colin Tucker Smith, Marton Koever, and Matthias Bluemke, "Implicit Measures of Attitudes and Political Voting Behavior," *Social and Personality Psychology Compass* 10, no. 4 (2016): 188–201, https://doi.org/10.1111/spc3.12246.

6 Samira Rajibi, *All My Friends Live in My Computer: Trauma, Tactical Media, and Meaning* (New Brunswick, NJ: Rutgers University Press, 2021), 30.

7 Lynn Fendler, "Others and the Problem of Community," *Curriculum Inquiry* 36, no. 3 (2006): 303, 319, https://doi.org/10.1111/j.1467-873X.2006.00360.x.

8 Silvia Cristina Bettez, "Critical Community Building: Beyond Belonging," *Educational Foundations (Ann Arbor, Mich.)* 25, nos. 3–4 (2011): 3–19.

9 See any number of Brene Brown books, most especially *The Power of Vulnerability: Teachings on Authenticity Connection, and Courage* (Boulder, CO: Sounds True, 2012).

10 Janice Omadeke, "The Best Leaders Aren't Afraid to Be Vulnerable," *Harvard Business Review*, July 22, 2022, https://hbr.org/2022/07/the-best-leaders-arent-afraid-of-being-vulnerable.

11 See for example, Carey Yazeed, "The Dangers of Courage Culture and Why Brene Brown Isn't for Black Folk," Dr. Cary Yazeed, December 12, 2021, https://drcareyyazeed.com/the-dangers-of-courage-culture-and-why-brene-brown-isnt-for-black-folk/.

12 Stella Ting-Toomey and Atsuko Kurogi, "Facework Competence in Intercultural Conflict: An Updated Face-Negotiation Theory," *International Journal of Intercultural Relations*, 22, no. 2 (1998): 196–97, https://doi.org/10.1016/S0147-1767(98)00004-2.

13 Hear Beth and Lydia's conversation in Julie Feng, "Community Is an Intentional Choice," Interrupting Privilege, September 30, 2023, https://ip.ccde.com.uw.edu/?p=2420.

14 L. A. Bell, "Theoretical Foundations for Social Justice Education," in *Teaching for Diversity and Social Justice*, ed. M. Adams, L.A. Bel, and P. Griffin, (New York: Routledge, 1997), 3.

15 Hear Addis and Corey's conversation in Julie Feng, "It's So Great to Have That Community," Interrupting Privilege, May 6, 2024, https://ip.ccde.com.uw.edu/?p=2940.

16 Gregory M. Walton and Shannon T. Brady, "The Many Questions of Belonging," in *Handbook of Competence and Motivation: Theory and Application 2nd Edition*, ed. A. J. Elliot, C. S. Dweck, and D. S. Yeager (New York: Guilford, 2017), 272.

17 john a. powell, "Clip 3: Institute Overview," April 14, 2023, https://public.3.basecamp.com/p/M6hGWyocUb8CTvhRLfrxkFNd.

18 Kaleb Germinaro, "Learning within Moments of Distress," Interrupting Privilege, May 18, 2022, http://ip.ccde.com.uw.edu/?p=1698.
19 Personal correspondence with Allison Briscoe Smith, February 19, 2024.
20 Mónica Guzmán, *I Never Thought of It That Way: How to Have Fearlessly Curious Conversations in Dangerously Divided Times* (Dallas: BenBella Books, 2022), 75.
21 Guzmán, *I Never Thought of It That Way*, 47.
22 Elizabeth S. Parks, "Dialogic Listening: Moving Beyond Idealism to Intercultural Ethical Praxis," *Listening (River Forest)* 56, no. 2 (2021): 126, https://doi.org/10.5840/listening202156219. Here we are following some of the tenets of dialogic listening, which is when "listeners must open themselves to a variety of perspectives that are held and a polyphony of voices that express, choosing to be inclusive of diverse standpoints while encountering new orientations of other and self that ultimately lead to expansiveness of thought and evolving social identities" (Korey Floyd, "Listening: A Dialogic Perspective," in *Listening and Human Communication in the 21st Century*, ed. Andrew D. Wolvin [West Sussex, UK: Blackwell Publishing, 2010], 127).
23 Zillah Eisenstein, "The Combahee River Collective Statement," 1978, reprinted in *Home Girls: A Black Feminist Anthology*, ed. Barbara Smith (New York: Kitchen Table: Women of Color Press, 1983), 270.
24 Kimberlé Crenshaw, "Demarginalizing the Intersection of Race and Sex: A Black Feminist Critique of Antidiscrimination Doctrine, Feminist Theory and Antiracist Politics," *University of Chicago Legal Forum* 1989, no. 1 (1989): 139–67.
25 Kimberlé Crenshaw, "Why Intersectionality Can't Wait," *Washington Post*, September 24, 2015, https://www.washingtonpost.com/news/in-theory/wp/2015/09/24/why-intersectionality-cant-wait/.
26 The nonprofit Fatal Encounters catalogues people "killed during interactions with law enforcement" (Fatal Encounters, homepage, n.d., accessed January 10, 2020, https://fatalencounters.org).
27 Kimberlé Crenshaw, "The Urgency of Intersectionality," TED Women, October 2016, 18:39, www.ted.com/talks/kimberle_crenshaw_the_urgency_of_intersectionality/up-next?language=en.
28 African American Policy Forum, "#SAYHERNAME," n.d., accessed June 1, 2021, https://aapf.org/sayhernamereport.
29 See, for example, P. R. Lockhart, "Living While Black and the Criminalization of Blackness," *Vox*, August 1, 2018, www. https://www.vox.com/explainers/2018/8/1/17616528/racial-profiling-police-911-living-while-black.
30 The conversation between April and Amanda can be found in jas moultrie, "On Sustaining and Being Ourselves in Community," Interrupting Privilege, April 27, 2022, http://ip.ccde.com.uw.edu/?p=1623.
31 Ting-Toomey and Kurogi, "Facework Competence," 206.
32 Tanja Dreher, "Eavesdropping with Permission: The Politics of Listening for Safer Speaking Spaces," *Borderlands E—Journal: new spaces in the humanities*, vol. 8, no. 1 (2009): 12.

33 Ting-Toomey and Kurogi, "Facework Competence," 206.
34 Allen and Joseph, "'This Space Works for Me.'"
35 Dagmar Heller, "Dia-Logos," in *Pathways for Ecclesial Dialogue in the Twenty-First Century: Revisiting Ecumenical Method*, ed. Mark D. Chapman and Miriam Haar (New York: Palgrave Macmillan, 2016), 11.
36 To this end, Martin Buber explains that dialogue means a person's "becom[ing] conscious of himself as . . . co-existing, and thus as being. . . . [A] person makes his appearance by entering into relation with other persons" (*I and Thou* [New York: Scribner, 1970], 130–31).
37 Buber, *I and Thou*, 97.
38 Interpersonal scholar Korey Floyd notes, "Buber suggests that dialogue requires active attentiveness to the particular, as the words that other people speak are directed to a distinct intention rather than an unspecified generality" ("Listening," 131).
39 See also Mikhail M. Bakhtin and Michael Holquist. *Dialogic Imagination: Four Essays* (Austin: University of Texas Press, 1981), 279.
40 Public opinion expert Daniel Yankelovich makes this distinction clear in his classic *The Magic of Dialogue: Transforming Conflict into Cooperation* (New York: Simon & Schuster, 1999), 39.
41 Parks, "Dialogic Listening," 126. Here we are following some of the tenets of dialogic listening, which is when "listeners must open themselves to a variety of perspectives that are held and a polyphony of voices that express, choosing to be inclusive of diverse standpoints while encountering new orientations of other and self that ultimately lead to expansiveness of thought and evolving social identities" (Floyd, "Listening," 127).
42 Guzmán, *I Never Thought of It That Way*, 208.
43 For more on dialogic listening, see James J. Floyd, "Listening: A Dialogic Perspective," in *Listening and Human Communication in the 21st Century*, ed. Andrew D. Wolvin (Hoboken, NJ: Wiley-Blackwell, 2010), 127–40; Nancy C. Cornwell and Mark P. Orbe, "Critical Perspectives on Hate Speech: The Centrality of 'Dialogic Listening,'" *International Journal of Listening* 13, no. 1 (1999): 75–96, https://doi.org/10.1080/10904018.1999.10499028.
44 Adrienne Dessel and Mary E. Rogge. "Evaluation of Intergroup Dialogue: A Review of the Empirical Literature," *Conflict Resolution Quarterly* 26, no. 2 (2008): 213, https://doi.org/10.1002/crq.230.
45 Patricia Gurin, Biren (Ratnesh) A. Nagda, and Ximena Zuniga, *Dialogue across Difference: Practice, Theory, and Research on Intergroup Dialogue* (Chicago: Russell Sage Foundation, 2013), 11–12.
46 Keri A. Frantell, Joseph R. Miles, and Anne M. Ruwe, "Intergroup Dialogue: A Review of Recent Empirical Research and Its Implications for Research and Practice," *Small Group Research* 50, no. 5 (2019): 654, doi:10.1177/1046496419835923.
47 Gordon W. Allport, *The Nature of Prejudice* (Cambridge, MA: Addison-Wesley, 1954).

48 Gordon W. Allport, *The Person in Psychology; Selected Essays* (Boston: Beacon Press, 1968).
49 Ximena Zuniga, Biren A. Nagda, Mark Chesler, and Adena Cytron-Walker, "Intergroup Dialogue in Higher Education: Meaningful Learning about Social Justice," *ASHE Higher Education Report* 32, no. 4 (2007): 15, https://doi.org/10.1002/aehe.3204.
50 Zuniga et al., "Intergroup Dialogue," 3.
51 Kate G. Willink, Robert Gutierrez-Perez, Salma Shukri, and Lacey Stein, "Navigating with the Stars: Critical Qualitative Methodological Constellations for Critical Intercultural Communication Research," *Journal of International and Intercultural Communication* 7, no. 4 (2014): 295, doi:10.1080/17513057.2014.964150.
52 Sara DeTurk, "Quit Whining and Tell Me About Your Experiences! (In)Tolerance, Pragmatism, and Muting," in *Intergroup Dialogue: The Handbook of Critical Intercultural Communication*, ed. Thomas K. Nakayama and Rona Tamiko Halualani (Hoboken, NJ: Wiley-Blackwell, 2010), 579.
53 Ruth King, *Mindful of Race: Transforming Racism from the Inside Out* (Boulder, CO: Sounds True, Inc., 2018), 138, 142.
54 Other critical dialogue–based fields that address power inequities include restorative justice and transformative justice. See Robert Yazzie, "Life Comes from It: Navajo Justice Concepts," *New Mexico Law Review* 24, no. 2 (1994): 175–90.
55 DeTurk, "Quit Whining," 579.
56 Paolo Friere, *Pedagogy of the Oppressed* (New York: Continuum, 2007), 89.
57 Allen and Joseph, "'This Space Works for Me.'"
58 Allen and Joseph, "'This Space Works for Me.'"
59 Anna Steen-Utheim and Anne Line Wittek, "Dialogic Feedback and Potentialities for Student Learning," *Learning, Culture and Social Interaction* 15 (2017): 4, https://doi.org/10.1016/j.lcsi.2017.06.002.
60 Melissa Winchell, Tricia Kress, and Ken Tobin, "Teaching/Learning Radical Listening: Joe's Legacy Among Three Generations of Practitioners," in *Practicing Critical Pedagogy: The Influences of Joe L. Kincheloe*, ed. Mary Frances Agnello and William Martin Reynolds (Berlin, Germany: Springer, 2015), 111.
61 Winchell, Kress, and Tobin, "Teaching/Learning," 111.
62 Winchell et al., 111.
63 Winchell et al., 112.
64 Ting-Toomey and Kurogi, "Facework Competence, 187.
65 Ting-Toomey and Kurogi, "Facework Competence, 207. Ting-Toomey and Kurogi encourage the mindful observation practices of ODIS (observe, describe, interpret, and suspend evaluation) as a way to engage in equitable dialoguing, particularly in the space of intercultural conflict.
66 The critical friend model was developed by the Annenberg Institute for School Reform at Brown University as a feedback mechanism for how to navigate through challenges; see J. Appleby, *Becoming Critical Friends: Reflections of an NSRF Coach* (Providence, RI: The Annenberg Institute for School Reform at

Brown University, 1998); K. Cushman, *How Friends Can Be Critical as Schools Make Essential Changes* (Oxon Hill, MD: Coalition of Essential Schools, 1998); D. Bambino, "Redesigning Professional Development: Critical Friends," *Educational Leadership* 59, no. 6 (2002): 25–27.

67 See, for example, The Posse Foundation, homepage, n.d., accessed March 23, 2025, www.possefoundation.org/.

68 Laura Irwin, "Acountabili-buddies," Interrupting Privilege, September 23, 2023, https://ip.ccde.com.uw.edu/?p=2258. The three of us wrote up this experience in Lando Tosaya, Laura Irwin, and Ralina L. Joseph, "Weaving a Web Together: How to Create Accountability and Support Structures for Graduate Students," *Preparing Publicly Engaged Scholars: A Guide to Innovation in Doctoral Education* (New York: American Council of Learned Societies, 2024), 48.

69 For more about community and collectivity, see Shardé M. Davis, "The 'Strong Black Woman Collective': A Developing Theoretical Framework for Understanding Collective Communication Practices of Black Women," *Women's Studies in Communication* 38, no. 1 (2015): 20–35, https://doi.org/10.1080/07491409.2014.953714.

EPILOGUE

1 Merriam-Webster.com Thesaurus, s.v. "reckoning," n.d., accessed August 22, 2024, www.merriam-webster.com/thesaurus/reckoning.

2 Joy A. Williamson, "A Tale of Two Movements: The Power and Purpose of Misremembering *Brown*," in *With More Deliberate Speed: Achieving Equity in Literacy: Realizing the Full Potential of Brown v. Board of Education*, ed. Arnetha F. Ball (Washington, DC: National Society for the Study of Education, 2007), 41–42.

3 While U.S. multiculturalism was a moment, it originated as state policy in 1970s Canada to cede rights to Quebecois. See Tariq Modood, *Multiculturalism: A Civic Idea* 2nd ed., (Cambridge, UK: Polity Press, 2013), 6, and Elke Winter, "Rethinking Multiculturalism After its 'Retreat': Lessons from Canada," *American Behavioral Scientist* 2015, 59, no. 6 (2015): 638.

4 Christine Sleeter and Peter McLaren, "Introduction: Exploring Connections to Build a Critical Multiculturalism," in *Multicultural Education, Critical Pedagogy, and the Politics of Difference*, ed. Christine E. Sleeter and Peter L. McLaren (Albany: State University of New York Press, 1995), 12.

5 Joseph, Postracial Resistance, 7–8.

6 Ralina L. Joseph, "What's the Difference With 'Difference'? Equity, Communication, and the Politics of Difference." *International Journal of Communication (Online)*, 2017, 3311–12.

7 Sarah J. Jackson, Moya Bailey, and Brooke Foucault Welles, *Hashtag Activism: Networks of Race and Gender Justice* (Boston: MIT Press, 2020), xxv.

8 Paolo Gaudiano, "Florida's DEI Bill Shows the Problem with Focusing on How People Feel," *Forbes*, May 17, 2023, www.forbes.com/sites/paologaudiano/2023/05/17/floridas-dei-bill-shows-the-problem-with-focusing-on-how-people-feel/?sh=33d5e3106dc5.

9 Lowery, "Why There Was No Racial Reckoning."
10 Gene Marks, "The Diversity, Equity, and Inclusion Backlash Explained," *The Hill*, April 5, 2023, https://thehill.com/opinion/civil-rights/3935747-the-diversity-equity-and-inclusion-backlash-explained/.
11 Doyinsola Oladipo, "Big Tech Layoffs May Further Disrupt Equity and Diversity Efforts," *Reuters*, January 5, 2023, www.reuters.com/business/sustainable-business/big-tech-layoffs-may-further-disrupt-equity-diversity-efforts-2023-01-05/.
12 Kelsey Butler, "Big Tech Layoffs Are Hitting Diversity and Inclusion Jobs Hard," *Bloomberg*, January 24, 2023, https://www.bloomberg.com/news/articles/2023-01-24/tech-layoffs-are-hitting-diversity-and-inclusion-jobs-hard. By another account, DEI programs in corporate America surged in 2020 and 2021 and stalled in 2022. Aaron Terrazas, "Who Cares about Diversity, Equity and Inclusion?" *Glassdoor*, November 29, 2022, www.glassdoor.com/research/who-cares-about-diversity-equity-and-inclusion.
13 Bradley, "Picturing Catastrophe," 162.
14 Sara Ahmed, *On Being Included: Racism and Diversity in Institutional Life* (Durham, NC: Duke University Press, 2012), 27.
15 Sonia Nieto, "Foreword," in *Occupying the Academy: Just How Important Is Diversity Work in Higher Education?*, ed. Christine Clark, Kenneth J Fasching-Varner, and Mark Brimhall-Vargas (Lanham, MD: Rowman and Littlefield, 2012), xiv–xv.

BIBLIOGRAPHY

Adams, Brooke. "Microaggression and Racial Battle Fatigue." @THEU, December 2, 2016. https://attheu.utah.edu/facultystaff/microaggression-and-racial-battle-fatigue/.
The ADOS Advocacy Foundation. N.d. Accessed August 14, 2022. https://adosfoundation.org.
African American Policy Forum. "#SAYHERNAME." N.d. Accessed June 1, 2021. https://www.aapf.org/sayhername.
Ahmed, Sara. *The Cultural Politics of Emotion*. New York: Routledge, 2004.
Ahmed, Sara. "Not in the Mood." *new formations: a journal of culture/theory/politics* 82 (2014): 16–17.
Ahmed, Sara. *On Being Included: Racism and Diversity in Institutional Life*. Durham, NC: Duke University Press, 2012.
Alexakos, Konstantinos, and Agnieska Pierwola. "Learning at the 'Boundaries': Radical Listening, Creationism, and Learning from the 'Other.'" *Cultural Studies of Science Education* 8, no. 8 (2013): 39–49.
Allen, Joel, and Ralina L. Joseph. "'This Space Works for Me': Fostering Reparative Dialogue in Institutions." In *Reconciliation: The Final Step in Achieving Nonviolent Social Change* edited by Amy Aldridge Sanford, Kathryn B. Golsan, Kristina M. Scharp, and Stephen A. Spates. Solana Beach, CA: Cognella Press, forthcoming.
Allport, Gordon W. *The Nature of Prejudice*. Cambridge, MA: Addison-Wesley, 1954.
Allport, Gordon W. *The Person in Psychology; Selected Essays*. Boston: Beacon, 1968.
Appleby, J. *Becoming Critical Friends: Reflections of an NSRF Coach*. Providence, RI: The Annenberg Institute for School Reform at Brown University, 1998.
Arnold, Jenna. *Raising Our Hands: How White Women Can Stop Avoiding Hard Conversations, Start Accepting Responsibility, and Find Our Place on the New Frontlines*. Dallas: BenBella Books, 2020.
Bailey, Moya. *Misogynoir Transformed: Black Women's Digital Resistance*. New York: New York University Press, 2021.
Bakhtin, Mikhail. *Speech Genres and Other Late Essays*. Translated by Vern W. McGee. Austin: University of Texas Press, 1986.
Bakhtin, Mikhail M., and Michael Holquist. *Dialogic Imagination: Four Essays*. Austin: University of Texas Press, 1981.
Bambino, Deborah. "Redesigning Professional Development: Critical Friends." *Educational Leadership* 59, no. 6 (2002): 25–27.

Beard, David. "How a Black Psychiatrist Shaped 'Sesame Street' as a Tool Against Racism." *Mother Jones*, June 5, 2019. www.motherjones.com/media/2019/06/recharge-56-sesame-street-anniversary-inclusion-chester-pierce/.

Befus, Deanna R., Megan Bennett Irby, Remy R. Coeytaux, and Donald B. Penzien. "A Critical Exploration of Migraine as a Health Disparity: The Imperative of an Equity-Oriented, Intersectional Approach." *Current Pain and Headache Reports* 22, no. 12 (2018): 79. doi:10.1007/s11916-018-0731-3.

Bell, L. A. "Theoretical Foundations for Social Justice Education." In *Teaching for Diversity and Social Justice*, edited by M. Adams, L. A. Bell, and P. Griffin, 1–31. New York: Routledge, 1997.

Bentley, Michelle. "Trigger Warnings and the Student Experience." *Politics* 37, no. 4 (2017): 470–85. https://doi.org/10.1177/0263395716684526.

Bettez, Silvia Cristina. "Critical Community Building: Beyond Belonging." *Educational Foundations (Ann Arbor, Mich.)* 25, nos. 3–4 (2011): 3–19.

Blackmore, Jill. "Academic Pedagogies, Quality Logics and Performative Universities: Evaluating Teaching and What Students Want." *Studies in Higher Education* 34, no. 8 (2009): 857–72. https://doi.org/10.1080/03075070902898664.

"Black Women and the Wage Gap." National Partnership for Women & Families, October 2022. www.nationalpartnership.org/our-work/resources/economic-justice/fair-pay/african-american-women-wage-gap.pdf.

Bloom, Paul. *Against Empathy: The Case for Rational Compassion*. New York: Ecco, 2016.

Bodie, Graham D. "Listening as Positive Communication." In *The Positive Side of Interpersonal Communication*, edited by Thomas J. Socha and Margaret J. Pitts, 109–25. New York: Peter Lang, 2012.

Boler, Megan. "A Pedagogy of Discomfort: Witnessing and the Politics of Anger and Fear." In *Feeling Power*, 175–202. New York: Routledge, 1999. https://doi.org/10.4324/9780203009499.

Bonilla-Silva, Eduardo. "Feeling Race: Theorizing the Racial Economy of Emotions." *American Sociological Review* 84, no. 1 (2019). https://doi.org/10.1177/0003122418816958

Bonilla-Silva, Eduardo. "The Linguistics of Color Blind Racism: How to Talk Nasty about Blacks without Sounding, 'Racist.'" *Critical Sociology* 28, no. 1–2 (2002): 41–64. https://doi.org/10.1177/08969205020280010501.

Bouchard, Kelley. "African-American Parents Say 'The Talk' Is a Life-and-Death Matter." *Portland Press Herald*, July 17, 2016. www.pressherald.com/2016/07/17/african-american-parents-say-the-talk-is-a-life-and-death-matter/.

Buber, Martin. *I and Thou*. New York: Scribner, 1970.

Buckner, Tyler W., and Nigel S. Key. "Venous Thrombosis in Blacks," *Circulation* 125, no. 6 (2012): 837–39. doi: 10.1161.

Butler, Kelsey. "Big Tech Layoffs Are Hitting Diversity and Inclusion Jobs Hard." *Bloomberg*, January 24, 2023. https://www.bloomberg.com/news/articles/2023-01-24/tech-layoffs-are-hitting-diversity-and-inclusion-jobs-hard.

Bradley, Rizvana. "Picturing Catastrophe: The Visual Politics of Racial Reckoning." *Yale Review* 109, no. 2 (2021): 158–77. doi:10.1353/tyr.2021.0044.

Brekke, Anjuli Joshi. "Listening across Difference: Mapping StoryCorps' Affective Archives." PhD diss., University of Washington, 2020.

Brekke, Anjuli Joshi. "Radical Listening: Cultivating A Feminist Ethics of Reception through Collective Listening." *Listening (River Forest)* 56, no. 2 (2021): 96–107. https://www.doi.org/10.5840/listening202156216.

Brekke, Anjuli Joshi, Ralina Joseph, and Naheed Gina Aaftaab. "'I Address Race Because Race Addresses Me': Women of Color Show Receipts through Digital Storytelling." *Review of Communication* 21, no. 1 (2021): 44–57.

Brown, Brené. *The Power of Vulnerability: Teachings on Authenticity Connection, and Courage.* Boulder, CO: Sounds True, 2012.

Carmack, Preston. "Roots and Wings: Emergent Listening and Attentiveness to Narrative Ground as a Unity of Contraries." *Listening (River Forest)* 56, no. 2 (2021): 148–56. https://www.doi.org/10.5840/listening202156221.

Carter, Robert T. "Racism and Psychological and Emotional Injury: Recognizing and Assessing Race-Based Traumatic Stress." *Counseling Psychologist* 35, no. 1 (2007): 13–105. doi:10.1177/0011000006292033.

Centers for Disease Control. "Racism and Health." June 20, 2024. www.cdc.gov/minority-health/racism-health/index.html.

Charleston, Larry. "Headache Disparities in African-Americans in the United States: A Narrative Review." *Journal of the National Medical Association* 113, no. 2 (2021): 223–29. doi:10.1016/j.jnma.2020.09.148.

Chartrand, Tanya L., and John A. Bargh. "The Chameleon Effect: The Perception-Behavior Link and Social Interaction." *Journal of Personality and Social Psychology* 76, no. 6 (1999): 893–910. doi:10.1037/0022-3514.76.6.893.

Chun, Wendy Hui Kyong. "Unbearable Witness: Toward a Politics of Listening." *differences: A Journal of Feminist Cultural Studies* 11, no. 1 (1999): 112–49.

Clark, Rodney, Norman B. Anderson, Vernessa R. Clark, and David R. Williams. "Racism as a Stressor for African Americans: A Biopsychosocial Model." *American Psychologist* 54, no. 10 (1999): 805–16. doi:10.1037/0003-066X.54.10.805.

Coleman Means, Robin R., and Jennifer McGee Reyes. "Assessing Programmatic Mentoring: Requiem for Carmen." *Communication, Culture & Critique* 14, no. 4 (2021): 675–81. doi:10.1093/ccc/tcab051.

Collins, Charles R., and Erin Watson. "Subverting Whiteness: A Systems Theoretical Approach to Anti-Racist Praxis." *Global Journal of Community Psychology Practice* 12, no. 3 (2021): 456–87.

Comas-Diaz, Lilian, Gordon Nagayama Hall, and Helen A. Neville. "Racial Trauma: Theory, Research and Healing: Introduction to the Special Issue," *American Psychologist* 74, no. 1 (2019): 1–5.

Cooper, Lisa A., Debra L. Roter, Rachel L. Johnson, Daniel E. Ford, Donald M. Steinwachs, and Neil R. Powe. "Patient-Centered Communication, Ratings of Care, and

Concordance of Patient and Physician Race." *Annals of Internal Medicine* 139, no. 11 (2003): 907–15. doi:10.7326/0003-4819-139-11-200312020-00009.

Cornwell, Nancy C., and Mark P. Orbe. "Critical Perspectives on Hate Speech: The Centrality of 'Dialogic Listening.'" *International Journal of Listening* 13, no. 1 (1999): 75–96. https://doi.org/10.1080/10904018.1999.10499028.

Cox, William Taylor Laimaka. "Developing Scientifically Validated Bias and Diversity Trainings That Work: Empowering Agents of Change to Reduce Bias, Create Inclusion, and Promote Equity." *Management Decisions* 61, no. 4 (2023): 1038–61. doi:10.1108/MD-06-2021-0839.

Crenshaw, Kimberlé. "Demarginalizing the Intersection of Race and Sex: A Black Feminist Critique of Antidiscrimination Doctrine, Feminist Theory and Antiracist Politics." *University of Chicago Legal Forum* 1989, no. 1 (1989): 139–67.

Crenshaw, Kimberlé. "The Urgency of Intersectionality." TED Women, October 2016. www.ted.com/talks/kimberle_crenshaw_the_urgency_of_intersectionality/up-next?language=en.

Crenshaw, Kimberlé, "Why Intersectionality Can't Wait." *Washington Post*, September 24, 2015. https://www.washingtonpost.com/news/in-theory/wp/2015/09/24/why-intersectionality-cant-wait/.

Cushman, K. *How Friends Can Be Critical as Schools Make Essential Changes.* Oxon Hill, MD: Coalition of Essential Schools, 1998.

Dahne, Jennifer R., Kelcey Stratton, Ruth Brown, Ananda Amstadter, Carl W. Lejuez, and Laura MacPherson. "Race as a Moderator of the Relationship between Distress Tolerance and Cigarette Smoking among Black and White Women." *Drug and Alcohol Dependence* 146 (2015): e256–e256. doi:10.1016/j.drugalcdep.2014.09.162.

DasGupta, Sayantani. "Listening as Freedom: Narrative, Health, and Social Justice." In *Health Humanities Reader*, edited by Therese Jones, Delese Wear, and Lester D. Friedman, 251–60. New Brunswick, NJ: Rutgers University Press, 2014.

Daughters, Stacey B., Stephanie M. Gorka, Jessica F. Magidson, Laura MacPherson, and C. J. Seitz-Brown. "The Role of Gender and Race in the Relation between Adolescent Distress Tolerance and Externalizing and Internalizing Psychopathology." *Journal of Adolescence (London, England)* 36, no. 6 (2013): 1053–65. doi:10.1016/j.adolescence.2013.08.008.

Davies, Bronwyn. *Listening to Children: Being and Becoming (Contesting Early Childhood).* New York: Routledge, 2014.

Davis, Angela Y. *Women, Culture, and Politics.* New York: Random House, 1984.

Davis, Shardé M. "The 'Strong Black Woman Collective': A Developing Theoretical Framework for Understanding Collective Communication Practices of Black Women." *Women's Studies in Communication* 38, no. 1 (2015): 20–35. https://doi.org/10.1080/07491409.2014.953714.

De Souza, Poppy, and Tanja Dreher. "Dwelling in Discomfort: On the Conditions of Listening in Settler Colonial Australia." *borderlands* 20, no. 2 (2021): 30–60. doi:10.21307/borderlands-2021-012.

Dessel, Adrienne, and Mary E. Rogge. "Evaluation of Intergroup Dialogue: A Review of the Empirical Literature." *Conflict Resolution Quarterly* 26, no. 2 (2008): 199–238. doi:10.1002/crq.230.

DeTurk, Sara. "Quit Whining and Tell Me About Your Experiences! (In)Tolerance, Pragmatism, and Muting." In *Intergroup Dialogue: The Handbook of Critical Intercultural Communication*, edited by Thomas K. Nakayama and Rona Tamiko, 565–84. Hoboken, NJ: Wiley-Blackwell, 2010.

DeTurk, Sara, and Elissa Foster. "Dialogue about Dialogue—Investigating Intersubjectivity in Interview Research." *Qualitative Research Journal* 8, no. 2 (2008): 14–27. https://doi.org/10.3316/qrj0802014.

Devine, Patricia G., and Tory L. Ashy. "Diversity Training Goals, Limitations, and Promise: A Review of the Multidisciplinary Literature." *Annual Review of Psychology* 73, no. 1 (2022): 403–49. doi:10.1146/annurev-psych-060221-122215.

Dictionary.com. S.v. "interrupt." N.d. Accessed August 22, 2024. www.dictionary.com/browse/interrupt.

Dictionary.com. S.v. "privilege." N.d. Accessed August 22, 2024. www.dictionary.com/browse/privilege.

Dimsdale, Joel, Chester Pierce, D. Schoenfeld, A. Brown, R. Zusman, and R. Graham. "Suppressed Anger and Blood Pressure: The Effects of Race, Sex, Social Class, Obesity, and Age." *Psychosomatic Medicine* 48, no. 6 (1986): 430–36. https://doi.org/10.1097/00006842-198607000-00005.

Dobbin, Frank, and Alexandra Kalev. "Why Doesn't Diversity Training Work? The Challenge for Industry and Academia." *Anthropology Now* 10, no. 2 (2018): 48–55. doi:10.1080/19428200.2018.1493182.

Dobson, Andrew. "Thick Cosmopolitanism." *Political Studies* 54, no. 1 (2006): 165–84. https://doi.org/10.1111/j.1467-9248.2006.00571.x.

Dovidio, John F., Susan Eggly, Terrance L. Albrecht, Nao Hagiwara, and Louis A. Penner. "Racial Biases in Medicine and Healthcare Disparities." *Testing, Psychometrics, Methodology in Applied Psychology* 23, no. 4 (2016): 635–38. www.tpmap.org/racial-biases-in-medicine-and-helathcare-disparities/.

Dreher, Tanja. "Eavesdropping with Permission: The Politics of Listening for Safer Speaking Spaces." *Borderlands E—Journal: new spaces in the humanities* 8, no. 1 (2009): 1–21.

Drollinger, T., Comer, L.B. and Warrington, P.T, "Development and Validation of the Active Empathetic Listening Scale." *Psychology & Marketing* 23, no. 2 (2006): 161–80. https://doi.org/10.1002/mar.20105.

DuGruy, Joy. *Post Traumatic Slave Syndrome: America's Legacy of Enduring Injury and Healing*. Portland, OR: Joy DeGruy Publications, 2017.

Dunbar-Ortiz, Roxanne. *An Indigenous Peoples' History of the United States*. Boston: Beacon, 2015.

Dutta, Urmitapa. "Decolonizing 'Community' in Community Psychology." *American Journal of Community Psychology* 62, no. 3–4 (2018): 272–82. https://doi.org/10.1002/ajcp.12281.

Eberhardt, Jennifer. *Biased: Uncovering the Hidden Prejudice That Shapes What We See, Think, and Do*. New York: Penguin Random House, 2019.
Eberhardt, Jennifer. "How Racial Bias Works—and How to Disrupt It." TED Talk, June 2020. www.ted.com/talks/jennifer_l_eberhardt_how_racial_bias_works_and_how_to_disrupt_i.
Eggly, Susan, Ellen Barton, Andrew Winckles, Louis A. Penner, and Terrance L. Albrecht. "A Disparity of Words: Racial Differences in Oncologist-Patient Communication about Clinical Trials." *Health Expectations, An International Journal of Public Participation in Health Care and Health Policy* 18, no. 5 (2015): 1316–26. https://doi.org/10.1111/hex.12108.
Eisenstein, Zillah. "The Combahee River Collective Statement," 1978. Reprinted in *Home Girls, A Black Feminist Anthology*, edited by Barbara Smith. 269–77. New York: Kitchen Table: Women of Color Press, 1983.
Elnour, Awatif, and Khadar Bashir-Ali. "Teaching Muslim Girls in American Schools." *Social Education* 67, no. 1 (2003): 62–64.
Eriksen, Kristin Gregers. "Discomforting Presence in the Classroom—The Affective Technologies of Race, Racism and Whiteness." *Whiteness and Education* 7, no. 1 (2022): 58–77. https://doi.org/10.1080/23793406.2020.1812110.
Essed, Philomena. *Understanding Everyday Racism: An Interdisciplinary Theory*, vol. 2. Thousand Oaks, CA: SAGE Publications, 1991. doi:10.4135/9781483345239.
Evans, Elizabeth, and Éléonore Lépinard, eds. *Intersectionality in Feminist and Queer Movements: Confronting Privileges*. New York: Taylor & Francis, 2020.
"An Examination of the 2016 Electorate, Based on Validated Voters." Pew Research Center, August 9, 2018. www.pewresearch.org/politics/2018/08/09/an-examination-of-the-2016-electorate-based-on-validated-voters/.
Fatal Encounters. Homepage, n.d. Accessed January 10, 2020. https://fatalencounters.org.
Fendler, Lynn. "Others and the Problem of Community." *Curriculum Inquiry* 36, no. 3 (2006): 303–26. https://doi.org/10.1111/j.1467-873X.2006.00360.x.
Fitzgerald, Pamela, and Ivan Leudar, "On Active Listening in Person-Centered, Solution-Focused Psychotherapy." *Journal of Pragmatics* 42, no. 12 (2010): 3188–98. https://doi.org/10.1016/j.pragma.2010.07.007.
Floyd, James J. "Listening: A Dialogic Perspective." In *Listening and Human Communication in the 21st Century*, edited by Andrew D. Wolvin, 127–40. Hoboken NJ: Wiley-Blackwell, 2010.
"The Forgotten Tale of How Black Psychiatrists Helped Make 'Sesame Street.'" *Daily Beast*, May 19, 2019. www.thedailybeast.com/chester-pierce-the-forgotten-tale-of-how-a-black-psychiatrist-helped-make-sesame-street.
Foy, Steven L., and Rayshawn Ray. "Skin in the Game: Colorism and the Subtle Operation of Stereotypes in Men's College Basketball." *American Journal of Sociology* 125, no. 3 (2019): 730–85. doi:10.1086/707243.
Frantell, Keri A., Joseph R. Miles, and Anne M. Ruwe. "Intergroup Dialogue: A Review of Recent Empirical Research and Its Implications for Research and Practice." *Small Group Research* 50, no. 5 (2019): 654–95. doi:10.1177/1046496419835923.

Friere, Paolo. *Pedagogy of the Oppressed*. New York: Continuum, 2007.
Friese, Malte, Colin Tucker Smith, Marton Koever, and Matthias Bluemke. "Implicit Measures of Attitudes and Political Voting Behavior." *Social and Personality Psychology Compass* 10, no. 4 (2016): 188–201. https://doi.org/10.1111/spc3.12246.
Fung, Victor C., and Joyce Eastlund Gromko. "Effects of Active versus Passive Listening on the Quality of Children's Invented Notations and Preferences for Two Pieces from an Unfamiliar Culture." *Psychology of Music* 29, no. 2 (2001): 128–38. https://doi.org/10.1177/0305735601292003.
Gabriel, Trip, and Dana Goldstein. "Disrupting Racism's Reach, Republicans Rattle American Schools." *New York Times*, June 1, 2021. www.nytimes.com/2021/06/01/us/politics/critical-race-theory.html.
Gaines, Jeannie, and John M. Jermier. "Emotional Exhaustion in a High Stress Organization." *Academy of Management Journal* 26, no. 4 (1983): 567–86. doi:10.5465/255907.
Garcia, Antero. "Centering Analog Literacy in an Era of Digital Harm." *Research in the Teaching of English* 54, no. 2 (2019): 192–94.
Gaudiano, Paolo. "Florida's DEI Bill Shows the Problem with Focusing on How People Feel." *Forbes*, May 17, 2023. www.forbes.com/sites/paologaudiano/2023/05/17/floridas-dei-bill-shows-the-problem-with-focusing-on-how-people-feel/?sh=33d5e3106dc5.
Gilbert, Paul. *The Compassionate Mind: A New Approach to Facing the Challenges of Life*. London: Constable Robinson, 2010.
Gilbert, Paul. "Evolution, Social Roles, and the Differences in Shame and Guilt." *Social Research: An International Quarterly* 70, no. 4 (2003): 1205–30. https://doi.org/10.1353/sor.2003.0013.
Gilligan, Carol, Renée Spencer, M. Weinberg, and Tatiana Bertsch. "On the Listening Guide: A Voice-Centered Relational Method." In *Qualitative Research in Psychology: Expanding Perspectives in Methodology and Design*, edited by P. M. Camic, J. E. Rhodes, and L. Yardley, 157–72. Washington, DC: American Psychological Association, 2003.
Glenn, Evelyn Nakano, ed. *Shades of Difference: Why Skin Color Matters*. Palo Alto, CA: Stanford University Press, 2009.
Goldstein, Drew, Manveer Grewal, Ruth Imose, and Monne Williams. "Unlocking the Potential of Chief Diversity Officers." McKinsey and Company, November 18, 2022. www.mckinsey.com/capabilities/people-and-organizational-performance/our-insights/unlocking-the-potential-of-chief-diversity-officers.
Greene, Bryan. "The Unmistakable Black Roots of Sesame Street." *Smithsonian Magazine*, November 7, 2019. www.smithsonianmag.com/history/unmistakable-black-roots-sesame-street-180973490/.
Griffith, Ezra H. *Race & Excellence: My Dialogue with Chester Pierce*. Iowa City: University of Iowa Press, 1998.
Gurin, Patricia, Biren (Ratnesh) A. Nagda, and Ximena Zuniga. *Dialogue across Difference: Practice, Theory, and Research on Intergroup Dialogue*. Chicago: Russell Sage Foundation, 2013.

Guzmán, Mónica. *I Never Thought of It That Way: How to Have Fearlessly Curious Conversations in Dangerously Divided Times.* Dallas: BenBella Books, 2022.

Hajir, Basma, and Kevin Kester. "Toward a Decolonial Praxis in Critical Peace Education: Postcolonial Insights and Pedagogic Possibilities." *Studies in Philosophy and Education* 39, no. 5 (2020): 515–32. https://doi.org/10.1007/s11217-020-09707-y.

Håkansson Eklund, Jakob, and Martina Summer Meranius. "Toward a Consensus on the Nature of Empathy: A Review of Reviews." *Patient Education and Counseling* 104, no, 2 (2021): 300–307. https://doi.org/10.1016/j.pec.2020.08.022.

Hall, Stuart. *Representation: Cultural Representations and Signifying Practices.* London: Sage in association with the Open University, 1997.

Harcup, Tony. *Listening to the Voiceless: The Practices and Ethics of Alternative Journalism.* New York: Routledge 2015.

Heller, Dagmar. "Dia-Logos." In *Pathways for Ecclesial Dialogue in the Twenty-First Century: Revisiting Ecumenical Method*, edited by Mark D. Chapman and Miriam Haar. New York: Palgrave Macmillan, 2016.

Herring, Cedric. *Skin Deep: How Race and Complexion Matter in the "Color-Blind" Era.* Urbana: University of Illinois Press, 2004.

Higginbotham, Evelyn Brooks. *Righteous Discontent: The Women's Movement in the Black Baptist Church, 1880–1920.* Cambridge, MA: Harvard University Press, 1993.

Hill Collins, Patricia. *Black Feminist Thought: Knowledge, Consciousness, and the Politics of Empowerment*, 2nd ed. New York: Routledge, 2009.

Hine, Darlene Clark. "Rape and the Inner Lives of Black Women in the Middle West." *Signs: Journal of Women in Culture and Society* 14, no. 4 (1989): 912–20. doi:10.1086/494552.

Holling, Michelle A. "'You Intimidate Me' as a Microaggressive Controlling Image to Discipline Womyn of Color Faculty." *Southern Communication Journal* 84, no. 2 (2019): 99–112. doi:10.1080/1041794X.2018.1511748.

Houter, Kate Den, and Ellyn Maese. "Mentors and Sponsors Make the Difference." Gallup, April 13, 2023. www.gallup.com/workplace/473999/mentors-sponsors-difference.aspx.

Huber, Lindsay Pérez, and Daniel G. Solórzano. "Racial Microaggressions: What They Are, What They Are Not, and Why They Matter." *Latino Policy & Issues Brief*, no. 30 (2015): 1–4.

Hudson Banks, Kira, Laura P. Kohn-Wood, and Michael Spencer. "An Examination of the African American Experience of Everyday Discrimination and Symptoms of Psychological Distress." *Community Mental Health Journal* 42, no. 6 (2006): 555–70. doi:10.1007/s10597-006-9052-9.

Huerta-Wong, Juan Enrique, and Richard Schoech. "Experiential Learning and Learning Environments: The Case of Active Listening Skills." *Journal of Social Work Education* 46, no. 1 (2010): 85–101. https://doi.org/10.5175/JSWE.2010.200800105.

Hunter, Margaret. *Race, Gender and the Politics of Skin Tone.* New York: Routledge, 2005.

Hutchinson, Darren Lenard. "Racial Exhaustion." *Washington University Law Review* 86, no. 4 (2009): 917–74.

Ignatiev, Noel. *How the Irish Became White.* New York: Routledge, 1995.
International Listening Association, "Definition of Listening," 2012. https://www.listen.org/listening-definition.
Jackson, John L., Jr. "The Strange Immortalities of Race." *Soundings: An Interdisciplinary Journal* 96, no. 1 (2013): 12–17. https://doi.org/10.5325/soundings.96.1.0012.
Jackson, Sarah J., Moya Bailey, and Brooke Foucault Welles. *Hashtag Activism: Networks of Race and Gender Justice.* Boston: MIT Press, 2020.
Jacobson, Matthew Frey. *Whiteness of a Different Color.* Cambridge, MA: Harvard University Press, 1999.
Jaschik, Scott. "Quantifying the Advantage of Legacy Applicants." *Inside Higher Ed,* August 20, 2017. www.insidehighered.com/admissions/article/2017/08/21/data-provide-insights-advantages-and-qualifications-legacy-applicants.
Jaworski, Adam. *The Power of Silence: Social and Pragmatic Perspectives, Language and Language Behaviors.* Newbury Park, CA: Sage Publishing, 1992.
Johnson, Gene. "Officers Face Charges in Restraint Death of Black Man." Associated Press, May 27, 2021. https://apnews.com/article/george-floyd-7dbbc0146d17f4c26aeae1616d8d66cf.
Johnson, Rachel L., Debra L. Roter, Neil R. Powe, and Lisa A. Cooper. "Patient Race/Ethnicity and Quality of Patient-Physician Communication during Medical Visits." *American Journal of Public Health* 94, no. 12 (2004): 2084–90. https://www.doi.org/10.2105/AJPH.94.12.2084.
Jones, Andrew M., and Anni Vanhatalo. "The 'Critical Power' Concept: Applications to Sports Performance with a Focus on Intermittent High-Intensity Exercise." *Sports Medicine (Auckland, N.Z.)* 47, no. 1 (2017): 65–78. doi:10.1007/s40279-017-0688-0.
Joseph, Ralina L. "Opinion: Skirting Death by Implicit Bias at the Doctors Office." *South Seattle Emerald* February 4, 2021. https://southseattleemerald.com/2021/02/04/opinion-skirting-death-by-implicit-bias-at-the-doctors-office/.
Joseph, Ralina L. *Postracial Resistance: Black Women, Media, and the Uses of Strategic Ambiguity.* New York: New York University Press, 2018.
Joseph, Ralina L. "What's the Difference with 'Difference'? Equity, Communication, and the Politics of Difference." *International Journal of Communication (Online)* 11 (2017): 3306.
Joseph, Ralina, and Allison Briscoe-Smith. *Generation Mixed Goes to School: Radically Listening to Multiracial Kids.* New York: TC Press, 2021.
Judd, Bettina. "Sapphire as Praxis: Toward a Methodology of Anger." *Feminist Studies* 45, no. 1 (2019): 178–208. https://dx.doi.org/10.1353/fem.2019.0003.
Kaiser Permanente. "Equity, Inclusion, and Diversity." N.d. https://about.kaiserpermanente.org/commitments-and-impact/equity-inclusion-and-diversity.
Kaufmann, Paul J. *Sensible Listening: The Key to Responsive Interaction,* 7th ed. Dubuque, IA: Kendall Hunt, 2015.
Kendall, Frances. *Understanding White Privilege: Creating Pathways to Authentic Relationships across Race.* New York: Routledge, 2013.
Kendi, Ibram. *How to Be an Antiracist.* London: Bodley Head, 2019.

Kenney, Greta. "Interrupting Microaggressions." College of the Holy Cross, Diversity Leadership & Education, October 2014. https://www.uua.org/files/pdf/g/gretakenney-interrupting-microaggressions.pdf.

Kester, Kevin. "Global Citizenship Education and Peace Education: Toward a Postcritical Praxis." *Educational Philosophy and Theory* 55, no. 1 (2023): 45–56. https://doi.org/10.1080/00131857.2022.2040483.

Kester, Kevin, and Hilary Cremin. "Peace Education and Peace Education Research: Toward a Concept of Poststructural Violence and Second-Order Reflexivity." *Educational Philosophy and Theory* 49, no. 14 (2017): 1415–27. doi:10.1080/00131857.2017.1313715.

Khalulyan, Allie, Katie Byrd, Jonathan Tarbox, Alexandra Little, and Henrike Moll. "The Role of Eye Contact in Young Children's Judgements of Others' Visibility: A Comparison of Preschoolers with and without Autism Spectrum Disorder." *Journal of Communication Disorders* 89 (2021). https://doi.org/10.1016/j.jcomdis.2020.106075.

Kimmel, Michael S., and Abby L. Ferber, eds. *Privilege: A Reader*. New York: Routledge, 2017.

King, Ruth. *Mindful of Race: Transforming Racism from the Inside Out*. Boulder, CO: Sounds True, 2018.

Kleit, Rachel Garshick. "HOPE VI New Communities: Neighborhood Relationships in Mixed-Income Housing." *Environment and Planning. A* 37, no. 8 (2005): 1413–41. https://doi.org/10.1068/a3796.

Kraybill, Ron. "Cooperation Skills." In *Conflict Transformation and Restorative Justice Manual*, 5th Ed., edited by M. E. Armster and L. S. Amstutz, 116–17. Akron, PA: Office on Justice and Peacebuilding (OJP), 2008.

Kuang Keng Kuek Ser. "Data: Hate Crimes against Muslims Increased after 9/11." *The World*, September 8, 2016. https://theworld.org/stories/2016/09/08/hate-crime-against-muslim-never-same-after-911.

Kvale, Steinar. "The Dominance of Dialogical Interview Research: A Critical View." *Barn—Forskning Om Barn Og Barndom i Norden* 23, no. 3 (2005): 89–105. doi:10.5324/barn.v23i3.4438.

Lanzoni, Susan. *Empathy: A History*. New Haven, CT: Yale University Press, 2018.

Lapakko, David. "Communication Is 93% Nonverbal: An Urban Legend Proliferates." *Communication and Theater Association of Minnesota Journal* 34, no. 1 (2015): 7–19. https://doi.org/10.56816/2471-0032.1000.

Laverty, Megan. "Philosophy for Children and Listening Education: An Ear for Thinking." In *Listening to Teach: Beyond Didactic Pedagogy*, edited by Leonard J. Waks, 53–68, Albany: State University of New York Press, 2015.

LeBaron, Michelle. "The Open Question." In *Conflict Transformation and Restorative Justice Manual*, 5th ed., edited by Michelle E. Armster and Lorraine Stutzman Amstutz, 123–24. Akron, PA: Office on Justice and Peacebuilding (OJP), 2008.

Lewis, Laurie. *The Power of Strategic Listening*. Lanham, MD: Rowman & Littlefield, 2019.

Linehan, Marsha M. *Building a Life Worth Living: A Memoir*. New York: Random House, 2020.

Linehan, Marsha M. *DBT Skills Training Handouts and Worksheets*, 2nd ed. New York: Guilford Press, 2015.

Linehan, Marsha M., and Chelsey R. Wilks. "The Course and Evolution of Dialectical Behavior Therapy." *American Journal of Psychotherapy* 69, no. 2 (2015): 97–110. doi:10.1176/appi.psychotherapy.2015.69.2.97.

Lipari, Lisbeth. *Listening, Thinking, Being: Toward an Ethics of Attunement*. University Park: Pennsylvania State University Press, 2014.

Livingston, Julie, and Andrew Ross. *Cars and Jails: Freedom Dreams, Debt, and Carcerality*. New York: OR Books, 2022.

Lockhart, P.R. "Living While Black and the Criminalization of Blackness." *Vox*, August 1, 2018. www. https://www.vox.com/explainers/2018/8/1/17616528/racial-profiling-police-911-living-while-black.

Lopez, German. "Black Parents Describe 'The Talk' They Give to Their Children about Police." *Vox*, August 8, 2016. www.vox.com/2016/8/8/12401792/police-black-parents-the-talk.

Lorde, Audre. *Sister Outsider: Essays and Speeches*. Trumansburg, NY: Crossing Press, 1984.

Lorde, Audre. "The Uses of Anger." *Women's Studies Quarterly* 25, no. 1/2 (1997): 278–85.

Louis, Bertin M., and Eric Joy Denise. *Conditionally Accepted: Navigating Higher Education from the Margins*. Austin: University of Texas Press, 2024. doi:10.7560/324882.

Lowery, Wesley. "Why There Was No Racial Reckoning: Systemic Problems Will Not Be Solved by Representational Victory." *The Atlantic*, February 8, 2023. www.theatlantic.com/ideas/archive/2023/02/tyre-nichols-death-memphis-george-floyd-police-reform/672986/.

Macadam, Alison. "Six Ways to Run a Listening Session." NPR Training, February 16, 2016. https://training.npr.org/2016/02/16/six-ways-to-run-a-listening-session/.

Magee, Rhonda. *The Inner Work of Racial Justice: Healing Ourselves and Transforming Our Communities through Mindfulness*. New York: Penguin Random House, 2019.

Manning, Kimberly D. "A Reckoning of Racial Reckoning." *The Lancet (British Edition)* 399, no. 10327 (2022): 784–85. doi:10.1016/S0140-6736(22)00317-8.

Mar, Raymond A. "Stories and the Promotion of Social Cognition." *Current Directions in Psychological Science* 27, no. 4 (2018): 257–62. https://doi.org/10.1177/0963721417749654.

Marks, Gene. "The Diversity, Equity, and Inclusion Backlash Explained." *The Hill*, April 5, 2023. https://thehill.com/opinion/civil-rights/3935747-the-diversity-equity-and-inclusion-backlash-explained/.

Marsh, Brett. "Post Traumatic Slave Syndrome: DeGruy Talks to Oakland Audience about the Lingering Trauma of African Diaspora." *Oakland North*, September 17, 2019. https://oaklandnorth.net/2019/09/17/post-traumatic-slave-syndrome-degruy-talks-to-oakland-audience-about-the-lingering-trauma-of-african-diaspora/.

Martinot, Steve. *The Machinery of Whiteness: Studies in the Structure of Racialization*. Philadelphia: Temple University Press, 2010.

McIntosh, Peggy. "Beyond the Knapsack." *Teaching Tolerance Magazine* 46 (Spring 2014). www.learningforjustice.org/magazine/spring-2014/toolkit-for-beyond-the-knapsack.

McIntosh, Peggy. "White Privilege: Unpacking the Invisible Knapsack." *ESED 5234—Master List*, January 1990. https://digitalcommons.georgiasouthern.edu/esed5234-master/51.

McKinsey & Company, "Women in the Workplace," 2023. https://sgff-media.s3.amazonaws.com/sgff_r1eHetbDYb/Women+in+the+Workplace+2023_+Designed+Report.pdf.

Mehrabian, Albert. *Nonverbal Communication*. Chicago: Aldine-Atherton, 1972.

Mehrabian, Albert. *Silent Messages: Implicit Communication of Emotions and Attitudes*, 2nd ed. Belmont, CA: Wadsworth, 1981.

Merriam-Webster.com Dictionary. S.v. "community." N.d. Accessed September 9, 2024. www.merriam-webster.com/dictionary/community.

Merriam-Webster.com Dictionary. S.v. "empathy." N.d. Accessed March 19, 2025. www.merriam-webster.com/dictionary/empathy.

Merriam-Webster.com Dictionary. S.v. "sympathy." N.d. Accessed March 19, 2025. www.merriam-webster.com/dictionary/sympathy.

Merriam-Webster.com Thesaurus. S.v. "reckoning." N.d. Accessed August 22, 2024, www.merriam-webster.com/thesaurus/reckoning.

Mettler, Kate, and Mark Berman. "Seattle Police Fatally Shoot Pregnant Woman." *Washington Post*, June 19, 2017. www.washingtonpost.com/national/seattle-police-fatally-shoot-pregnant-woman/2017/06/19/628fc2c0-4fcf-11e7-be25-3a519335381c_story.html.

"Microaggressions," Buzzfeed, n.d. Accessed August 14, 2024. www.buzzfeed.com/au/tag/microaggressions.

Modood, Tariq. *Multiculturalism: A Civic Idea*, 2nd edition. Cambridge, UK: Polity Press, 2013.

Molina-Markham, Elizabeth. "Finding the 'Sense of the Meeting': Decision Making through Silence among Quakers." *Western Journal of Communication* 78, no. 2 (2014): 155–74. doi:10.1080/10570314.2013.809474.

Molina-Markham, Elizabeth. "Listening Faithfully with Friends: An Ethnography of Quaker Communication Practices." PhD diss., University of Massachusetts, Amherst, 2011.

Moore, Shannon A. "Radical Listening: Transdisciplinarity, Restorative Justice and Change," *World Futures* 74, no. 74 (2018): 471–89.

Morrison, Aaron. "Racism of Rioters Takes Center Stage in Jan 6. Hearing." AP News, July 28, 2021. https://apnews.com/article/joe-biden-government-and-politics-riots-race-and-ethnicity-capitol-siege-b3eb4a7f1a0d183c9db89a08c84a70cb.

Mosley, Della V., Helen A. Neville, Nayeli Y. Chavez-Dueñas, Hector Y. Adames, Jioni A. Lewis, and Bryana H. French. "Radical Hope in Revolting Times: Proposing a Culturally Relevant Psychological Framework." *Social and Personality Psychology Compass* 14, no. 1 (2020). doi:10.1111/spc3.12512.

Myllyneva, Aki, and Jari K. Hietanen. "The Dual Nature of Eye Contact: To See and to Be Seen." *Social Cognitive and Affective Neuroscience* 11, no. 7 (2016): 1089–95. https://doi.org/10.1093/scan/nsv075.

Naz, Saiqua, Romilly Gregory, and Meera Bahu. "Addressing Issues of Race, Ethnicity and Culture in CBT to Support Therapists and Service Managers to Deliver Culturally Competent Therapy and Reduce Inequalities in Mental Health Provision for BAME Service Users." *Cognitive Behavior Therapist* 12, no. e22 (2019). doi:10.1017/S1754470X19000060.

Neacsiu, Andrada D., Shireen L. Rizvi, and Marsha M. Linehan. "Dialectical Behavior Therapy Skills Use as a Mediator and Outcome of Treatment for Borderline Personality Disorder." *Behaviour Research and Therapy* 48, no. 9 (2010): 832–39. doi:10.1016/j.brat.2010.05.017.

Nelson, Jacqueline K., Kevin M. Dunn, and Yin Paradies. "Bystander Anti-Racism: A Review of the Literature." *Society for the Psychological Study of Social Issues* 11, no. 11 (2011): 263–84. doi:10.1111/j.1530-2415.2011.01274.x.

Nieto, Sonia. "Foreword." In *Occupying the Academy: Just How Important Is Diversity Work in Higher Education?*, edited by Christine Clark, Kenneth J. Fasching-Varner, and Mark Brimhall-Vargas. Lanham, MD: Rowman and Littlefield, 2012.

Obama, Michelle. *The Light We Carry: Overcoming in Uncertain Times.* New York: Crown, 2022.

O'Donnell, Penny, Justine Lloyd, and Tanja Dreher. "Listening, Pathbuilding and Continuations: A Research Analysis of Listening." *Continuum: Journal of Media & Cultural Studies* 23, no. 4 (2009): 423–39.

Oladipo, Doyinsola. "Big Tech Layoffs May Further Disrupt Equity and Diversity Efforts." *Reuters*, January 5, 2023. www.reuters.com/business/sustainable-business/big-tech-layoffs-may-further-disrupt-equity-diversity-efforts-2023-01-05/.

Omadeke, Janice. "The Best Leaders Aren't Afraid to Be Vulnerable." *Harvard Business Review*, July 22, 2022. https://hbr.org/2022/07/the-best-leaders-arent-afraid-of-being-vulnerable.

Omadeke, Janice. "What's the Difference between a Mentor and a Sponsor?" *Harvard Business Review*, October 20, 2021. https://hbr.org/2021/10/whats-the-difference-between-a-mentor-and-a-sponsor.

Omi, Michael, and Howard Winant. *Racial Formation in the United States*, 3rd ed. New York: Routledge, 2014.

Ozias, Moira L. "White Women's Affect: Niceness, Comfort, and Neutrality as Cover for Racial Harm." *Journal of College Student Development* 64, no. 1 (2023): 31–47. doi:10.1353/csd.2023.0000.

Painter, Nell Irvin. *The History of White People.* New York: W.W. Norton, 2011.

Parks, Elizabeth. "Introduction." *Listening* 56, no. 2 (2021): 92–95. https://doi.org/10.5840/listening202156215.

Parks, Elizabeth, Meara Few, and Laura Lane, *Listening: The Key Concepts.* New York: Routledge Press, 2024. https://doi.org/10.4324/9781003410775.

Parks, Elizabeth S. "Dialogic Listening: Moving beyond Idealism to Intercultural Ethical Praxis." *Listening (River Forest)* 56, no. 2 (2021): 126–36. https://doi.org/10.5840/listening202156219.

Parks, Elizabeth S. "Listening with Empathy in Organizational Communication." *Organization Development Journal* 33, no. 3 (2015): 9–22.

Peavey, F. "Strategic Questions as a Tool for Rebellion." In *The Wisdom of Listening*, edited by M. Brady, 168–89. Boston: Wisdom Publishers, 2003.

Pereira, Maria do Mar. "Uncomfortable Classrooms: Rethinking the Role of Student Discomfort in Feminist Teaching." *European Journal of Women's Studies* 19, no. 1 (2012): 128–35. https://doi.org/10.1177/1350506811426237c.

Perez, Christopher M., Bonnie C. Nicholson, Eric R. Dahlen, and Melanie E. Leuty. "Overparenting and Emerging Adults' Mental Health: The Mediating Role of Emotional Distress Tolerance." *Journal of Child and Family Studies* 29, no. 2 (2020): 374–81. doi:10.1007/s10826-019-01603-5.

Petrovic, Sanja, Daphne Lordly, Susan Brigham, and Mary Delaney. "Learning to Listen: An Analysis of Applying the Listening Guide to Reflection Papers." *International Journal of Qualitative Methods* 14, no. 5 (2015). doi:10.1177/1609406915621402.

Petulla, Sam, Tammy Kupperman, and Jessica Schneider. "The Number of Hate Crimes Rose in 2016." CNN, November 13, 2017. www.cnn.com/2017/11/13/politics/hate-crimes-fbi-2016-rise/index.html.

Pierce, Chester. "Offensive Mechanisms." In *The Black Seventies*, edited by F. B. Barbour, 265–82. Boston, MA: Porter Sargent, 1970.

Pierce, Chester M. "Psychiatric Problems of the Black Minority," in *American Handbook of Psychiatry*, edited by Silvano Arieti, 515. New York: Basic Books, 1974.

Pierce, Chester M., and Gail B. Allen. "CHILDISM." *Psychiatric Annals* 5, no. 7 (1975): 15–24. https://doi.org/10.3928/0048-5713-19750701-04.

Pierce, Chester M., Jean V. Carew, Diane Pierce-Gonzalez, and Deborah Wills. "An Experiment in Racism: TV Commercials." *Education and Urban Society* 10, no. 1 (1977): 61–87. https://doi.org/10.1177/001312457701000105.

Pierson, Ashley M., Vinushini Arunagiri, and Debra M. Bond. "'You Didn't Cause Racism, and You Have to Solve It Anyways': Antiracist Adaptations to Dialectical Behavior Therapy for White Therapists." *Cognitive and Behavioral Practice* 29, no. 4 (2022): 796–815. doi:10.1016/j.cbpra.2021.11.001.

powell, john a. "Clip 3: Institute Overview." April 14, 2023. https://public.3.basecamp.com/p/M6hGWyocUb8CTvhRLfrxkFNd.

Quilty, Aideen. "Queer Provocations! Exploring Queerly Informed Disruptive Pedagogies within Feminist Community-Higher-Education Landscapes." *Irish Educational Studies* 36, no. 1 (2017): 107–23. https://doi.org/10.1080/03323315.2017.1289704.

Rajibi, Samira. *All My Friends Live in My Computer: Trauma, Tactical Media, and Meaning*. New Brunswick, NJ: Rutgers University Press, 2021.

Ratcliffe, Krista. *Rhetorical Listening: Identification, Gender, Whiteness*. Carbondale: Southern Illinois Press, 2005.

Reed, Wernie. "Framing the Discussion of Racism." In *Africana Cultures and Policy Studies: Scholarship and the Transformation of Public Policy*, edited by Z. Williams, 55–72. New York: Palgrave Macmillan, 2009.

Reiss, Helen. "The Science of Empathy." *Journal of Patient Experience* 4, no. 2 (2017): 74–77. doi:10.1177/2374373517699267.

Richeson, Jennifer A., and Sophie Trawalter. "Why Do Interracial Interactions Impair Executive Function? A Resource Depletion Account." *Journal of Personality and Social Psychology* 88, no. 6 (2005): 934–47.

Robertson, Kathryn. "Active Listening: More Than Just Paying Attention." *Australian Family Physician* 34, no. 12 (2005): 1053–55. doi:10.3316/informit.366629010280498.

Robinson, Dylan. *Hungry Listening: Resonant Theory for Indigenous Sound Studies*. Minneapolis: University of Minnesota Press, 2020.

Rogers, Carl R., and Richard E. Farson. *Active Listening*. Mansfield Centre, CT: Martino Publishing 2015.

Rosenboom, Helen, and Ralina L. Joseph. "'What Makes You Think I'm African American?': Identity Performance, Code Switching and the Strong Black Woman on Love Is Blind." *Critical Studies in Media Communication* 41, no. 3 (2024): 2–6. doi: 10.1080/15295036.2024.2385459.

Rost, Michael, and J. J. Wilson. *Active Listening: Research and Resources in Language Teaching*. New York: Routledge, 2013.

Rothstein, Richard. *The Color of Law: A Forgotten History of How Our Government Segregated America*. New York: Liveright, 2017.

Sabater, Mariona Massip, and Edda Sant. "Gendering Citizenship Education. Feminist-Relational Approaches on Political Education." *Revista de investigación en didáctica de las ciencias ociales* no. 11 (2022). doi:10.17398/2531-0968.11.35.

Sanders, Matthew L., and Matthew A. Koschmann. *Understanding Nonprofit Work: A Communication Perspective*. United Kingdom: Wiley-Blackwell, 2020.

Schneider, Dona, David E. Lilienfeld, and Wansoon Im. "The Epidemiology of Pulmonary Embolism: Racial Contrasts in Incidence and In-Hospital Case Fatality." *Journal of the National Medical Association* 98, no. 12 (2006): 1967–72.

Seattle Times Staff. "Here's How Seattle Voters' Support for Trump Compared to Other Cities." *Seattle Times*, November 17, 2016. www.seattletimes.com/seattle-news/politics/heres-how-seattle-voters-support-for-trump-stacks-up-to-other-u-s-cities/.

Sensoy, Özlem, and Robin DiAngelo. *Is Everyone Really Equal? An Introduction to Key Concepts in Social Justice Education*. New York: TC Press, 2017.

Siminoff, Laura A., Graham, Gregory C., and Gordon, Nahida H. "Cancer Communication Patterns and the Influence of Patient Characteristics: Disparities in Information-Giving and Affective Behaviors." *Patient Education and Counseling* 62, no. 3 (2006): 355–60. https://doi.org/10.1016/j.pec.2006.06.011.

Sims-Schouten, Wendy, and Patricia Gilbert. "Revisiting 'Resilience' in Light of Racism, 'Othering,' and Resistance." *Race & Class* 64, no. 1 (2022): 84–94. doi:10.1177/03063968 221093882.

Siry, Christina, Michelle Brendel, and Roger Frisch. "Radical Listening and Dialogue in Educational Research." *International Journal of Critical Pedagogy* 7, no. 20 (2016): 119–35. https://hdl.handle.net/10993/29848.

Sleeter, Christine, and Peter McLaren. "Introduction: Exploring Connections to Build a Critical Multiculturalism." In *Multicultural Education, Critical Pedagogy, and the Politics of Difference*, edited by Christine E. Sleeter and Peter L. McLaren, 5–32. Albany: State University of New York Press, 1995.

Smith, Clint. *How the Word Is Passed: A Reckoning with the History of Slavery across America*. New York: Little, Brown, 2021.

Smith, William A. "Foreword." In *Racial Battle Fatigue in Faculty: Perspectives and Lessons from Higher Education*, edited by Nicholas D. Hartlep and Daisy Ball, xix–xxii. New York: Routledge, 2020.

Smith, William A., Walter R. Allen, and Lynette L. Danley. "'Assume the Position . . . You Fit the Description': Psychosocial Experiences and Racial Battle Fatigue among African American Male College Students." *American Behavioral Scientist* 51, no. 4, (2007): 551–78.

Smooth, Jay. "How I Learned to Stop Worrying and Love Discussing Race." TEDx Talks, November 15, 2011. www.youtube.com/watch?v=MbdxeFcQtaU.

Sobande, Francesca, Akane Kanai, and Natasha Zeng. "The Hypervisibility and Discourses of 'Wokeness' in Digital Culture." *Media, Culture & Society* 44, no. 8 (2022): 1576–87. doi:10.1177/01634437221117490.

Solorzano, Daniel, Miguel Ceja, and Tara Yosso. "Critical Race Theory, Racial Microaggressions, and Campus Racial Climate: The Experiences of African American College Students." *Journal of Negro Education* 69, no. 1/2 (2000): 60–73.

Spencer, Michael. "Dialoguing across Difference: Listening with Ting." Zoom lecture, University of Washington Graduate School, January 10, 2023.

Springfield, Sparkle, Feifei Qin, Haley Hedlin, Charles B. Eaton, Milagros C. Rosal, Herman Taylor, Ursula M. Staudinger, et al., "Modifiable Resources and Resilience in Racially and Ethnically Diverse Older Women: Implications for Health Outcomes and Interventions." *International Journal of Environmental Research and Public Health* 19, no. 12 (2022): 7089. doi:10.3390/ijerph19127089.

Steen-Utheim, Anna, and Anne Line Wittek. "Dialogic Feedback and Potentialities for Student Learning." *Learning, Culture and Social Interaction* 15 (2017): 18–30. https://doi.org/10.1016/j.lcsi.2017.06.002.

Stenberg, Shari. "Cultivating Listening: Teaching from a Restored Logos." In *Silence and Listening as Rhetorical Arts*, edited by Cheryl Glenn and Krista Ratcliffe. 250–63. Carbondale: Southern Illinois University Press, 2011.

Stolberg, Sheryl Gay. "'Pandemic within a Pandemic': Coronavirus and Police Brutality Roil Black Communities." *New York Times*, June 7, 2020. www.nytimes.com/2020/06/07/us/politics/blacks-coronavirus-police-brutality.html.

Sturgis, Meshell, and Darius Presley. "B(l)ack Talk: An Auto-Ethno-Bio-Mytho-Graphic." N.d. Accessed April 22, 2025. https://meshellsturgis.com/posts/black-talk.

Sturgis, Meshell L., and Ralina L. Joseph. "'You're the Whitest Black Person I Know': Speaking Back to Microaggressions through the Poetics of Interruption." *Women's Studies in Communication* 45, no. 3 (2022): 358–77. https://doi.org/10.1080/07491409.2021.2020193.

Sue, Derald Wing. *Race Talk and the Conspiracy of Silence: Understanding and Facilitating Difficult Dialogues on Race*. New York: Wiley, 2015.

Tang, Sandra, Vonnie C. McLoyd, and Samantha K. Hallman. "Racial Socialization, Racial Identity, and Academic Attitudes among African American Adolescents: Examining the Moderating Influence of Parent-Adolescent Communication." *Journal of Youth and Adolescence* 45, no. 6 (2016): 1141–55. doi:10.1007/s10964-015-0351-8.

Tansey, Janeta F. "Existential Listening as Ethical Distancing: The Meaningfulness of Imposterism, Fear and Shame in Relation." *Listening (River Forest)* 56, no. 2 (2021): 137–47. https://doi.org/10.5840/listening202156220.

Terrazas, Aaron. "Who Cares about Diversity, Equity and Inclusion?" *Glassdoor*, November 29, 2022. www.glassdoor.com/research/who-cares-about-diversity-equity-and-inclusion.

The Microaggressions Project. "Microaggressions: Power, Privilege, and Everyday Life." N.d. Accessed August 14, 2024. www.microaggressions.com/.

The Posse Foundation. Homepage, n.d. Accessed March 23, 2025. https://www.possefoundation.org/.

"This Week's Profile: Rev. James Lawson." Memphis Public Libraries, n.d. Accessed April 16, 2025. www.memphislibrary.org/diversity/sanitation-strike-exhibit/sanitation-strike-exhibit-march-17-to-23-edition/this-weeks-profile-rev-james-lawson/.

Thurber, Amie, and Robin DiAngelo. "Microaggressions: Intervening in Three Acts." *Journal of Ethnic & Cultural Diversity in Social Work* 27, no. 1 (2018): 17–27. doi:10.1080/15313204.2017.1417941.

Ting-Toomey, Stella. "Identity Negotiation Theory: Crossing Cultural Boundaries." In *Theorizing about Intercultural Communication*, edited by William B. Gundykunst, 211–33. Thousand Oaks, CA: Sage College Publishing, 2005.

Ting-Toomey, Stella, and Atsuko Kurogi. "Facework Competence in Intercultural Conflict: An Updated Face-Negotiation Theory." *International Journal of Intercultural Relations* 22, no. 2 (1998): 187–225. https://doi.org/10.1016/S0147-1767(98)00004-2.

To, Alexandra, Wenxia Sweeney, Jessica Hammer, and Geoff Kaufman. "'They Just Don't Get It': Towards Social Technologies for Coping with Interpersonal Racism." *Proceedings of the ACM on Human-Computer Interaction* 4, no. CSCW1 (2020): 1–29. doi:10.1145/3392828.

Tobin, Kenneth. "Tuning into Others' Voices: Radical Listening, Learning from Difference, and Escaping Oppression." *Cultural Studies of Education* 4, no. 3 (2009): 505–6.

Tosaya, Lando, Laura Irwin, and Ralina L. Joseph. "Weaving a Web Together: How to Create Accountability and Support Structures for Graduate Students." In *Preparing Publicly Engaged Scholars: A Guide to Innovation in Doctoral Education*, 48–54. New York: American Council of Learned Societies, 2024.

"Trump Holds Listening Session with Students on Mass Shootings." ABC News, February 21, 2018. https://abcnews.go.com/Politics/trump-holds-listening-session-students-mass-shootings/story?id=53245367.

Vilson, Jose Luis. "The Need for More Teachers of Color." *American Educator* 39, no. 2 (2015): 27–31.

Vittrup, Brigitte. "Color Blind or Color Conscious? White American Mothers' Approaches to Racial Socialization." *Journal of Family Issues* 39, no. 3 (2018): 668–92. https://doi.org/10.1177/0192513X16676858.

Walton, Gregory M., and Shannon T. Brady. "The Many Questions of Belonging." In *Handbook of Competence and Motivation: Theory and Application, 2nd Edition*, edited by Andrew J. Elliot, Carol S. Dweck, and David S. Yeager, 272. New York: Guilford, 2017.

Way, Amy K., Robin Kanak Zwier, and Sarah J. Tracy. "Dialogic Interviewing and Flickers of Transformation: An Examination and Delineation of Interactional Strategies That Promote Participant Self-Reflexivity." *Qualitative Inquiry* 21, no. 8 (2015): 720–31. doi:10.1177/1077800414566686.

Weisleder, Pedro. "Moral Distress, Moral Injury, and Burnout: Clinicians' Resilience and Adaptability Are Not the Solution." *Annals of the Child Neurology Society* 1, no. 4 (2023): 262–66. doi: 10.1002/cns3.20048.

Williams, Monnica T. "Microaggressions: Clarification, Evidence, and Impact." *Perspectives on Psychological Science* 15, no. 1 (2020): 3–26. https://doi.org/10.1177/1745691619827499.

Williams, Sheena S. "Racial Reckoning: I Am Exhausted." *Nursing Management* 54, no. 4 (2023): 6–7. doi.10.1097/01.NUMA.0000921896.45611.ed.

Williamson, Joy A. "A Tale of Two Movements: The Power and Purpose of Misremembering *Brown*." In *With More Deliberate Speed: Achieving Equity in Literacy: Realizing the Full Potential of Brown v. Board of Education*, edited by Arnetha F. Ball, 41–42. Washington, DC: National Society for the Study of Education, 2007.

Willink, Kate G., Robert Gutierrez-Perez, Salma Shukri, and Lacey Stein. "Navigating with the Stars: Critical Qualitative Methodological Constellations for Critical Intercultural Communication Research." *Journal of International and Intercultural Communication* 7, no. 4 (2014): 289–316. doi:10.1080/17513057.2014.964150.

Winchell, Melissa, Tricia Kress, and Ken Tobin. "Teaching/Learning Radical Listening: Joe's Legacy among Three Generations of Practitioners." In *Practicing Critical Pedagogy: The Influences of Joe L. Kincheloe*, edited by Mary Frances Agnello and William Martin Reynolds, 99–102. Berlin, Germany: Springer, 2015.

Wing Sue, Derald, Christina M. Capodilupo, Gina C. Torino, Jennifer M. Bucceri, Aisha M. B. Holder, Kevin L. Nadal, and Marta Esquilin. "Racial Microaggressions in Everyday Life: Implications for Clinical Practice." *The American Psychologist* 62, no. 4 (2007): 271–86. https://doi.org/10.1037/0003-066X.62.4.271.

Winter, Elke. "Rethinking Multiculturalism after Its 'Retreat': Lessons from Canada." *American Behavioral Scientist* 59, no. 6 (2015): 637–57.

Wolvin, Andrew D., and Carolyn Gwynn Coakley. "Appreciative Listening." In *Listening*, 2nd ed. Dubuque, IA: Wm. C. Brown Company, 1996.

Yankelovich, Daniel. *The Magic of Dialogue: Transforming Conflict into Cooperation*. New York: Simon & Schuster, 1999.

Yazeed, Carey. "The Dangers of Courage Culture and Why Brene Brown Isn't for Black Folk." Dr. Cary Yazeed, December 12, 2021. https://drcareyyazeed.com/the-dangers-of-courage-culture-and-why-brene-brown-isnt-for-black-folk/.

Yazzie, Robert. "Life Comes from It: Navajo Justice Concepts." *New Mexico Law Review* 24, no. 2 (1994): 175–90.

"You Look Different," MTV, n.d. Accessed August 14, 2024. www.youtube.com/playlist?list=PLBPLVvU_jvGssvzwax_GijPAnZqbiQqyB.

Zembylas, Michalinos, and Megan Boler. "On the Spirit of Patriotism: Challenges of a 'Pedagogy of Discomfort.'" *Teachers College Record* 104, no. 5 (2022): 1–27.

Zheng, Lily. *DEI Deconstructed: Your No-Nonsense Guide to Doing the Work and Doing It Right*. Oakland, CA: Berrett-Koehler Publishers, 2022.

Zuniga, Ximena, Biren A. Nagda, Mark Chesler, and Adena Cytron-Walker. "Intergroup Dialogue in Higher Education: Meaningful Learning about Social Justice." *ASHE Higher Education Report* 32, no. 4 (2007): 1–128. https://doi.org/10.1002/aehe.3204.

INTERRUPTING PRIVILEGE CLIP BIBLIOGRAPHY

Brekke, Anjuli. "Let's Talk About the Angry Black Woman." Interrupting Privilege, December 2, 2020. https://ip.ccde.com.uw.edu/?p=405.
Brekke, Anjuli. "Talking to Your Family About Race." Interrupting Privilege. September 10, 2024. https://ip.ccde.com.uw.edu/?p=3385.
Feng, Julie. "Community is an Intentional Choice." Interrupting Privilege, September 30, 2023. https://ip.ccde.com.uw.edu/?p=2420.
Germinaro, Kaleb. "Being Brave and Humble." Interrupting Privilege. May 14, 2022. http://ip.ccde.com.uw.edu/?p=1673.
Germinaro, Kaleb. "Breathing for Resistance." Interrupting Privilege, May 11, 2022. https://ip.ccde.com.uw.edu/?p=1660.
Germinaro, Kaleb. "Learning Within Moments of Distress." Interrupting Privilege, May 18, 2022. http://ip.ccde.com.uw.edu/?p=1698.
Germinaro, Kaleb. "Making Space for Self Compassion." Interrupting Privilege, May 11, 2022. http://ip.ccde.com.uw.edu/?p=1662.
Germinaro, Kaleb. "On the Meaning of Words Like Resilience." Interrupting Privilege, May 16, 2022. http://ip.ccde.com.uw.edu/?p=1679.
Germinaro, Kaleb. "Stop Calling Us Resilient." Interrupting Privilege, May 16, 2022. https://ip.ccde.com.uw.edu/?p=1677.
Irwin, Laura. "Acountabili-buddies." Interrupting Privilege, Sept 23, 2023. https://ip.ccde.com.uw.edu/?p=2258.
Irwin, Laura. "Being Black in the Greek System," Interrupting Privilege, July 1, 2021. https://ip.ccde.com.uw.edu/?p=782.
Irwin, Laura. "The Black Tax." Interrupting Privilege, July 1, 2021. http://ip.ccde.com.uw.edu/?p=788.
Irwin, Laura. "Changing the Systems." Interrupting Privilege, March 11, 2022. http://ip.ccde.com.uw.edu/?p=1536.
Irwin, Laura. "I Went and Got Someone Who Could Interrupt the Problem." Interrupting Privilege, September 8, 2021. https://ip.ccde.com.uw.edu/?p=1425.
Irwin, Laura. "Managing the Toll of Resistance on Our Bodies." Interrupting Privilege, March 11, 2022. http://ip.ccde.com.uw.edu/?p=1539.
Irwin, Laura. "Processing Microaggressions." Interrupting Privilege, September 7, 2021. https://ip.ccde.com.uw.edu/?p=1385.
Irwin, Laura. "Race and Gender in the Greek System." Interrupting Privilege, July 1, 2021. https://ip.ccde.com.uw.edu/?p=782.

Irwin, Laura. "Speaking Up is a Gift for People." Interrupting Privilege, March 11, 2021. http://ip.ccde.com.uw.edu/?p=1532.

Irwin, Laura. "Transnational Microaggressions." Interrupting Privilege, August 12, 2021. https://ip.ccde.com.uw.edu/?p=1144.

Irwin, Laura. "When Should You Interrupt Privilege." Interrupting Privilege, September 2, 2021. https://ip.ccde.com.uw.edu/?p=1338.

moultrie, jas. "On Sustaining and Being Ourselves in Community." Interrupting Privilege, April 27, 2022. http://ip.ccde.com.uw.edu/?p=1623.

INDEX

Page numbers in italics indicate photos

Aaftaab, Gina, 52
AARP. *See* American Association of Retired Professionals
ableism, 9, 107
accountabilibuddy, 152
accountability, for racial microaggressions, 122–23
active listening, 39–41, 44–45, 71
ADOS. *See* American Descendants of Slavery
advertising, racial microaggressions in, 97
affirmative action, 4, 159–60
African immigrants, racial experiences of, 22
Against Empathy (Bloom), 73
Ahmed, Sara, 42, 71, 112, 160
Allen, Joel, 127
Allport, Gordon, 145
allyship: as active state, 109; friction and, 68; racial microaggressions and, 110–11; white racial exhaustion and, 8–9
American Association of Retired Professionals (AARP), 37
American Descendants of Slavery (ADOS), 22, 149
analytical empathy, 190n58
Angry Black Woman stereotype: as anti-Black women stereotype, 65–66; misogynoir and, 66; racial microaggressions and, 64; radical speaking and, 87–89

Angry White Woman, 123–26
anti-racism, xi, 33, 186n1
Anti-racism Response Training (ART), 33
anti-"woke" movement: denial of racism as element of, 26; political support for, 26–27; in schools, 27; Stop Woke Act, 26–27; in workplaces, 27
appreciative listening, 40
Arbery, Ahmaud, 158
ART. *See* Anti-racism Response Training
Asian Americans, 1–2, 91, 115
attentive listening, 39–41
attunement, 42–43, 48

Bahu, Meera, 70
Bailey, Moya, 158
Bakhtin, Mikhail, 94, 141
Bell, L. A., 134
Bettez, Silva, 133
bias, implicit, 26
BIPOC populations (Black, Indigenous, and People of Color populations), 1–2. *See also* Black people and populations; Indigenous people and populations; people of color
Black feminism: pedagogies of discomfort and, 65; power matrix of domination and, 2
Black Freedom Struggle, 156
Black Lives Matter movement (BLM movement), 138, 156; school programs and, 9; in Seattle, x

Blackness: African immigrant experience and, 22; American Descendants of Slavery and, 22; authenticity of, 149–50; Black race talk from, 2; construction of, 2; legacy Black, 22; racial exhaustion and, 2

Black people and populations: African immigrant experience and, 22; American Descendants of Slavery, 22, 149; Black tax for, 64, 66; emotional exhaustion of, 70–71; Juneteenth, 58; legacy Black experiences, 22; "living while Black," 139; politics of respectability for, 194n20; state-sanctioned violence against, ix; as term of description, 1–2. *See also* Blackness; Black women

Black Power movements, 156

Black race talk, from construction of Blackness, 2

Black racial exhaustion: for Black women, 83; fatigue thresholds for, 5; grind culture and, 5; health effects of, 3–4; racial battle fatigue from, 3

Black tax, 64, 66

Black women: Angry Black Woman stereotype, 64–66, 87–89; devaluation of, 19; intersectionality and, 137–39; misogynoir and, 66, 118; mothering practices of, 18; Post Traumatic Slave Syndrome and, 18; racial exhaustion for, 83; racial microaggressions against, 64, 81; resilience of, 82; Say Her Name movement, 138; state-sanctioned violence against, 138; Strong Black Woman stereotype, 81

Blake, Jacob, 25, 55

Bland, Sandra, 138

BLM movement. *See* Black Lives Matter movement

Bloom, Paul, 73

Boler, Megan, 64–65, 67, 73

Bonilla-Silva, Eduardo, 62

Boyd, Rekia, 138

Bradley, Rizvana, 25

Brady, Shannon T., 135

Brazile, Donna, 173n2

Brekke, Anjuli, 49–51, 66, 183n38

Briscoe-Smith, Allison, 136

Brown, Brene, 133

Brown, Michael, 138, 156

Buber, Martin, 141, 201n36

burnout, sitting with discomfort and, 68–71. *See also* racial exhaustion

Canada, multiculturalism policies in, 203n3

Carmack, Preston, 183n53

Castile, Philando, 138

casual racism, 98

Chisholm, Shirley, x, 173n2

Chun, Wendy, 44

Civil Rights Act of 1964, U.S., 156

Civil Rights movement, 145, 156

classical racism, 4

Clinton, Hillary, 22–23

cognitive empathy, 73

Coleman, Robin Means, 11–12

collective witnessing, 66

colleges and universities: DEI initiatives at, 26–27; racial microaggressions in, 117–18. *See also* University of Washington

Collins, Charles R., 84

Collins, Patricia Hill, 2, 89

color blind/color mute approach, in white race talk, 62

color-conscious approach, in white race talk, 62

colorism, 9, 173n5. *See also* pigmentocracy

Comas-Diaz, Lilian, 51–52

Combahee River Collective, 137

communication, models of: Encoding/Decoding, 15; nonverbal, 41. *See also* critical communication of race

communities and neighborhoods: belonging in, 135–36; bridging in, 136; critical, 133; egalitarian, 134; expectations of, 132; geographic, 132; intersectional community-building, 137–40; LGBTQ+ populations in, 133–34; multicultural, 132–33; norms in, 136, *137*; power in, 133; racial gentrification of, 8; radical listening and, 136; radical speaking spaces, 137–40; reparative dialoguing in, 127, 131–36, 151–52; vulnerability in, 133–34
compassion, distress tolerance and, 60
compliments, as racial microaggressions, 103
Confronting Prejudiced Responses model (CPR model), 197n69
contact hypothesis, 145
counterspaces, in critical race scholarship, xii–xiii
COVID-19 pandemic, 158; BIPOC communities affected by, 10–11; Interrupting Privilege program during, 24–25; racialized impact of, ix; racial reckoning and, 171
CPE. *See* critical peace education
CPR model. *See* Confronting Prejudiced Responses model
Cremin, Hilary, 192n94
Crenshaw, Kimberlé Williams, 137–39. *See also* intersectionality
critical communication of race, ix, *12*; dialogue and, 144–45; Interrupting Privilege program and, 11; learning as element of, 28; pedagogies of discomfort and, 68; race talk and, 2; radical listening and, 54–55; radical speaking and, 95, 152; reparative dialoguing and, 152; sitting with discomfort and, 68. *See also* Interrupting Privilege program
critical friend model, 202n66
critical peace education (CPE), 188n27

critical race scholarship, counterspaces in, xii–xiii
Cusseaux, Michelle, 138

Daughters, Stacey, 76
Davis, Angela, 45
Davis, Sharde, 81
DBT. *See* Dialectical Behavioral Therapy
declarative statement, for racial microaggressions, 116–19
defensiveness mode, in radical listening, 36
DEI initiatives. *See* Diversity, Equity, and Inclusion initiatives
Denise, Eric Joy, 105
DeSantis, Ron, 26
DeTurk, Sara, 146
Dialectical Behavioral Therapy (DBT), 75–77, 79–80
dialogic feedback, 147–48, 150
dialogic listening, 200n22, 201n41
dialogue: critical communication of race, 144–45; debate compared to, 141–42; etymology of, 141; intergroup, 145–48; through relationality, 141. *See also* reparative dialoguing
DiAngelo, Robin, 19, 108–10
discomfort. *See* pedagogies of discomfort; sitting with discomfort
discriminative listening, 40
dissemblance, 194n20
distress tolerance: compassion and, 60; definition of, 76; in Dialectical Behavioral Therapy, 75–77, 79–80; Interrupting Privilege program and, 78; mindfulness and, 60, 78–79; naming racism and, 79; racial justice and, 77; radical acceptance and, 76–77; Resistance through Resilience project, 78, 80–85; sitting with discomfort and, 13, 60, 75–80; synthesis of acceptance and change in, 76–77
diversity, 25, 160

Diversity, Equity, and Inclusion initiatives (DEI initiatives): at colleges and universities, 26–27; corporate expansion of, 25; guiding principles of, 102, 157; historical context for, 156–57; multiculturalism and, 156–57; racial exhaustion and, 158–59; racial reckoning era and, 26. *See also* anti-"woke" movement; post-DEI era

Dobbs v. Jackson Women's Health Organization, 160

Dobson, Andrew, 190n55

Dreher, Tanja, 42, 67, 74, 140

DuGruy, Joy, 18, 177n38

Eberhardt, Jennifer, 13, 67–68
Ellis, Manuel, 173n6
emotional empathy, 73
emotional exhaustion, 70–71, 189n40
empathy: active listening and, 71; analytical, 190n58; cognitive, 73; definition of, 71–72; emotional, 73; passive, 73; sitting with discomfort and, 71–75; white women and, 73; witnessing and, 72
empathy-into-action, 74
employment. *See* workplaces
Encoding/Decoding model of communication, 15
equality, 142–43, *144*
equity, *144*; definition of, 25, 143; equality compared to, 142–43; school development courses on, 9–10

Farson, Richard E., 40
feedback. *See* dialogic feedback
feminism. *See* Black feminism
Fendler, Lynn, 132
Floyd, George, 11, 25, 31, 55, 155–56. *See also* racial reckoning
Floyd, Korey, 201n38
Folino, Alexandria, 170

friction: allyship and, 68; sitting with discomfort and, 13, 67–68
Friere, Paulo, 147

Garner, Eric, 55, 156
Garrison, William Lloyd, 91
gender: microaggressions and, 103, 112; racial microaggressions and, 106. *See also* Black women; white women; women
Generation Mixed project, 50
gentrification, racial, 8; reparative dialoguing and, 127–29
Gilbert, Paul, 69
Gilligan, Carol, 43
The Giving Tree (Silverstein), 143
Gonzalez, Emma, 39
Gregory, Romilly, 70
grind culture, 5
guilt, sitting with discomfort and, 68–71
Guzmán, Monica, 136, 142

Hall, Mya, 138
Hall, Stuart, 15
Harris, Kamala, 161
hashtag activism, 158
hate crimes, during Trump presidency, 10
hate speech, during Trump presidency, 10
hearing to the root, 46, 48
Helper, Laura, 42
Hersey, Tricia, 5
Higginbotham, Evelyn Brooks, 194n20
Hill, Andre Maurice, 55
Hine, Darlene Clark, 194n20
Holling, Michelle, 104, 106
homophobia, 9, 107
Hope 6 program, 127
How to Be an Antiracist (Kendi), 186n1
Hutchinson, Darren, 4

implicit bias, 26, 54
inclusion, definition of, 25
incredulity mode, in radical listening, 36

Indigenous people and populations: talking about race by, 91; Tarahumara Natives, 97
inequality, *143*
institutional diversity, 160
institutional listening, 37–39
intentionality, of racial microaggressions, 99–106
intergroup dialogue, 145–48
interlistening, 180n9
International Listening Association, 40
interpersonal power, 2
interpersonal racism, 8, 131; intersectionalism in, 11; police violence and, 30
Interrupting Privilege program, 9, *161*; during COVID-19 pandemic, 24–25; critical communication of race and, 11; distress tolerance and, 78; education administrators' role in, 20–21; establishment of, 20; expansion of, 20–21; Families of Color Seattle, 168; goals of, 10, 20–21; interracial meetings for, *21*; intra-racial versions of, 24; LGBTQ+ populations, 22, 171–72; methodological approach to, 27–28; pedagogies of discomfort and, 66; privilege defined in, 17; purpose of, 10, 20–21; racial demographics of participants, 21–22; racial microaggressions and, 114–15, 120–21, 123, 198n70; radical listening in, 49; radical speaking and, 88–89, 193n10; reaction to Trump election, 23–24; researchers for, 172; Resistance through Resilience project, 60, 74, 78, 80–85, 169–70; sample dialogue prompts, 167–72; in Seattle, 21; sitting with discomfort and, 57, 60
interruption of privilege: definitions within, 15; guiding principles of, 179n64; as term, 15
interruption strategies, for racial microaggressions, 107–8, 110, 113–23, *115*, *117*, *119–21*

intersectionality: in interpersonal racism, 11; radical speaking and, 94
intersectional racism, structural, 11
Ishiyama, Ishu, 113, 197n67
Islamophobia, 112

Jackson, John L., 29
Jackson, Sarah J., 158
Jacobson, Matthew Frye, 2
Jefferson, Ataina, 138
Jennings, Helen, 179n64
Jim Crow, 99, 105
Joseph, Naima, 171
Judd, Betinna, 89
Juneteenth, 58
justice, *145*; listening and, 43; restorative, 202n54; social justice liberals, xi; transformative, 202n54. *See also* racial justice

Kendi, Ibrahim X., 186n1
Kennedy, Megan, 78–79
Kenney, Greta, 114
Kester, Kevin, 192n94
Kinchole, Joe, 46
King, Martin Luther, Jr., 98
King, Ruth, 16, 29, 60, 79, 95, 146, 174n4; on racialized stress, 13–14
Kleit, Rachel, 127
Kurogi, Atusko, 134, 140, 148–49, 190n58

Lanzoni, Susan, 72
Latine people, Latine populations and: labor abuse of, 106; talking about race by, 91; as term of description, 1–2
Laverty, Megan, 45
Lawson, James, Jr., 99
legacy Black experiences, 22
Lewis, Laurie, 37, 40
LGBTQ+ populations: in communities, 133–34; Interrupting Privilege program and, 22, 171–72; reparative dialoguing and, 149–50. *See also* homophobia; transphobia

Linehan, Marsha, 75–78
Lipari, Lisbeth, 42, 180n9
listening: active, 39–41, 44, 71; appreciative, 40; attentive, 39–41; attunement and, 42–43; centering of justice and, 43; through critical race lens, 44; dialogic, 200n22, 201n41; discriminative, 40; eye contact and, 41–42; gender factors for, 43; hearing to the root, 46, 48; institutional, 37–39; interlistening, 180n9; mindful, 42; neutral, 36, 39–41; passive, 181n15, 181n20; for power, 41–47; research for, 36–37; rhetorical, 43, 183n42; voice-centered Listening Guide, 43. *See also* radical listening
"The Listening Project," 43
"living while Black," 139
Lorde, Audre, 90–91, 118
Louis, Bertin M., Jr., 105
Loving v. Virginia, 173n3
Lowery, Wesley, 159
Lyles, Charleena, 173n6

macroaggressions, 98. *See also* microaggressions; microaggressions, racial
Magee, Rhonda, 77
Manning, Kimberly D., 26
Martin, Trayvon, 138, 156
mass media, racial microaggressions in, 97
McDonald, Michele, 194n15
McIntosh, Peggy, 19
McLaren, Peter, 157
Mehrabian, Albert, 41
microaggressions, 195n30; with accents, 111–12; gendered, 103, 112; sexualized, 112; transphobia and, 103
microaggressions, racial, 14; accountability for, 122–23; in advertising, 97; allyship and, 110–11; amplification strategies for, 118–19; Angry Black Woman trope and, 64; against Asian American women, 115; Black tax and, 64; against Black women, 64, 81; as casual racism, 98; coding of, 100; in colleges and universities, 117–18; compliments and, 103; declarative statements for, 116–19; definition of, 98, 102, 104; deniability of, 99–106; forms of, 100–101; gender and, 106; identification of, 100; intentionality of, 99–106; Interrupting Privilege program and, 114–15, 120–21, 123, 198n70; interruption strategies, 107–8, 110, 113–23, *115, 117, 119–21*; Islamophobia and, 112; in mass media, 97; minoritization processes as result of, 112; misogynoir as, 118; Pierce and, 96–98, 106; preference statements for, 120–21; punting responses to, 121–22; race confession and, 111; racial exhaustion from, 101, 105, 108; radical listening and, 101; radical speaking and, 93, 96–123; scope of, 64; shame as result of, 99–100, 117; sitting with discomfort and, 64, 66–67; skepticism about, 105; unintentional, 102; against white people, 103; white supremacy and, 98; white women and, 101, 109, 112
mindful listening, 42
mindfulness, 146; distress tolerance and, 60, 78–79; race and, 29
misogynoir, 66, 118
Molina-Markham, Elizabeth, 42, 47
monologic radical speaking, 94
Moore, Kayle, 138
Moore, Susan, 55
mothering practices, maternal behaviors and, by race, 18
multicultural communities, 132–33
multiculturalism, 156–57, 203n3
multigenerational reparative dialoguing, *151*

NAAM. *See* Northwest African American Museum
naming of race/racism: distress tolerance and, 79; radical speaking and, 90–91; sitting with discomfort and, 68–70
Native Americans, 1–2, 22
Naz, Saiqa, 70
Nelson, Jacqueline, 114
neutral listening (power-evasive listening), 36, 39–41
Nieto, Sonia, 160
non-Black emotional exhaustion, 70–71. *See also* white racial exhaustion
nonverbal communication, 41
Northwest African American Museum (NAAM), 21, 22, 24, 168–69

Obama, Barack, *xiii*, 22–23, 156–57, 179n64. *See also* post-racialism
Obama, Michelle, 106
Omakdeke, Janice, 133
Omi, Michael, 2, 174n7
Ozias, Moira L., 109

Parkland High School, 38–39
Parks, Elizabeth, 42, 136, 180n8
passive empathy, 73
passive listening, 181n15, 181n20
passive racism, 58; during holidays, 129–30
pedagogies of discomfort, 13; anti-Black women stereotypes and, 65–66; Black feminism and, 65; collective witnessing and, 66; conceptual approach to, 65; critical communication of race and, 68; culture of inquiry and flexibility, 65–66; Interrupting Privilege program and, 66; mentorship programs and, 67; peace education and, 188n27; racial exhaustion and, 59–60, 64–68; Resistance through Resilience project and, 80–85; self-reflection in, 65–66

people of color (POC): emotional exhaustion for, 189n40; methodological approach to, 1–2; racial exhaustion for, 34, 60–64; radical listening and, 34; as term of description, 1–2. *See also* Black people and populations; Indigenous people and populations; Latine people; Native Americans; POC racial exhaustion
Pierce, Chester, 96–98, 106, 174n9
Pierson, Ashley, 78
pigmentocracy, class privilege through, xii
POC racial exhaustion, 34; from discrimination, 61; sitting with discomfort and, 60–64; white racial exhaustion as distinct from, 69. *See also* Black racial exhaustion
police violence, interpersonal racism and, 30. *See also* Floyd, George; racial reckoning; *specific people*
politics of expression/impression, 44
polygenesis theory, racism and, 31
post-DEI era, 155–61
post-racialism, 156
postracialism, postracial era and: abandonment of, xiv; election of Obama, B., as symbol of, 156–57; after racial reckoning, xiv
Post Traumatic Slave Syndrome, 18, 177n38
powell, john a., 135
power: abuse of, 174n4; context for, 47; definitions of, 2; interpersonal, 2; radical listening for, 34, 41–48; reparative dialoguing and, 141–48; as situational, 47; structural, 2
power-evasive listening. *See* neutral listening
Predominately White Institutions (PWIs), 34
preference statements, for racial microaggressions, 120–21

privilege: definition of, 15–17; DiAngelo and, 19; in educational spaces, 19–20; in Interrupting Privilege program, 17; metaphors for, 19; praise as, 17–18; Simmel and, 19; as unearned, 17–18; visibility of, 19–20; whiteness as, 15–17; white racial exhaustion and, 14
punting responses, to racial microaggressions, 121–22
PWIs. *See* Predominately White Institutions

Quiggin, Robynne, 63

race: listening and, 44; mindfulness and, 29; mothering practices informed by, 18; radical listening and, 34; school development courses on, 9–10; as social construct, 2; traumatic stress and, 3. *See also* Blackness; naming of race/racism; race talk; whiteness; *specific topics*
race confession, 111
race scholarship, race as construct, 2
race silence, xii; white-perpetrated, 4
race talk, language about race and: critical communication of race, 2; hate speech, 10; racial dialoguing projects, 6–10; radical speaking and, 91; in white spaces, xi. *See also* racial fluency; reparative dialoguing
racial battle fatigue (RBF), 3
racial categorization, in U.S., 31
racial changemaking, 11
racial dialoguing projects, 6–10
racial exhaustion: Blackness and, 2; case studies in, 6–10; conceptual approach to, ix–xiv, 1, 3–5; definition of, 3; DEI initiatives and, 158–59; embodiment of, 3–4; geography as factor for, x–xi; history of, 155; in medical contexts, 53–54; methodological approach to, 13–15; pedagogies of discomfort and, 59–60, 64–68; racial battle fatigue, 3;

from racial microaggressions, 101, 105, 108; reparative dialoguing and, 151–52; silence and, 70. *See also* Black racial exhaustion; POC racial exhaustion; radical listening; radical speaking; reparative dialoguing; sitting with discomfort; white racial exhaustion; *specific topics*
racial fluency, xiv. *See also* critical communication of race
racial gentrification. *See* gentrification
racialization: of ableism, 9; of colorism, 9; as historical process, 2; of homophobia, 9; of sexism, 9; of transphobia, 9. *See also* racism
racialized stress, 13–14
racialized structures, 2. *See also* colleges and universities; schools; workplaces
racialized systems, oppression through, 2
racial justice, distress tolerance and, 77
racial microaggressions. *See* microaggressions, racial
racial reckoning: COVID-19 pandemic and, 171; DEI initiatives and, 26; globalization of, xiv; political backlash against, 26–27; postracialism after, xiv; sitting with discomfort and, 57
racial socialization, xi–xii
racial trauma, radical listening and, 51–52
racism: affirmative action as response to, 4; apologies for, 107; casual, 98; classical, 4; denial of, 26; as individual issue, 83; interpersonal, 8, 11, 30, 131; "living while Black," 139; naming of, 79; passive, 58, 129–30; polygenesis theory and, 31; resource hoarding and, 7–8; silencing of, 3; structural intersectional, 11; systemic, 156; in therapy, 74; during Trump presidency, 10; from white racial exhaustion, 10. *See also* bias; naming of race/racism; race talk; racial exhaustion; racial reckoning; *specific topics*

racist, as label: fear of, 1; white racial exhaustion and, 84
radical acceptance, 76–77
radical listening, 12, 179n64; academic theories of, 39; active listening and, 39–41, 44–45; appreciative listening and, 40; attentive listening and, 39–41; attunement in, 48; for change, 47–48; community-based research principles in, 49; conceptual approach to, 33–34; as context-dependent, 113; critical communication of race and, 54–55; defensiveness mode, 36; definition of, 45; difference and, 46–48, 56; discriminative listening and, 40; as form of resilience, 52; Generation Mixed project and, 50; hearing as physiological process and, 40; hearing to the root in, 46, 48; incredulity mode, 36; institutional listening and, 37–39; in Interrupting Privilege program, 49; as lifesaving act, 52–56; listening research and, 36–37; in medical contexts, 53–54; methodological approach to, 14–15; neutral listening and, 36, 39–41; Parkland High School and, 38–39; participants in, 49–50; POC racial exhaustion and, 34; power and, 34, 41–48; in Predominately White Institutions, 34; purpose of, 48; to race, 34; race-based stress and, 51–52; racial microaggressions and, 101; racial trauma and, 51–52; radical speaking and, 102; reparative dialoguing and, 147, 149, 152; sessions in, 48–52, 50–51; silence as element of, 34; as space-dependent, 113; strategic ambiguity and, 52; as time-dependent, 113; what-about-me mode, 36; white privilege and, 36; white racial exhaustion and, 34
radical speaking, 12, 179n64; in academic contexts, 93; Angry Black Woman stereotype and, 87–89; Angry White Woman and, 123–26; Buddhist origins of, 95; changemaking and, 93; critical communication of race and, 95; definition of, 89–90; as fear-based, 91; Interrupting Privilege program and, 88–89, 193n10; intersectional identities and, 94; monologic, 94; naming of race/racism and, 90–91; as pedagogical exercise, 94–95; purpose of, 90–92; racial microaggressions and, 93, 96–123; radical listening and, 102; talking about race and, 91; white racial exhaustion and, 124–26
RAIN technique, 194n15
Ratcliffe, Krista, 43
RBF. *See* racial battle fatigue
Reiss, Helen, 72
reparative dialoguing, 12, 179n64; as active process, 148–53; American Descendants of Slaves and, 149; attending to power, 146–48; without attending to power, 141–45; community building through, 127, 131–36, 151–52; conditions for, 147; critical communication of race and, 152; dialogic feedback and, 147–48, 150; in educational spaces, 147–48; Hope 6 program, 127; intergroup dialogue, 145–48; LGBTQ+ populations and, 149–50; methodological approach to, 14; multigenerational, *151*; racial exhaustion and, 151–52; radical listening and, 147, 149, 152; sitting with discomfort and, 149, 152; in spaces of gentrification, 127–29
resilience: for Black women, 82; radical listening as form of, 52; Resisting through Resilience project, 60
resistance, to structural intersectional racism, 11
Resistance through Resilience project, 60, 74, 169–70; distress tolerance and, 78, 80–85; pedagogy of discomfort and, 80–85

resource hoarding, in schools, by white people, 7–8
restorative justice, 202n54
Reyes, Jennifer, 11–12
rhetorical listening, 43, 183n42
Rice, Tamir, 138
Roe v. Wade, 160
Rogers, Carl R., 40
Rosenbloom, Helen, 81
Ruth, Tony, 143, *143–45*

Say Her Name movement, 138
SBW stereotype. *See* Strong Black Woman stereotype
schools, educational spaces and: anti-"woke" movement in, 27; Black Lives Matter movement and, 9; Interrupting Privilege program in, 20–21; Parkland High School, 38–39; privilege in, 19–20; race and equity development courses in, 9–10; racial animus in, xii; radical speaking in, 93; reparative dialoguing in, 147–48; resource hoarding by white people in, 7–8; white racial exhaustion in, 8–10, 74. *See also* colleges and universities; University of Washington
Scott, Walter, 138
Seattle, Washington: anti-racism in, xi; Black Lives Matter movement in, x; during COVID-19 pandemic, 169; diverse social groups in, xiii; Families of Color Seattle, 168; Interrupting Privilege program in, 21; Northwest African American Museum in, 21, 22, 24, 168–69; racial exhaustion in, x–xi; whiteness of, x–xi
sexism, 9, 107
shame: racial microaggressions and, 99–100, 117; sitting with discomfort and, 68–71
silence: racial exhaustion and, 70; racism and, 3; radical listening and, 34. *See also* race silence

Silverstein, Shel, 143
Simmel, Michael, on privilege, 19
Siry, Christina, 94
Sister Outsider (Lorde), 90
sitting with discomfort, 12, 179n64; avoidance behaviors and, 70; burnout and, 68–71; collective witnessing and, 66; as conscious act, 57; critical communication of race and, 68; distress tolerance and, 13, 60, 75–80; diversity of environments as element of, 59; empathy and, 71–75; friction in, 13, 67–68; guilt and, 68–71; Interrupting Privilege program and, 57, 60; naming race/racism, 68–70; passive racism and, 58; pedagogies of discomfort, 13, 59–60, 64–68; for people of color, 59; POC racial exhaustion and, 60–64; racial microaggressions and, 64, 66–67; racial reckoning and, 57; reparative dialoguing and, 149, 152; Resilience Lab and, 60; Resisting through Resilience project, 60; shame and, 68–71; silence and, 70; Strong Black Woman stereotype, 81; white racial exhaustion and, 59–64
Sleeter, Christine, 157
Smith, William, 3, 174n9, 195n32
Smooth, Jay, 16, 114
socialization, racial, xi–xii
social justice liberals, xi
Southwest Asian North African population (SWANA), 1–2, 22, 91
de Souza, Poppy, 42, 67, 74
speaking. *See* dialogue; race talk; radical speaking; reparative dialoguing; *specific topics*
Spencer, Michael, 34
state-sanctioned violence: against Black people, ix; against Black women, 138. *See also* police violence
Steen-Utheim, Anna, 147
Stenberg, Shari, 68

Sterling, Alton, 138
Stop Woke Act, 26–27
stress. *See* Post Traumatic Slave Syndrome; racial battle fatigue; racialized stress
Strong Black Woman stereotype (SBW stereotype), 81
structural intersectional racism, 11
structural power, 2
Students for Fair Admissions, Inc. v. President and Fellows of Harvard, College/University of North Carolina et. al., 159–60
Sturgis, Meshell, 103, 106, 130, 196n48
SWANA. *See* Southwest Asian North African population
systemic racism, 156

Tansey, Janeta, 44–45
Tarahumara Natives, 97
Taylor, Breonna, 25, 55, 138, 158
Thurber, Amie, 108–10, 113
Ting-Toomey, Stella, 34, 42, 134, 140, 148–49, 190n58
To, Alexandra, 100–101, 122
Tobin, Ken, 46–48
transformative justice, 202n54
transphobia: apologies for, 107; microaggressions and, 103; racialization of, 9
trauma. *See* Post Traumatic Slave Syndrome; racial trauma
Trump, Donald, 39, 112, 160–61; hate crimes/speech under, 10; political rejection of, 23; racism under, 10
Tubman, Harriet, 91

unintentional racial microaggressions, 102
United States (U.S.): Civil Rights Act of 1964, 156; codification of racial categories in, 31; Voting Rights Act of 1965, 156. *See also* Asian Americans; Native Americans; *specific topics*
universities. *See* colleges and universities

University of Washington, Resilience Lab, 60
U.S. *See* United States

violence. *See* police violence; state-sanctioned violence
Vittrup, Brigitte, 62
Voting Rights Act of 1965, U.S., 156

Walensky, Rochelle, 3
Wallace, David Foster, 19
Wallace, Michele, 81
Walton, Gregory M., 135
Watson, Erin, 84
Welles, Brooke Foucault, 158
whiteness: academic studies on, 19; geographic homogeny of, xi; as race privilege, 15–17; of Seattle, x–xi. *See also* white privilege
white people, white populations and: emotional exhaustion for, 189n40; interracial interactions as influence on cognitive functions, 4; race silence by, 4; racial microaggressions and, 103; resource hoarding by, 7–8; talking about race by, 91; as term of description, 1–2. *See also* white race talk; white racial exhaustion; white women; *specific topics*
white privilege, 15–16; white racial exhaustion and, 74
white race talk, 2; color blind/color mute approach in, 62; color-conscious approach in, 62
white racial exhaustion: allyship and, 8–9; emotional regulation and, 60–61; expressions of, 4; within families, 61, 63; modeling of, 62; POC racial exhaustion as distinct from, 69; privilege and, 14; racism perpetuated through, 10; racist labeling and, 84; radical speaking and, 124–26; in schools, 8–10, 74; self-examination as

white racial exhaustion (cont.)
    element of, 61; sitting with discomfort and, 59–64; among students, 74; white privilege and, 74
white supremacy, 98
white women: Angry White Woman, 123–26; empathy and, 73; mothering practices of, 18; racial microaggressions and, 101, 109, 112
Wilks, Chelsey, 76–77
Williams, Monnica, 102, 195n32
Williams, Sheena S., 26
Williamson-Lott, Joy, 156
Willink, Kate, 146
Winant, Howard, 2, 174n7
Wing Sue, Derald, 14, 93, 99, 102, 104
witnessing: collective, 66; empathetic, 72
Wittek, Anne Line, 147
women, emotional exhaustion for, 189n40. *See also* Black women; gender; white women
workplaces, employment spaces and: anti-"woke" movement in, 27; racial animus in, xii

X, Malcolm, 116

Yankelovich, Daniel, 201n40

Zheng, Lily, 173n1
Zuniga, Daphne, 146

ABOUT THE AUTHOR

RALINA L. JOSEPH is a scholar, teacher, and facilitator of race and communication. She is Vice Provost of Inclusive Excellence and Professor of African American Studies at the University of California, Los Angeles. Ralina is the author of three other books including *Postracial Resistance* (2018), which was the International Communication Association's Outstanding Book of 2019.